NETWORKING NT
Using Windows NT™ in the
Corporate LAN Environment

NETWORKING NT

Using Windows NT™ in the Corporate LAN Environment

Christopher Monro

 VAN NOSTRAND REINHOLD
_____ New York

Library of Congress Catalog Card Number 93-49069
ISBN 0-442-01829-0

I(T)P   Van Nostrand Reinhold is an International Thomson Publishing company.
ITP logo is a trademark under license.

Printed in the United States of America.

Van Nostrand Reinhold
115 Fifth Avenue
New York, NY 10003

International Thomson Publishing GmbH
Königswinterer Str. 418
53227 Bonn
Germany

International Thomson Publishing
Berkshire House,168-173
High Holborn, London WC1V 7AA
England

International Thomson Publishing Asia
221 Henderson Bldg. #05-10
Singapore 0315

Thomas Nelson Australia
102 Dodds Street
South Melbourne 3205
Victoria, Australia

International Thomson Publishing Japan
Kyowa Building, 3F
2-2-1 Hirakawacho
Chiyoda-ku, Tokyo 102
Japan

Nelson Canada
1120 Birchmount Road
Scarborough, Ontario
M1K 5G4, Canada

ARCFF   16   15   14   13   12   11   10   9   8   7   6   5   4   3   2   1

Library of Congress Cataloging in Publication Data

Monro, Christopher.
    Networking NT : using Windows NT in the corporate LAN environment
    / Christopher Monro.
        p.   cm.
    Includes bibliographical references and index.
    ISBN 0-442-01829-0
    1. Windows NT. 2. Networking Basics
QA76.76.O63M64   1994
005.7' 1369--dc20   93-49069
                                                                        CIP

Contents

Trademarks

The following terms used in this publication are registered trademarks or service marks of Microsoft Corporation:

Microsoft
Windows
Windows NT
Windows NT Advanced Server
Windows for Workgroups
Remote Access Service
Excel
Project
PowerPoint
Winword

The following terms used in this publication are registered trademarks or service marks of Novell, Inc.

NetWare
Novell

Dedication

This book is published in memory of my mother, Pamela Bennett Macpherson Monro, who died in June of 1993. She was a woman who was far too young and far too wise to leave this world.

This book is dedicated to a small but very important group of people in many different places who, sometimes without even knowing it, made this book possible. Officer Fisor of the Ottawa Hills Police Department, Chaplain William Stafford of Mohican Youth Center, my grandparents, Mr. and Mrs. James G. Macpherson, and my aunt, Julie Hancock.

Finally, I want to personally thank Jamal and Tammy Khatib, president and vice president of Cedar Computer Center, who gave me the opportunity to write this book. Thanks, Jamal and Tammy!

*If there's one thing in my life that's missing
it's the time that I spend alone, sailing on
the cool and bright clear water . . .
- Little River Band*

62 foot Custom C&C

*There are no problems, only issues.
-Jamal Khatib*

GO NAVY!

Preface

The revolution has begun! You know, I read that statement almost every week in some trade magazine that is extolling the latest technological advance in PC to food processor communication or some other equally abstract subject. The revolution actually began when the ancient Romans created an abacus for simple math. Everything we have done in computers is really an improvement on that basic machine. Over the last 12 years we have seen tremendous advances in micro technology; smaller, faster, and more capable hardware has led the market.

The downside is that capitalism has the uncanny ability to create diversity. If you want to sell something, it had better be different than other products, so that you can carve a niche for your sales. The problem with that is that in the computer industry, *diversity* traditionally has meant incompatibility. However, the wide varieties of products and platforms in the computer industry exemplifies a thriving market which, through its perpetual mutation, produces new innovations that we all come to use and need.

With all of the different platforms, protocols, operating systems, and applications, however, it's a wonder that any one system can talk to another. The biggest market in the networking industry will always be the products that connect one data source to another. We spent nearly five decades creating different types of systems, and now we have to make them all work together. It is not surprising that in the global marketplace of computers and technology, the biggest selling point of any product, whether hardware or software, is compatibility with both de facto and recognized standards. The product must be upgradable and must be able to connect to nearly everything else on this planet to gain market acceptance. Computer operating systems are no exception.

The term *operating system* would lead you to believe that it is the core of the entire machine. While that may be true in some ways, the true test of an operating system these days is in its ability to change to fit a given set of circumstances. It has to be modular, so you can "plug in" options, third-party products, and modifications. Today's operating system has to be not just a core, but must also include the other components such as networking, mass storage control, security, and so on. We have no idea what will be available next week, but the operating system had better be able to work with it. That flexibility is the core of Windows NT.

Windows NT is perhaps the finest operating system ever devised. There is little doubt that Windows NT will see revision after revision and will probably change names several times too. The difference is that Windows NT doesn't just define how your computer will execute commands or handle multiprocessing, but define how computers in general will work in the future. In that sense, Windows NT *is* a revolution. Just as for nearly twelve years DOS defined how computers would work (though I am sure we wish it weren't so, now), Windows NT defines how computers will work, independent of hardware platform, and open to almost any new innovations. I have heard many people say that Windows NT, like anything else, will be obsolete soon. While the version may become obsolete, the underlying technology will have a long-term impact on computer technology and the way we work on systems for a long time to come.

As stated before, one of the most important aspects of any computer product is its ability to connect with other non-related products. Windows NT is a prime example of a product that connects to nearly anything. It was built with connectivity and compatibility in mind. As you will see throughout the course of this book, Windows NT can connect and has some remarkable capabilities. Follow along and I will show you how to make Windows NT act the way you want in a corporate environment where there are many different standards for data, protocols, topologies, and operating systems stretching from one side of the world to the other. (Of course, if you're running nothing but a two-station LAN with Windows NT, that can be done too!)

Because there are so many standards available and in use for protocols and topologies, there isn't any easy way to streamline the process of installing and maintaining connections with other systems. The services

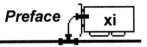

and capabilities available to a given machine when connected to another varies greatly depending on the method used to connect them.

Networking NT is designed to walk you through the process of connecting Windows NT to the world's prominent network operating systems and help you to tune performance and functions for the most productive operation.

Introduction

READ THIS!!!!

I had to put that there because so many people skip the introduction. Unfortunately, in order to get the most out of this book, you need to know how it is put together and why.

As you know if you read the preface, the idea is to address the multiple possible configurations of Windows NT in a network environment. Several books are available about Windows NT, and the Microsoft manuals that come with NT aren't bad at all. The manuals don't go far enough, though, and the Windows NT Resource Kit is almost too much information. *Networking NT* is designed for two types of people:

First, the book contains many screen shots and is full of real-life experience; not just how the operating system is supposed to work, but what happens when something doesn't work. This design makes it superb for the Windows NT student. If you don't have access to Windows NT but need to know how it works in a network, this book is for you.

Secondly, for network administrators, MIS department heads, and others connecting Windows NT to a wire, this book is full of the information you need, not the stuff you don't need. Granted, I did include some background information on the OSI reference model, but other than that, it's all the stuff that you need to know, taking you right through the process and explaining the Windows NT concepts and functions that are pertinent to your projects.

Read the first four chapters straight through, then pick from Chapters 5 through 9 depending on the project you want to accomplish, then familiarize yourself with the security and maintenance of NT as it relates to networking by reading Chapters 10 through 14.

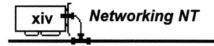
All text that denotes a button, menu option, or typed text will appear in 12-point bold courier typeface as shown below:

TEXT, MENU COMMAND, BUTTON...

Good luck and enjoy. You'll be up and running Windows NT in no time! If you're ready, let's get started. First stop, an overview of Windows NT.

Part One

Overview of
Windows NT

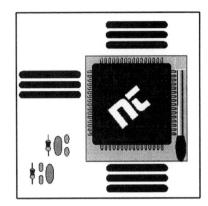

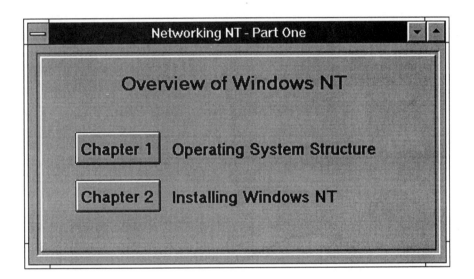

Chapter 1

Operating System Structure

For those of you who are just starting with Windows NT, Part 1 is devoted to an overview of NT. We'll cover the operating system structure and installation, and other basic topics. If you are a Windows 3.x user moving up to Windows NT, It is recommended that you read this section, since many of the concepts later in the book deal with vocabulary and concepts that are discussed here.

There were many objectives for the creation of Windows NT. The operating system needed to solve a host of different problems in order to become a market force; many of them had never been tackled before. Here is a list of the major design goals that Windows NT needed to satisfy and how each has been accomplished:

Compatibility: Windows NT needed to be able to run DOS, Windows, POSIX, and OS/2 applications in addition to the new Win32-based NT applications.

Solved: Windows NT has a new file system called NTFS for New Technology File System, which can accommodate the existence of OS/2, DOS, POSIX, and NT applications and files all in the same disk partition. NTFS supports uppercase and lowercase letters and file names of up to 254 characters. Each is automatically converted to a DOS-style 8.3 file name and also exists in its native form to accommodate DOS and 16-bit Windows applications (applications written for Windows 3.x) which couldn't understand 254-character file names.

To run these different application types, Windows NT uses what are called *environment subsystems*. Users access their applications and files from the File Manager or the command line without regard to what types of applications they are. Windows NT will determine the correct type and launch the appropriate subsystem to handle the application. Windows NT has three subsystems: OS/2, POSIX, and Win32. The DOS and 16-bit Windows applications run as part of the Win32 subsystem.

There are some limitations to the subsystems for OS/2 and POSIX applications however. OS/2 applications must be 16-bit character mode applications and they can only run on Intel based x86 systems like the i386, i486, or Pentium. The RISC hardware platform does not support OS/2 applications. POSIX applications must conform to an IEEE standard 1003.1 and usually must be compiled on an NT machine before they will work correctly.

Security: To compete in the government market and mission-critical roles in corporate environments, Windows NT needed to have an ironclad security subsystem that would be implemented at the core of the operating system, in which every function and operation was checked for security, instead of the security features just lying on top as in most applications and operating systems previously.

Solved: Windows NT was designed from the ground up as a secure operating system. The OS was designed to meet or exceed DoD C-2 level security ratings. Security will be discussed more deeply, later on in the book. Initially, you should know that the security is created at the root of the operating system so that every function can be checked and verified. Since Windows NT runs multiple environment subsystems, the security is implemented at the core so that authentication and other security functions can be passed on to secure application in the OS/2 and POSIX subsystems, as well as native 32-bit Windows NT applications.

Portability: NT needed to run some of the most powerful software applications ever: scientific and data-gathering applications, high-end database applications, graphics, and engineering applications. In the engineering field, Intel x86-based machines like the 386 or 486 are not the machines of choice because they don't have the power needed. Workstations such as the DEC Alpha and MIPS R4000 RISC-based machine are more qualified to run such high-end apps. To garner that market, Windows NT needed to run on Intel chips *and* the higher-end platforms like those mentioned above. This was a difficult task — to say the least — as Windows NT should work the same across all platforms; yet the platforms themselves are tremendously different from a hardware standpoint, and Microsoft did not want to write different versions of NT for each new platform.

Solved: One of the most remarkable features of Windows NT is a new layer, which is the very beginning of the OS, called the HAL or Hardware Abstraction Layer. This was designed so that a small piece of code could serve as an interpreter between all the functions of Windows NT and the individual hardware features of each platform. Figure 1-1 contains a simple illustration of this concept.

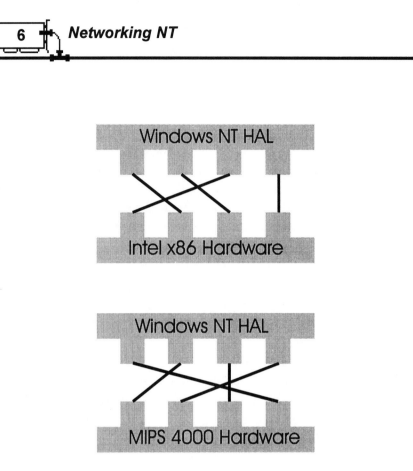

Figure 1-1
Hardware Abstraction Layer Function

The figure is an oversimplification but it illustrates the basic idea. Features for hardware interaction with the operating system are in different places on different platforms, and the HAL smooths this process so that NT interacts with the HAL. The HAL then figures out where to go with the commands and how to talk to the individual hardware types.

The manufacturers of the individual hardware platforms write the HAL, though Windows NT does include all PC-based HALs for ISA, EISA, and Micro Channel architectures as well several multiprocessing HALs.

Internationalization: To establish NT as a standard in the global marketplace, it was imperative that Windows NT be able to operate in other countries using different languages and character sets such as Chinese and Japanese.

Solved: Microsoft utilized Unicode, an improvement over ASCII (American Standard Code for Information Interchange) which could address only 256 characters. Unicode can address 65,536 characters. The implementation of internationalization in Windows NT is a very complex system. Font information and the appearance of a character is separated from the actual character.

Network connectivity: This objective was to build networking into the core of the operating system, making it inherently networkable, with multiple protocols and network cards. Host connectivity with IBM and other mainframes was also important, and OS should be designed to accept these innovations from the beginning, not just later add-ons.

Solved: Windows NT networking is built into the operating system or OS at the very start. NT was designed from the start to be a networking operating system. That means that network functions are not just riding on top of the OS or doing something funky with the OS, like DOS, to get networking functions. Windows NT supports multiple network cards and multiple protocols like TCP/IP, IPX, and NetBIOS.

Multiprocessing and scalability: Because NT would be running very powerful applications, an efficient method of sharing processor time was needed. Support for multiple processors in machines such as the MIPS R4000 was also a requirement. This scalability would give Windows NT the ability to execute one application on one processor and another application on a second, third, or fourth processor.

Physical RAM
Process 1, Page 1
Process 1, Page 3
Process 1, Page 2
Process 2, Page 1
Process 2, Page 2
Process 1, Page 4
Process 2, Page 3

Process 1

Process (2GB)
System (2GB)

Process 2

Process (2GB)
System (2GB)

Figure 1-2
Memory Allocation

Solved: These functions are implemented at the kernel and HAL levels. To address machines that have the ability to operate with more than one processor, the HAL and modifications to the kernel allow the OS to execute threads —which are individual execution commands passed to the processor— on multiple processors. For multitasking which is the ability of the OS to execute multiple threads seemingly at once, Windows NT uses preemptive multitasking. What that means is that every thread is given a priority, and if a lower-priority thread is executing on the processor when a higher-priority thread is executed, the higher-priority thread is given access to the processor. NT has 32 levels of priority.

Reliability: Given all the roles that Windows NT was destined to fill, the operating system needed to be *very* stable. Poorly written applications and errors by users or network communications could not be allowed to hurt the operating system and cause a crash. Errors needed to be either self-corrected or nondestructive to any other process on the system.

Solved: Reliability has been achieved through several different mechanisms. First, Windows NT uses a flat memory model. Memory is not segmented as in DOS which has 640K in conventional memory and then expanded and extended memory. Windows NT looks at RAM as a flat structure and can address more RAM than you can possibly hope to use in the near future. Each process in Windows NT is given 4 GB of potential RAM to use. If you noticed something funny about that statement, bear with me; it's how reliability is achieved.

A process is, essentially, an application that is running. Excel is an example of a process. Each process in Windows NT is given its own address space *to run in*. Every interaction with the operating system is verified to protect the OS. Two applications running under Windows NT are running in completely separate spaces of memory, not overlapped or combined. If an error occurs in an application, it can sabotage its own address space, not the operating system or any other application. In addition, Windows NT employs *Structured Exception Handling,* which is a fancy way of saying that errors that occur are trapped by the OS or by the application in a more efficient manner and the program can react to the error, in many cases solving the problem itself. Figure 1-2 illustrates the basic idea behind the flat memory model as well as showing that hard drive space can be used in the form of paging files to emulate RAM as a temporary memory-storage area. Items in memory that are not being used at a particular time can be "paged" to the hard drive while it's not in use.

One other part of the reliability of Windows NT stems from its use of multiple message queues. The message queue is the medium by which Windows NT communicates with applications and applications communicate with NT. If there is only one queue and an application crashes, sending electronic garbage into this queue, the system is hung since nothing else in the system can talk to the OS and vice versa. OS/2 v2.1 suffers from a single message queue. Windows NT has a message queue for each process, thus protecting other applications and the operating system from poorly written programs.

Extensibility: DOS was designed with what programmers at the time viewed as "limitless" capabilities, though many of the functions that we use computers for now, are far beyond what was deemed as a necessity for DOS. Windows NT had to do the impossible: be able to utilize technology that hadn't even been invented. Five years from now, all of us will be using computers in radically different ways, many of which haven't even been thought of yet. NT needed to provide universal hooks for new hardware, software, and network innovations so as not to make the OS obsolete.

Solved: Windows NT has been designed from the ground up to solve problems imposed upon users and developers by older operating systems. Ask any Windows, or DOS-based programmer what problem is dealt with most, and the answer is usually a diatribe on limitations that are inherent to the operating system. Memory is one of the biggest problems in development. Additionally, the BIOS or Basic Input/Output System of Intel x86 processors places limitations on disk operations and bus I/O, as well as several other aspects. As stated in the Preface, the ideal operating system in today's market is one that can adapt to fit a given set of circumstances and not be encumbered by arbitrary limitations. For the first basic view of Windows NT, take a look at Figure 1-3.

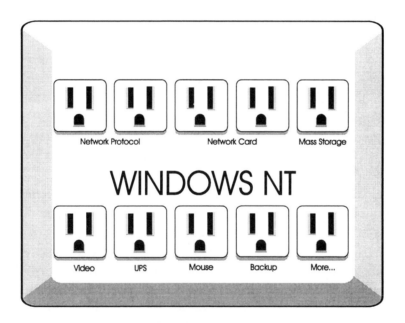

Figure 1-3
Modular Design of Windows NT

In simplest terms, the Windows NT core is a power strip, which alone does nothing spectacular, but when it is plugged with the options shown, it becomes very powerful. The modularity will be discussed again on the next page and applies just as much to new I/O methods as to backup options and UPS implementations.

Looking over the proceeding list, Windows NT had some very lofty goals, and little or no model from which to build the structure needed. While the functionality of UNIX and VMS were helpful, what NT does goes far beyond anything to date. Happily, all of the goals have been met. What is perhaps most striking about Windows NT is that it is very familiar. NT looks just like Windows 3.1 and interaction with the interface is essentially identical as well. The interface has caused many people at trade shows to simply walk past Windows NT machines because they thought it was Windows 3.1. However, beneath the smooth and familiar exterior lies a whole new beast.

Modularity

The beauty of the OS is that it is entirely modular. From simple things like mouse drivers to high-level network protocols, you can plug in the solution that works for you. The Win32 API or Application Programming Interface that defines the functions and procedures to write software for Windows NT has the tools to create device drivers for virtually any hardware or software device. Many of you who are Windows v3.1 users may be saying: "What's the big deal? Windows 3.1 already does it like that." There is a difference —in fact, a big difference. The difference lies in the way in which Windows NT handles the device drivers. In Windows v3.1, if a device driver fails, the game is over. You usually have to reboot the machine and try again because the device driver has affected some other part of the environment and so you crash. Not in Windows NT. The NT operating system is structured in such a way that every device driver is a process to be stopped and started. If the device driver fails to load, the only affected functions are those that the device driver directly manipulates. If the device driver fails in progress, the process is stopped and an error is written to the event log for NT. The device cannot interfere with any other portion of the OS because NT holds private virtual address space for each process. Any communication with another portion of the OS is granted or denied based on security and, as strange as it seems, the intentions of the communicator. NT protects itself from drivers.

Security

Security is at the heart of Windows NT, and its footprint can be found in nearly every part of the operating system and its components. NT really had two goals for security. The first was to meet the DoD (Department of Defense) C-2 security rating for use in government installations and the second was to meet a much broader corporate security standard.

To the government, security is very important, and the C-2 rating which Windows NT strives to meet has several specific requirements which are illustrated in Figure 1-4.

Understand that the DoD C-2 rating defines more than just the software. Hardware, software, installation, location and many other aspects which, by nature, a software operating system cannot affect, are part of the "Orange Book" that the DoD calls the *Department of Defense Trusted Computer System Evaluation Criteria*. Windows NT, if it receives recognition as a C-2 level operating system, is only one part of an entire plan that implements C-2. A computer that is placed in a reception area with open access by anyone cannot be a C-2 installation even if the operating system is C-2 rated.

Figure 1-4
DoD C-2 Security Specifications

I'll touch briefly on each of these requirements so that you can get an idea of what kind of security you can expect from Windows NT.

Discretionary Access Control

Discretionary Access Control specifies that users of a system may have access only to objects for which they are authorized. The creator or owner of an object has the ability to grant or deny access to other users or groups.

Authentication

Authentication means that any user who wishes to use a system must log onto the system first, entering a user name, and a password. When a new user is created on a Windows NT system, the user name and password are tied to a SID, or Security Identifier. Regardless of changes to a user name or password, the SID is the same so that changing attributes of a user does not prevent a user from being able to access objects they have created or have been granted access to. Let's say you have a secretary whose name is Cindy, and she has created several objects and has been granted access to several objects. If Cindy is promoted, and a new person, Ivy, takes over her position, changing Cindy's user name and password over to Ivy will give Ivy access to all the objects that Cindy used, which is necessary for her job. The SID is the same.

Object Reuse Protection

If you create a user with a particular SID and then delete that user, the SID should not be able to be reused, so a user cannot have access to a previous user's objects. If you create a user called Rhonda and she has several files that she has created and then the user is deleted, creating another user called Rhonda will not give the new user access to the old Rhonda's files. The SID is unique. This is object reuse protection.

Auditing

The auditing requirement is an obvious one. It requires that a log be available to record access and attempted access to protected objects such as secure files.

These are the basic requirements for DoD C-2 security. As mentioned earlier, there was another goal of Windows NT security: to meet requirements of commercial users. While the most important aspect from the government is security, the security should not be an impediment to user productivity. For this reason, the entire security subsystem is transparent to the user after logon. Access to files, applications, system resources, administrative functions, E-mail, and many other objects are granted or denied based on the user's rights determined during logon.

The process of authenticating a user on an Intel-based machine involves pressing the **[CTRL] + [ALT] + [DEL]** key sequence. Microsoft recommends that even if you walk up to a machine that has a logon dialog box displayed, you should still press the **[CTRL] + [ALT] + [DEL]** key sequence to ensure that the logon program is not a Trojan horse program that looks like the logon screen but actually records your user name and password.

Fault Tolerance

From a broad perspective, fault tolerance is the ability of a computer to recover from a potentially disastrous hardware failure. The most basic level of fault tolerance is a solid, secure, and frequent backup for data. A tape drive or other mass storage device should be implemented and used regularly. Beyond this basic level, fault tolerance takes on a wide array of problems dealing with critical hardware and different methods of protecting it.

The most extensive portion of fault tolerance is disk fault tolerance. Windows NT has many different methods of protecting the integrity of data on NT local drives. When working with and protecting hard drives,

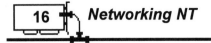

there are two areas of vulnerability: the hard drive itself and the hard drive controller.

Disk mirroring is the function of keeping two drives identical during operation and in the event that one drive should fail, the operating system will recognize this and continue operating with the one functional hard drive. The vulnerability in this scheme is that mirroring is dependent on a single controller. If the hard drives function perfectly, the controller could still fail, taking down the entire system.

Disk duplexing is the next level of disk fault tolerance; it mirrors drives across multiple controllers. The mirrored drives exist on separate controllers so a failure on one drive or controller will not take the system down.

Windows NT employs both of these methods for fault tolerance. One additional method which is more advanced but does not necessarily afford any more protection is called "disk stripping with parity," also known as the RAID 5 specification. RAID 5 is only available in the Windows NT Advanced Server product. This method allows a user to connect same-size partitions on multiple physical disks together so that they appear as one drive and leave a final same-size partition that stores the value of information on the other disks. As a simple example, if you store a 5 on partition one, a 3 on partition two, and a 9 on partition three, the final partition or parity partition stores the value 17 which is the total. If the second partition fails, a simple calculation can replace the second partition information. This is an oversimplification, but the theory is the same.

Two additional fault tolerance features are the UPS monitor and the SCSI tape backup program.

NT ships with a serial port UPS monitor for AC line fault tolerance. Most local area network-based UPS products have a serial cable that goes from the UPS to a computer to communicate the status of the UPS. Information such as charge level, length of time the battery will operate, UPS temperature, and loading can all be sent back to the computer. Intelligent drivers on the computer will interpret signals from the UPS and do certain things based on the information. The primary function of this capability is to notify the operating system that power has been interrupted and that the battery is discharging. The OS can then take steps to shut itself down "cleanly," without corrupting files by running a command file, or it can simply notify the user of the system that the power is lost and the system will be going down in x minutes. See Figure 1-5.

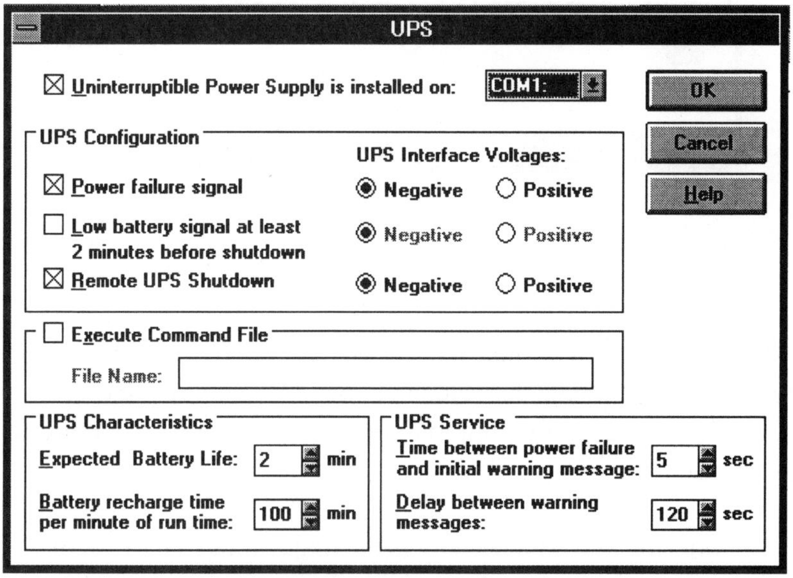

Figure 1-5
UPS Configuration Screen

Another component is the SCSI tape backup utility. The backup is not for enterprise-wide backup but rather for local or workgroup-based backup. The utility works with the Maynard tape system. The interface is very easy to use and provides for normal, incremental, and differential backup schemes. The backup utility is shown in Figure 1-6.

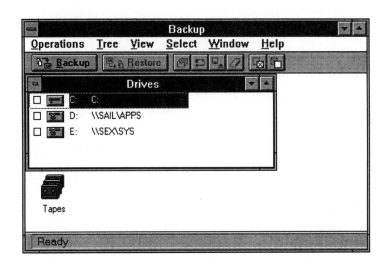

Figure 1-6
Backup Utility

Looking back over this chapter, we can see that a truly unique and robust operating system has taken shape. The features and abilities of Windows NT exceed anything to date and leave a solid structure for future enhancements.

Networking and connectivity is the major focus of this book and we will get to all the juicy details soon. But first, to close this first section on the Windows NT overview, the next chapter covers the installation process and options for installation.

Chapter 2

Installing Windows NT

The last chapter focused on the overall structure of Windows NT and the major features of the environment. Most of these topics are universal to Windows NT on any hardware platform, with the exception of support for environment subsystems. Installation, however, does differ, depending on the hardware platform you intend to install to and the method you wish to use. We'll get to the specifics in a moment.

In keeping with the goals of Windows NT, the installation program for the operating system is remarkably similar to the installation program for Windows v3.1. A character-based installation routine is followed by a graphical routine and the screens are very similar.

RISC-based computers, though varied in construction, generally have one thing in common: a CD-ROM drive. You should know up front that your computer, if RISC-based, must either be supported by drivers contained in the Windows NT box or the computer's manufacturer must supply you with a HAL. HAL, an acronym for the Hardware Abstraction Layer of Windows NT, makes the hardware differences among different architectures transparent to the Windows NT operating system. The list of fully supported RISC machines for which HALs are included in the Windows NT box is found in the *Hardware Compatibility Guide* that accompanies Windows NT. All RISC installations are performed by CD-ROM drive. Intel x86-based computers, including the i386, i486, and Pentium processor lines, which constitute the bulk of the personal computer industry, have three installation options: diskette, CD-ROM, or network-based installations.

Before you start the installation process, there are a few things you need to have ready. Most installations of Windows NT are to existing

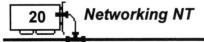

DOS and OS/2 systems. There's good news and bad news. Windows NT in its initial release supports FAT and HPFS from existing systems. That's the good news. The bad news is that the "DoubleSpace" technology for disk compression, which Microsoft has included in DOS version 6.x, is not supported. Windows NT will see the uncompressed drive with the large compressed drive file, but that's all. Keep this in mind, as any existing applications and data files that exist on the compressed drive will be unavailable. If you have standard FAT or OS/2 HPFS partitions, you can select to keep the partitions, and all data and programs will remain intact.

You should also consider how you want to use Windows NT. The OS supports multiple boot configurations, so that the machine can run DOS, OS/2, and Windows NT, where you choose the OS to boot with when the machine starts. In order to do this though, you have some restrictions on the file system you can use as the boot drive. The following chart shows the options and applicable file systems. Bear in mind that these options apply only to Intel x86-based machines, as RISC-based machines cannot run OS/2 or DOS.

| | | Operating System Options | | | |
		Windows NT	Windows NT and DOS	Windows NT and OS/2	Windows NT, DOS, and OS/2
Possible Boot Drive Partitions	NTFS (Windows NT File System)	X			
	HPFS (High Performance File System)	X		X	
	FAT (File Allocation Table)	X	X	X	X

Figure 2-1
File System Options Based on Operating System

Taking these items into consideration before you install Windows NT will save you lots of headaches after you're up and running. As you may expect, OS/2 and DOS cannot read or even identify an NTFS drive. One solution for a system that already has DOS on it is to leave the FAT partition intact, and as an option, add an additional drive for an NTFS volume. NT will install just fine to FAT or HPFS but you won't have the file and directory security features that NTFS offers. NTFS is the only choice when you need user and group level security of your files and directories. NTFS also allows for auditing of files. Another option is to backup all DOS data and then repartition the drive as FAT for the boot drive and create an additional partition for NTFS.

With all of these disk and partition options decided, there are a few more items that require attention before you install the operating system. I am not going to go out on a limb and date this book by suggesting the minimum requirements for running Windows NT, because these requirements have changed regularly depending on the documentation you are reading and the version you are running. I will, however, describe the ideal Windows NT machine.

The following specification will give you the best level of performance, compatibility, and options, using currently available technology.

- Intel Pentium 66-Mhz computer
- 450+ kb/s CD ROM Drive
- Adaptec 154x or 174x SCSI controller
- (2) 400 MB+ SCSI-2 hard drives
- 32-MB RAM
- 16-bit Ethernet or Token Ring network card

Windows NT will run on a system having less than these options, but consult your Windows NT documentation for the minimums.

Before you start the installation, know your equipment. Determine the hardware settings of installed options like SCSI cards and network card, as well as sound cards and I/O ports like your COM ports and parallel ports. Many of these settings, such as the IRQ (interrupt) and base I/O address, are important to enable Windows NT to run.

The installation instructions are going to focus on the Intel x86-based platform since this represents the largest group of Windows NT

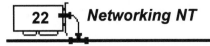

installations. The RISC-based install is dependent on the hardware manufacturer and therefore would severely restrict the usability of this chapter for the largest population of Windows NT users.

Diskette Install

If you are going to install Windows NT from diskette, place the Windows NT Disk 1 in your boot drive and power on the machine. After loading the micro-kernel or miniature of the NT operating system and looking at the hardware in your system, you are presented with the first of several character-based setup screens. Comprehensive help is available at every step of the install process. Just press the F1 function key. On this opening screen, notice an important option. The installation program is also the means by which you can repair a corrupted installation of Windows NT with the "R" option. The blank disk that is used during the installation is used by the repair option. We'll cover the emergency disk later in this chapter.

You are presented with a screen that is familiar for Windows users, which allows you to choose an express setup or a custom setup. The express setup option bypasses many of the choices given for installation options. I think it ought to be a standard, that when given the choice between an express and custom setup, the user be informed of exactly what they're missing if they choose "express." Most manuals will tell you "When in doubt, choose the express installation." As a systems integrator, I can tell you the opposite is usually true. I'll walk you through the entire installation routine, and show where the custom and express options differ.

SCSI Detection Phase

After selecting the custom or express option, the Windows NT install program will attempt to determine the existence of and, if found, the model and settings of the SCSI card. You should consult the most recent hardware compatibility list for Windows NT to determine which cards are supported by NT right out of the box. If you have a SCSI card that is not supported by drivers in the Windows NT box, but whose manufacturer provides NT drivers, you must choose the custom install option. The express option will look for supported SCSI cards, and if one is not found, the install program continues. With the custom install, the program will tell you what it found, if anything, and then will give you the opportunity to load a manufacturer's driver and find additional SCSI cards.

System Options Phase

After the SCSI detect phase the installation program attempts to determine the basic system settings. CPU type, display type, mouse type, keyboard type, and layout are all detected by the program. Using the custom install option, you have the opportunity to change the detected settings. With the express install, the program assumes that it's detections are correct and does not give you the chance to change any settings. All machines based on the Intel x86 chip are not the same; BIOS chips and other support chips vary depending on the manufacturer, and the HAL for each of these variations of the architecture is different. The installation program was designed in conjunction with hundreds of hardware manufacturers to determine ways for the install program to detect their hardware and it is very accurate. Once the system options have been detected or specified, the Windows NT installation program will ask for Disk 2.

Disk and Partition Phase

After loading files from Disk 2, the Windows NT installation program will begin setting up your disk. Up to this point, Windows NT has loaded every file that it has read into memory. What happens at this point depends entirely on the state of your system before you began the install of Windows NT. The installation will detect FAT, HPFS, and NTFS partitions, and you can format any partition as NTFS or FAT. Both express and custom install options offer the same choices. During the partition setup, you can define an unlimited number of partitions. Also, be aware that, although you may ask the installation program to format a partition as NTFS, initially, it will be FAT. The setup program will convert it to NTFS later in the installation.

After you select partition specifications, you need to select the default root directory that Windows NT will be installed to. The default is **WINNT**. After that, the installation program will start asking for disks until it reaches Disk 9 at which point you will be asked to remove the disk and reboot the system. The rest of the setup is graphical.

Software Options Phase

Once the system has rebooted, you must enter your name and company, and select a computer name. The computer name is important because, in a workgroup of Windows NT and Windows for Workgroup machines as well as in a LAN Manager-based network, this computer name is what will identify your computer to other users. The name shouldn't be the same as the workgroup or domain name. If you are not familiar with domains or workgroups, don't worry; we'll cover all of that later in Part Two.

Next you have to choose a language/locale for your system. This determines some of the international settings for your system like currency format, units of measure, and so on.

If you selected custom install, the installation program presents you with a dialog box in which you can choose whether or not to install networking, select printers, search the hard drive for existing applications, and set up specific components of Windows NT. The components are like those in Windows 3.1 You can choose to install accessories, readme files, wallpaper, etc. The express install does not give you these options.

The next setup option is for virtual memory. This also appears only if you have selected custom install. In an express installation, the virtual memory settings are determined by the installation program based on available disk space and the amount of physical memory in the computer. The virtual memory settings for Windows NT are similar to the swap file that is used by Windows 3.1 in 386 Enhanced mode. Virtual memory acts like physical RAM, but it uses space on the hard drive to do it. The difference is that in Windows 3.1, a swap file was optional. Windows NT requires virtual memory. Windows NT sets up a special file on the hard drive that acts like memory. If you set up a 30-MB virtual memory file, Windows NT sees it as 30 MB of additional physical RAM. The rule of thumb for determining the best size of the virtual memory file is roughly twice the size of true physical RAM. If you have 16 MB of RAM, your virtual memory file should be about 32 MB. The virtual memory file is used by NT to store information from true RAM that is not currently needed. When physical RAM is full of information, items of lesser priority are "swapped" to the virtual memory file while higher priority functions are executed. Once complete, the swapped data is moved back to physical RAM for continued execution. Virtual memory files can be placed on multiple drives to improve performance. Placing two files on the same physical drive would slow things down, because writing would have to take place to both files, alternately. By placing the files on separate drives, each can work at its own speed, essentially writing twice as much data at one time as could be accomplished with a single file. If you are writing 10 MB worth of information, each drive can write 5 MB, which occurs simultaneously, rather than having one drive write all 10 MB.

Next up is printer selection. This option appears on express installations, and also if you selected to install a printer during the software options selections of a custom installation. You type in a name to identify the printer. It should be a unique name, as it will appear as the printer resource name to other computers in a workgroup or LAN Manager network.

Network Options

Windows NT will attempt to detect the type and model of any network card that is present in your system. You should consult the latest hardware compatibility list from Microsoft to determine what network cards are supported right out of the box. Similar to the SCSI detection phase, both installations will prompt you with a detected network card and ask you to confirm the settings of the card. The custom installation will ask if it has found the correct card, ask whether or not to search for additional cards, and gives you the opportunity to install drivers that are not provided with Windows NT. The express option assumes that it has found the correct card and only wants you to confirm the settings from the card such as IRQ and base I/O address. If, in either installation, you can select **CANCEL** from the dialog box, and the network setup will be cancelled.

The custom install also gives you the choice to install specific protocols and network services like server and workstation services and Remote Procedure Call (RPC) ability. This is the point at which you can install TCP/IP and other included network options. In general, most network options that are from third-party vendors should be installed after the initial installation of NT. The express installation will setup NetBEUI, Workstation, Server, and RPC services. These are the basic options needed to get NT working in a workgroup or domain-based network.

Disk Feeding Phase

After the network configuration, you start feeding disks. Disk 21 is the last disk; the time is approximately two minutes per disk.

Network Setup Phase II

After all the disks have been fed, the install program goes back to network settings, where you can confirm the installed adapters, protocols, and software, and check the network bindings. Bindings are a reference to the manner in which NT handles network services. Windows NT, like many network services for Novell and Microsoft, layer the different modules of a particular service. Look at it this way: A car traveling down the highway can be used as an example of binding. Four major items must be present for the car to travel; a car, driver, gasoline, and an engine. Considering the end result, none of these items are worth much alone, but when they are combined, they form a bound entity. Binding in Windows NT is similar.

The order in which these items are bound makes a big difference. The lowest-order binding is always the network card. Three bindings are present in the default setup of Windows NT. They are the NetBEUI protocol service, Workstation Service, and Server Service. Each of these eventually depends on the network card to function. These options and protocols in general will be covered in greater depth in Part Two.

If you chose the express installation, the network configuration will appear and then disappear after NT fills in the default information.

Next stop is the Workgroup/Domain setup dialog box. This appears regardless of which installation option you chose. A more lengthy discussion of workgroups and domains appears in the next chapter but for now, I'll give you an overview. Windows NT has the ability to be part of a workgroup or domain of PCs. If you have Windows for Workgroups or other Windows NT machines that you wish to connect to, you may already have a workgroup or domain name. If this is the case, you should enter the name in the boxes provided. I have a workgroup of 4 NT machines that is called "SAIL." When I setup a new Windows NT machine, I enter **SAIL** as the workgroup name so that the new machine will be included in the existing workgroup. If I give it a different name, the new machine will not see the existing machines and vice versa. It can be done, but different names usually imply different locations or a division of users who wouldn't normally interact. Domains are a bit more complicated, but the idea is the same.

If you are setting up the first machine in a relatively small group of PCs running either Windows NT or Windows for Workgroups, you can apply any name you like to the workgroup name. All subsequent machines that are set up must also have the same workgroup name in order to talk to one another.

If you are setting up the first machine in a large group of PCs that has Windows NT Advanced Server present as a domain, you can set up a domain name to connect to, and optionally specify a user name and password in the domain user accounts database. (This DOES NOT apply to machines connecting to a LAN Manager network since Windows NT sees LAN Manager as a workgroup.) This will be used to log you onto the specified domain so the account must already exist. NT will check to be sure it exists before you can continue. If you don't know the name or password, just leave it alone. You can come back to it later. Also, for NT machines connecting to a LAN Manager server, the domain name should be entered in the workgroup name edit box, not the domain edit box. We'll cover this in more detail in Chapter 7.

Environment Setup

Once all the networking stuff is complete, The install program goes into autopilot for a while, setting up the program manager, creating the groups, and inserting the icons for the groups. If you are running the express install, Windows NT searches for existing programs on the hard drive and creates an "Applications" group in the Program Manager. On an empty machine, the express install will find one program, Microsoft Quick Basic, which comes with the pseudo-DOS in Windows NT.

You may or may not have noticed something distinctly different when NT was setting up the Program Manager. That's the dual cursor, showing an hourglass and pointer at the same time. This is a representation of Windows NT's ability to multitask. The multi-pointer shows that the system is busy doing something but that it can also accept other processes. The pointer in this state is still active, unlike a solid hourglass. You may continue using the mouse, clicking to your heart's content while the system is in this state.

Next, Windows NT wants to know the name of the administrator for this machine, and the name of the everyday user of the machine. These user accounts will exist only on the system being set up. Both account names will have supervisory rights on the system. It is possible, though not recommended, to set up the accounts without passwords.

Users who specify the custom setup will then have the opportunity to select which drives to search in pursuit of already-installed software applications.

Emergency Disk Phase

Windows NT next creates an emergency repair disk. This disk holds the information stored in the registry as well as some other vital information about the system. You must provide a blank disk, formatted or not. Windows NT will format the disk, and place the information on it. The disk is used in conjunction with the "R" option of the installation program. If you select **R** from the opening screen of the install program, Windows NT will search for SCSI adapters, then ask for Disk 2 of the Windows NT disk set, and then ask for the emergency disk. Windows NT will restore all default settings to ensure the integrity of the registry. After all information is transferred off the emergency disk, Windows NT will usually request Disk 9 and continue copying default configuration files and executable files to make sure they are fresh and uncorrupted. The disks that are requested depend on the specific problem you are having, but Disk 9 and Disk 15 are the most common requests. During routine operations and in the first occurrence of its kind on any of my machines, the KERNAL32.DLL failed repeatedly to load. The repair operation solved the problem. After disk 9, Windows NT will ask for disk 15. The amount of available space on the Windows NT partition is important because although Windows NT will be replacing files, not creating new ones, the temporary storage of these files requires additional disk space which will be cleaned up at the end of the repair. Windows NT will try to find "orphaned" files to delete, which are files no longer associated with the system and marked for deletion, as a means of gaining any and all available disk space.

Next, Windows NT will want to know whether or not to reinstall the default security database and configuration database. Only do this after much forethought, because users and groups will be restored to their original configurations and any new users added will be wiped out. Also, specific drivers in the system configuration that have been added since the emergency disk was created will no longer be loaded. All other avenues for restoring the system to working order should be tried before you do this. We'll talk about crash recovery in Chapter 14 using such topics as "Last Known Good" and using the system backup to recover.

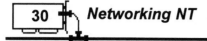

Once the emergency disk is created, NT will prompt you for date, time, and time-zone information as well as determine whether you would like to have NT automatically change the system time for daylight savings, an American biannual adjustment of local time for more hours of sunlight.

Reboot Phase

This one is pretty simple. Shut down. When you restart, what happens depends on the configuration information you specified for your disks. If you asked to format for an NTFS volume, the Windows NT operating system will read the queued request for conversion to NTFS and will convert the specified partition. Although you may have specified NTFS, the entire installation takes place with the drive in FAT format, to avoid the security and other system-related overhead during the installation. Now that the whole system is in place, the drive can be converted. The process is relatively short; about two minutes on 486/25 with a 120-MB drive. The system will reboot two more times by itself during the conversion phase. The conversion involves associating security attributes for all files in the system.

If your install called for only a FAT installation, Windows NT will start up immediately, but without the security and fault-tolerant features of NTFS.

You're done with the installation of Windows NT. If you are using one of the other methods of installation, stay tuned for the specifics of CD and network-based installs.

CD-ROM Installation

The CD-ROM-based install is nearly identical to the disk-based install except that instead of starting the installation of NT with Disk 1 from the Windows NT disks, you insert your CD-ROM into the CD-ROM drive and insert the CD-ROM boot disk, included with Windows NT, in the boot drive and start the machine. Windows NT will attempt to identify your CD-ROM drive and begin accessing files from it for the installation. All other aspects of the install and configuration are the same as the diskette-based install.

Network Installation

The network install option has a number of important advantages for sites that will have large quantities of Windows NT machines. The first advantage is speed. Other advantages include customization and compatibility. Let's look at how this is done.

At sites that have an existing network, such as LAN Manager, Novell NetWare, LANtastic, or NetWare Lite, you can use the network as a central storage area for the Windows NT files. From an existing Windows NT machine, you can upload the entire contents of the 21 Windows NT disks or the Windows NT CD-ROM to a central directory on an existing MS-DOS-based network like those mentioned above. What you wind up with is a directory on the target server or network that contains everything that was on the disks or CD-ROM— a total of 1072 files including a tiny OS2 directory with two files in it, totalling nearly 28 MB of hard drive space.

From that point, new machines can connect to the network using DOS. As an example, you bring in a new HP Vectra VL and set it up to boot to a Novell network. Once you reach the **F:\LOGIN>** prompt, you simply log onto and go to the directory holding the Windows NT files. You run the **WINNT.EXE** program and the first thing that happens is that a boot disk is created with a blank floppy you supply. Next, Windows NT will copy all needed files to your system, into a directory called **WIN_NT.~LS**. You are instructed to reboot with the new floppy disk and the installation program takes over, moving the files that are already on your local hard drive to the correct locations.

Bear in mind that doing this requires that your new machine must first be connected to a network holding the Windows NT files and running MS-DOS. The core files for Windows NT cannot initially be up-

loaded to the network without at least one NT machine having access to the net. The command line to upload the files is:

```
SETUP /n /i initial.inf /s A:\ /d <destination>
```

This must be run from a Windows NT machine with access to the network where the destination is a drive letter that points to the network. The command line will upload all the disks to the destination.

Next, go to the machine that will be the new NT machine. Make certain that it meets the minimum system requirements, format the local hard drive as FAT, and load DOS, if it isn't already there. The drive should have at least 85 MB of free space. Remember that Windows NT does not understand DoubleSpace compressed drives so do not use that option when installing DOS 6.x. Next, connect to the network using the normal means you would to connect any DOS-based machine to the network. Once connected, run the **WINNT.EXE** program from the directory where you installed the Windows NT files. The boot disk is created. You reboot with the new boot disk in the floppy drive, run the setup, and you're up and running. It is very easy. The initial time it takes to upload the files to the network and the time to create the boot disk and copy the files down from the network is significantly outweighed by the quickness of the installation when you consider the time to set up twenty machines.

Potential Problems

One problem you may have with this is that your new machines may have no problems connecting to the DOS-based network to set up the program, but once NT takes over, the card you are using may not be supported. Make certain you have drivers for the card or that it is supported out of the box by Windows NT. Another potential pitfall is that the network you are trying to connect to may not be supported after you install Windows NT. If you got your files from a Novell or Banyan network while still running DOS, for example, once Windows NT is set up, your machine will not be able to access the network until you load the requester software for the network in question. One rather ungraceful solution to this problem is to leave dual-boot functionality in your system so that if you need to get to the network from time to time, you can boot up with DOS and connect to the network as a DOS machine, get your files or run an application, and then reboot back to NT when you are finished.

Computer Profile Setup

A fourth option for installation of Windows NT, called Computer Profile Setup (CPS) does exist but is not widely used. A program in the Windows NT Resource Kit allows an administrator to create a default profile of a Windows NT machine, store all configuration information and file information about that machine, and subsequently use the profile to install pre-configured Windows NT on new machines. All machines receiving this preconfigured Windows NT must be identical! Any slight variation in the BIOS version; video BIOS version; installed options; or hard drive size, type, and configuration can ruin any chance of a smooth installation. The creation of a profile must be completed on a single Windows NT machine whose configuration is *identical* to the machines that you wish to use the profile on. The installation of the profile will ask only for a domain name, if it is necessary, and a specific computer name. Everything else will be the same as the configuration of the "master" NT machine where the profile was created. As of the writing of this book, the "Computer Profile Setup" or CPS was not available for testing so no other information can be provided.

As a final feature of this chapter, Figure 2-3 shows the command-line options available for the Setup program in Windows NT.

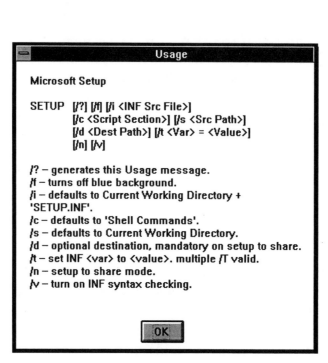

Figure 2-2
Setup Program Command Line Options

Next stop, networking concepts written in plain English. You need to know this stuff, so stick with me. I promise more pictures.

Part Two

Networking Basics

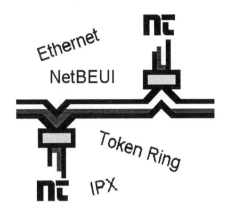

Ethernet
NetBEUI
Token Ring
IPX

Networking NT - Part Two

Networking Basics

| Chapter 3 | Networking Concepts and Design |

| Chapter 4 | Windows NT Protocols and Services |

Chapter 3

Networking Concepts and Design

Windows NT and the entire Microsoft family of networking products use two different network structures: workgroups and domains. Some of the products have both abilities and some have only one. Windows NT, by itself, is a workgroup-based operating system. The Windows NT Advanced Server product is a domain-based operating system. The Windows NT package can connect to a domain, but cannot establish one; in the same way, DOS machines can connect to a Novell LAN but it require the NetWare software in order to establish the LAN.

In this chapter we'll take a look at workgroups and domains and the advantages and disadvantages of both structures. If you're from the Novell camp, this may be interesting to you—understanding how the other half lives. Before we get into it though, it's important that we look at Windows NT networking from a generic point of view, aside from topologies, and understand how Windows NT does networking.

Networking Functions of Windows NT

Beneath the mild mannered interface of Windows NT, there beats the heart of a multi-protocol animal with capabilities to connect to just about anything. The Microsoft view of networking is very impressive! If I were building a network from scratch, I'd build with NT and Advanced Server. I do not, however, live in a vacuum and I was a Certified NetWare Engineer (CNE) long before I was a Microsoft Certified Professional (MCP). NetWare is everywhere and fortunately, Windows NT connects to NetWare. Later, we'll look at how the NetWare connection is made.

Windows NT supports multiple network cards, running multiple protocols. If you recall, during the installation of Windows NT, you were asked about what network card was present, what the configuration was and what networking software services should be loaded. To change any of these settings you can use the control panel under the Network icon.

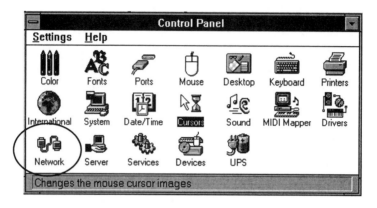

Figure 3-1
Network Control Panel

Well, almost any of them. The Server, Services, and Devices icons do play a role in the NT networking scheme, but they are secondary to the Network icon. We'll cover them next. For now, click on the network icon to take you into the primary network configuration screen, shown in Figure 3-2.

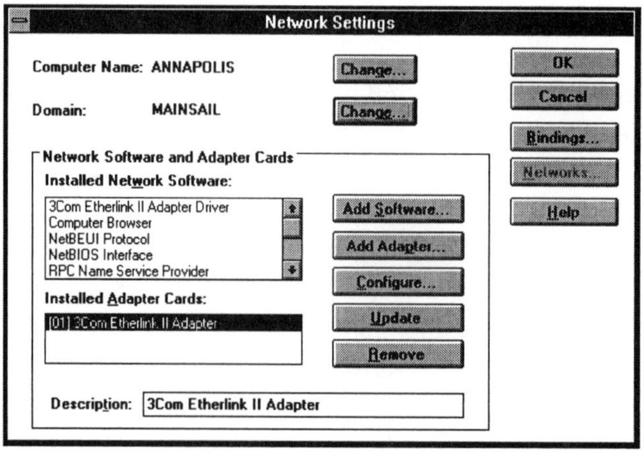

Figure 3-2
Network Settings Dialog Box

The machine from which this screen shot was taken was an Advanced Server machine with a 3Com 3C503 card in it. This would be a good time to remind you that Windows NT and Windows NT Advanced Server are nearly identical, with Advanced Server having the additional ability to establish and manage a domain.

As you can see from Figure 3-2, there are many different software drivers loaded. The machine is running NetBEUI, NetBIOS, and several other drivers. Some are protocols and some are services. These software drivers control what Windows NT can communicate with. The next chapter covers the protocols and services in much greater detail.

You will notice that this machine has only one network card installed. Adding cards to the machine is easy. Just click on the **Add Adapter...** button and select either a driver from the list of provided drivers, or, if your driver is not on the list and has been provided by a third-party vendor, select the **<Other>** option and insert the disk containing the NT driver for your network card.

Figure 3-3
Adding Network Adapters

With multiple network cards in a single machine you can dramatically increase performance by delegating specific communications to specific cards. For instance, card 1 can be talking TCP/IP protocol and card 2 can be talking NetBEUI/NetBIOS. The possibilities are nearly limitless. I'll show you that in just a minute.

Configuring a network card is a very easy process using Windows NT. If you are using a "smart" network card, there's no reason to open

your computer. The `Configure` option of the dialog box is to configure the hardware settings of the network card. These settings tell Windows NT how to talk to your card. If more than one is present, select the appropriate card from the list box before pressing `Configure`. Figure 3-4 shows the hardware options for a 3Com card.

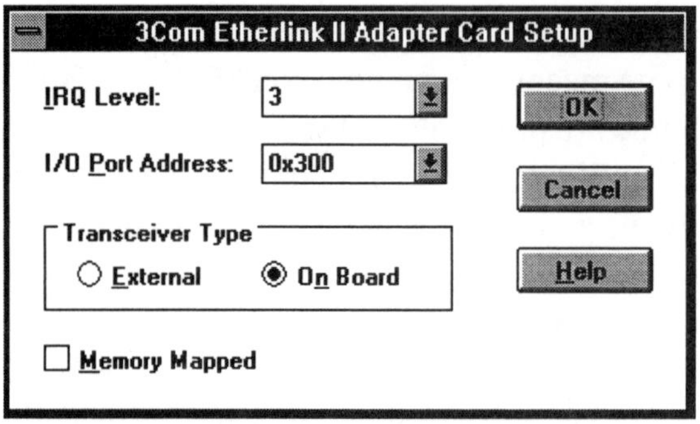

3Com Etherlink II Adapter Card Setup

I<u>R</u>Q Level: 3

I/O <u>P</u>ort Address: 0x300

┌ Transceiver Type ┐
  ○ <u>E</u>xternal   ◉ O<u>n</u> Board

☐ <u>M</u>emory Mapped

OK
Cancel
<u>H</u>elp

Figure 3-4
Network Hardware Configuration

When a vendor issues new network drivers for either software or hardware, you use the `Update` option. Just select either a software component or adapter card to be updated and click on update. You'll be prompted to insert a disk containing the updated software.

On the right side of the dialog box you'll find the `Bindings...` button. It is an informational look at how the network services in you workstation or server are put together and gives you the ability to enable or disable particular services for a network card. Earlier, I mentioned two network cards running different services—this is where you would enable this function.

Bindings give the Windows NT operating system modularity. Rather than designing one monolithic driver that controls all functions of a card for a protocol, bindings are a way to divide the driver into separate, manageable parts. There's a driver for the card itself and additional drivers for each of the services and protocols, which can be combined with the card driver to provide a functional service. The manufacturer of a network card only has to write a driver to the Windows NT Application Programming Interface (API). An API is a set of functions and commands for a particular environment; the means in which you write software to interact with the system.

All the additional protocols and services are a separate unit. The NetBEUI protocol is the same whether you using a 3C503 or an NE2000 network card, so why make a hardware driver with the protocol included? Remember our discussion on the HAL? The network drivers are similar. The card driver is written to a common standard so that any driver, protocol, or service in Windows NT can attach to that card. You don't need a separate self-contained driver for each different protocol or service. All the pieces fit together to form a service or function.

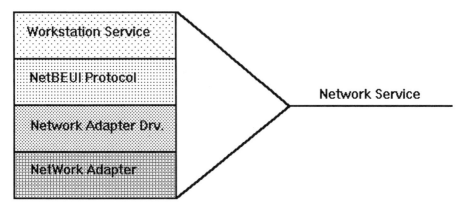

Figure 3-5
Binding Concept

Figure 3-5 illustrates the concept of bindings. Multiple modules are combined or bound together to form a service. If you are a NetWare administrator, and are not currently using Open Datalink Interface drivers (ODI), then using the WSGEN or SHGEN programs from Novell gets pretty tiring every time Novell releases a new version of their shell software. You have to go back and regenerate a whole new workstation driver because the protocol and hardware driver are combined. With the bindings in Windows NT, you just update the specific driver that is af-

fected. If the NetBEUI protocol has been updated, that's the only driver you need to deal with. The ODI drivers in NetWare are very similar to this.

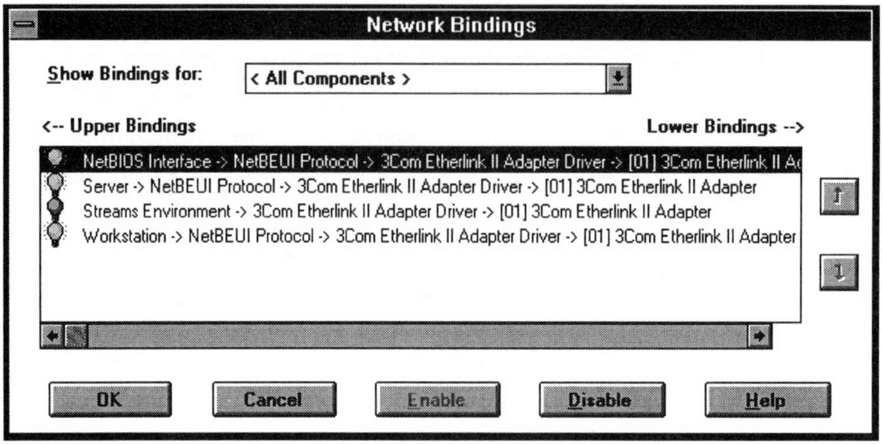

Figure 3-6
Network Bindings

Figure 3-6 shows the binding for a 3Com card. There are four services that the card normally runs. I currently have the Streams Environment service disabled. As you can see, each service is a series of drivers linked together in a hierarchical fashion. The lowest order of the binding is always the card itself.

The grayed out **Networks...** button of the network control panel is for selecting the order in which Windows NT browses different types of networks. If you are connecting to several type of networks and want to establish a priority for one network or another, this is the dialog box to do it in.

Be aware that just about anything you change in the network configuration dialog box will require you to shut down the machine before the changes take effect. While it is possible to start and stop a particular driver or service without restarting, changing the domain name, computer name, adding new protocols, changing hardware settings, and several other functions, all require you to restart for the changes to take effect.

You may be wondering what happens if you configure something incorrectly. If the hardware settings are wrong or you remove a network software service that is vital to the system, Windows NT will let you know about it, but in a stable manner, giving you the ability to review the errors and trace the real cause of the problem. A far cry from the cryptic error messages of the past, Windows NT documents everything that goes wrong, and each error is specific.

Your first indication that something has gone wrong is a discreet dialog box, like the one shown in Figure 3-7

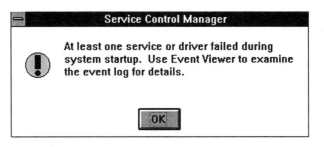

Figure 3-7
Something Didn't Work

At that point, locate the Event Viewer utility in the Adminstrative Tools group of the Program Manager. This utility helps to show what happened. It is shown in Figure 3-8. The root of networking problems usually can be traced back to the network card and improper settings.

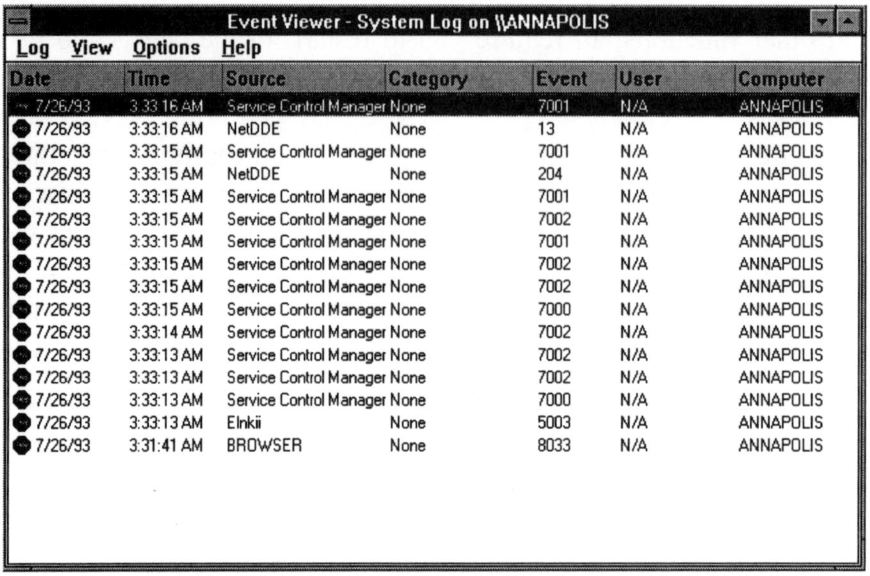

Figure 3-8
Errors in the Event Viewer

Your best bet is to work your way to the bottom of the list. Generally speaking, one service or process fails because another service was not available. Looking at the bottom of the list of recent errors will usually give you the root cause of the problem. In this case the "Elnkii" or EtherLink II driver failed because the settings were wrong for the card. All the errors above that were caused by the fact that the network card could not be accessed. All you have to do is go back to the Network control panel and change the settings on the network card using the **Configure** option. Problem solved!

Microsoft Networking

As stated in the overview of Windows NT, networking was built into NT at the beginning. NT was always conceptualized as a network operating system. For many, the term "Network Operating System" may invoke the image of an isolated PC, sitting in a wiring closet, without a monitor and usually without a keyboard—like Novell's NetWare v3.1x or 4.x. This is known as a dedicated server network, where the server

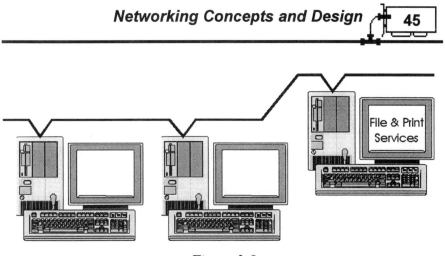

Figure 3-9
Dedicated Server Networking

does nothing but perform file, print, and I/O services for communications with external systems. Dedicated server systems have their advantages: chief among these is the significant reduction in the possibility that a user could crash the network. With no person sitting at the server, there is a very low probability that a user will kick the box or lock it up due to an error. Windows NT can be dedicated, but the second most popular network structure, Peer-to-Peer, is the primary design behind Windows NT.

Workgroups and Peer-to-Peer Networking

Windows NT contains both workstation and server services. This means that a Windows NT machine can use another machine's resources as well as offer its own resources to other machines. These resources

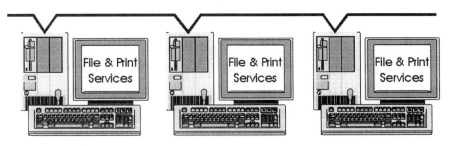

Figure 3-10
Peer-to-Peer Networking

include file and print services primarily. That is the concept behind peer-to-peer networking. As far as Windows NT is concerned, peer-to-peer computing is the same as workgroup computing. Workgroup-based computing is part of Windows NT and Windows for Workgroups. Using workgroups is a way of breaking up computers into smaller, more manageable, and logical groups of machines. Setting up workgroups among the sales staff, accounting staff, and so on keeps similar users together: those who will be working on the same files and applications and printing to the same printers. There are three primary objections to peer-to-peer or workgroup-based networking. They are:

Central Storage

The biggest objection that network integrators have to peer-to-peer networks is a lack of manageability. Rather than storing all files and maintaining all relevant services on a single dedicated machine, applications, printing, and data files are spread out across the network. This is, indeed, a valid concern. Users need to be aware of the structure and function of the network in order to properly operate. Network administrators can make it somewhat easier, but the core reality exists that there is no way to centrally administrate a peer-to-peer network. Helping users locate where they stored files and educating them about paths and directories is mandatory.

Being able to share hard drives and printers gives users the flexibility needed for workgroups, something that is much more difficult to establish and maintain in a dedicated server network, where administration of users, rights, printers, and many other resources is centralized.

Security

Security or the lack of it is another large concern with workgroups. In a small group of trusted people, this is usually not a concern, and if your network will be a small one, then security concerns shouldn't rule your decision to install a peer-to-peer network.

In Windows NT, user accounts and groups are managed at the machine level. Users who wish to access resources on another NT or WFW machine must pass the security of the machine they want to access. In a workgroup, an NT user logs onto his or her machine. The security authentication he or she passes through during logon only establishes the rights at that machine. The user of a machine has the right to share or not share resources on that machine and to set the number of users that can share that resource at any one time. Unless the administrator sets up standards on every machine in the workgroup (by physically configuring each one), The availability of shared resources is up to each user.

To give you an example of a potential problem area, let's say that Cindy has some sales figures on her local hard drive that she has been working on. If Cindy goes home and shuts off her machine, you can't access those files. If you can't start the machine, you can't share the files. If the system were to go down, you would be in the same situation: unable to access needed files. In general, it's not a very good idea to put the productivity of the network in the hands of all the users. Things happen.

An alternative to this problem is to set up a "dedicated" Windows NT or WFW machine to hold all relevant files and applications. The machine will still be part of a workgroup but all necessary shares can be administered from one point. Peer-to-peer functionality still exists for convenience, but isn't the backbone of the network. Printing can either be handled at this "dedicated" server or at the individual workstations.

Shares are resources such as a directory on a hard drive or a printer. An example of a share is **D:\WIN31**. The share would offer the **WIN31** directory as a shareable resource that other users in the workgroup can access from their machines.

Shared resources in a workgroup have only three settings:

- Read-only
- Change
- Full Control

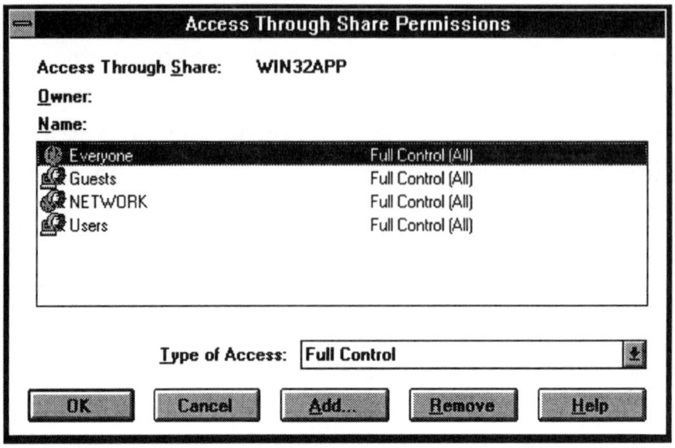

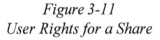

Figure 3-11
User Rights for a Share

Each of these rights is established and maintained on each individual machine. The control of groups and users is fairly robust, but is cumbersome at times due to the lack of central administration. As there are no groups or user accounts for Windows for Workgroups, if you limit access of an NT resource to a particular group—any group—the WFW machines cannot access it. Only when a shared resource has one of the groups "Everyone," "Guests," "Users," or "NETWORK" defined with rights in its permissions list will a WFW machine be able to get at the resource. In doing so, you leave the door wide open for anyone on the net to access the resource, because these groups require no special membership. We'll get into users and groups and rights later in the book, in Part Four.

The bottom line on security is that if your network includes WFW machines, you may have some difficulties, and overall, the administration of security is not very efficient in a workgroup-based network with a large number of machines.

Performance

Windows NT machines in a workgroup environment suffer very little in terms of performance. That last sentence may raise a few eyebrows, but I fully intend to back it up. You see, "traditional" peer-to-peer networks run on top of an operating system that was never designed to work on a network. The fact that peer-to-peer networks work at all on DOS-based machines is truly a credit to the programmers who have written them. The performance of machines in these networks generally suffer because each shared resource and the host processor must each take time to handle remote requests while maintaining its own operations. Now, Windows NT has the same duties, but within an operating system that was designed to work that way. The truth is, NT machines in a peer-to-peer arrangement see very little decrease in performance. The system is inherently multitasking. Obviously, the system would run slightly faster if it didn't have to share anything, but the performance hit is minimal.

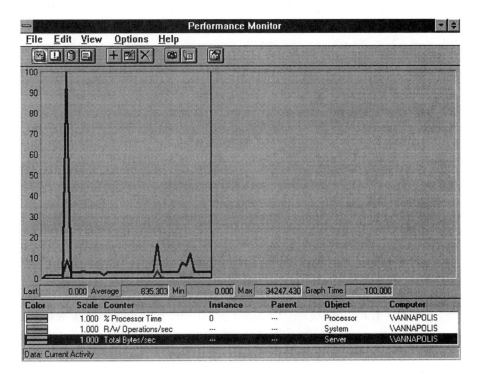

Figure 3-12
Windows NT Network Performance

Figure 3-12 shows the Windows NT Performance Monitor in action during a read from the hard disk by another workgroup machine. The very large spike that goes to 100 represents the server service, but notice the tiny spike inside of it that goes only to about 9. That is the processor. The last resource here, the system, didn't even budge during the operation. Windows NT does a great job of sharing its resources!

Finally, one other note of interest regarding workgroup-based computing with Windows NT. Workgroups have names which define a logical grouping of machines like "SALES" or "ACCOUNTING." Windows NT machines can access shared resources in other workgroups, but not by point-and-click. It has to be done manually by typing in the UNC name for the resource you want to access. UNC stands for Universal Naming Convention; it is a standard and the way that resources are referred to in Windows NT. **\\SAIL\CD-ROM** is a valid UNC name for the server **SAIL** and the resource name **CD-ROM** in that server. The browser does not see the other server because it is not on the same workgroup. Access is the same as in any other resource; it just has to be done manually.

So what do we have? We've got dedicated server networks and peer-to-peer networks. One focuses on a single, all-powerful machine dedicated to the network, the other gives the same abilities to all users on a network. The advantage of peer-to-peer networks is their flexibility, and the advantage of dedicated servers is fault tolerance, central administration, and central storage. In point of fact, a cross between the two is the best arrangement.

Large corporate networks have groups of users working on similar projects and files. Generally in close proximity to one another, it is the perfect environment for quickly sharing printers, programs, and data files. In the larger picture, however, users need to be tied together from across the company for database sharing, centralized administration, and more.

It is possible to set up a Windows NT machine to be a print server and file server: a machine that nobody uses. This would resemble a dedicated-server network. Security would still be a problem when you consider the limitation of WFW machines in that network. If the network were entirely made up of Windows NT machines, security would not really be an issue because of the Windows NT ability to handle groups and individual users when granting access to shared resources.

Domains

The next level up in the Windows NT networking structure is the domain. The domain has been part of Microsoft's networking strategy in nearly all of their networking products. A domain has features and abilities over and above the features offered by workgroup-based networks. Domains are made up of a logical grouping of multiple servers and workstations, similar in concept to workgroups. However, domains can maintain a master security database, replicate security databases among domain controllers, share resources, and trust other domains. It's the best of both worlds. Peer-to-peer functionality is still available, but with the advantage of centralized administration of security and corporate-wide sharing of resources.

You should realize up front that you cannot set up a domain with a Windows NT machine. In order to establish a domain, you must be using the Windows NT Advanced Server product. Windows NT machines can be members of a domain, but cannot establish one.

For many who are familiar with the NetWare environment, Novell did not have this kind of functionality until NetWare 4.x. Prior to that

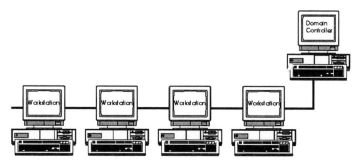

Figure 3-13
Basic Domain—Similar to NetWare

release, Novell servers stood alone, from an administrative standpoint. While it is very easy to connect multiple servers into a larger Novell LAN, administration, security, and all other points of configuration were based on each individual server.

Domains are much closer to the dedicated server network design since, in many cases, the domain controllers are unattended machines. In order to have a domain, the network must have a domain controller. The options beyond that point are numerous and complicated. A single domain with a domain controller and workstations is the closest to a Novell v3.1x network.

The domain controller, which must be an Advanced Server, holds the security database for the domain. When you create a user or a group, or modify security permissions, the changes occur on the domain controller. A domain can have only one domain controller, but can have many servers. What this means is that when you create a user, you can give that user rights to any resource, contained on any server in the domain. When a user logs into the network, he or she is logging into a domain. The domain security sets up access or denial of access for all domain resources. If your domain contains three servers—a database on one server, a spreadsheet on another server, and a graphics application on yet another server—you can grant access to all of them through one logon. Using resources on another server does not require additional logons. You can't think of a network as a single server but as a domain; a group of connected resources that you log onto with one authentication.

The security database that resides on the domain controller can also be replicated or copied. After the first Advanced Server in a domain, which takes the role of a domain controller, each additional Advanced Server in a domain becomes a receptor to the domain security database. In a LAN Manager 2.x domain this is known as a backup domain controller. If the domain controller is busy or unavailable, any other Advanced Server in the domain can authenticate users and process logon requests. Although you make changes to the domain security database from any Advanced Server, the changes all go back to the domain controller. Every five minutes, the other Advanced Servers in the domain ask the domain controller if any changes have been made to the security database. If changes have been made, the domain controller sends the requesting server a copy of the changes. Only the changes are transmitted, not the entire database.

Domains are a great way to organize your network. Servers that have many different applications and functions can be split into several servers each performing specific roles, thus lightening the load on any one server.

Joining domains together builds on the organizational strength of the whole network. Domains have the ability to "trust" one another. It means that one domain can use resources on another domain if a trust relationship is established. The relationship can be one-way as well. The MIS department that oversees all LAN operations may want unlimited access to all domains in the company, but the MIS managers don't want users in the individual domains to have any access to the MIS domain. That's a one-way trust relationship. When establishing a trust relationship, the domain that is trusting can gain access to the security database of that domain. You can have a domain that has all the security for all domains contained on it. All other domains trust the security domain, and thus, even among multiple domains, you can still have centralized administration.

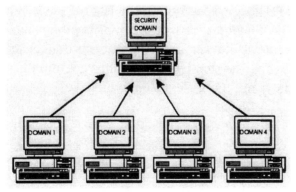

Figure 3-15
Security Domain for Multiple Domains

All of the domains represented above trust the security domain, and as a result, they can access the user and group list of the security domain. All security can be administered at the security domain for all domains. Very powerful!

Workgroups and domains can coexist on the same wire, and workgroups appear identical to domains. After that it gets kind of complicated, so pay attention. For simplicity's sake I've broken it down into two categories: a Windows NT machine connected to a domain and a Windows NT machine connected to a workgroup.

A Windows NT Machine Connected to a Domain

The NT machine can connect to, browse, and use resources on the domain and workgroups connected to the same wire. The workgroups appear as just another domain, and from a browsing standpoint, there is no way to tell that it is a workgroup, rather than a domain.

A Windows NT Machine Connected to a Workgroup

The machine can interact with its own workgroup and other workgroups but cannot access a domain except as a "Guest."

In later chapters we'll cover the specifics of users, groups, rights, accessing remote resources, configuring machines for workgroup or server usage, and more. Stay tuned. If you are implementing an NT machine in a LAN environment other than workgroup- or domain-based, such as NetWare, hang on. The step-by-step sections get into the nitty-gritty of establishing the connection. Next stop, protocols.

Chapter 4

Windows NT Protocols and Services

As mentioned throughout this book, Windows NT can connect to just about anything. Windows NT comes out of the box supporting a few well-selected protocols. The primary mover of information in the networked Windows NT environment is NetBEUI. NetBEUI is a modification of the NetBIOS interface, now implemented as a protocol. Before we get into the guts of these methods of communication, I need to lay some groundwork for the reader's benefit.

In order to understand networking, and why there are tremendous difficulties with networking, you need to understand that a network is not just a cable connecting two machines together. If that's all there was to it, books like this wouldn't be needed. To communicate with another machine, there are many different factors to consider. In the mid-fifties, when networking was just beginning to make a showing in the computer industry as a means of connecting terminals to mainframe computers, there wasn't anybody to tell companies how to go about it. IBM and DEC had to make up the designs as they went along. As a result, the process to communicate from a mainframe to a terminal was entirely defined by those companies. As you might expect, the DEC and IBM "standards" didn't interoperate. Now, as we approach the millennium, the number of different ways that one computer can talk to another is staggering. At times, one wishes that there were only two different methods, like there were in the fifties.

The OSI Model

To answer the screams of network vendors and end-users, who cried for a standard by which computers connect to one another, the International Standards Organization, or ISO, stepped in to help. What the ISO came up with is a model that defines the different functions of communication between computers. It is known as the OSI model, which stands for Open Systems Interconnection. The OSI model, which is more of a guide for development of networking services than a standard that developers write to, has become the backbone of networking. It is a way to describe the services that a particular driver, protocol, or process provides.

The OSI model is broken down into seven layers of functionality. Each layer has a specific function. Figure 4-1 shows what the OSI model looks like:

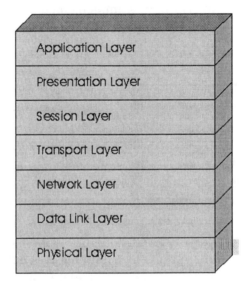

Application Layer

Presentation Layer

Session Layer

Transport Layer

Network Layer

Data Link Layer

Physical Layer

Figure 4-1
The OSI Model

The top of the model is the layer that a user sees: the layer that is the interface. The bottom of the model is the physical hardware: the cable, the connectors. What happens in between these layers is how networking works. The top is the database application you run every day; the bottom is the network card and cable attached to the back of your machine. Everything else is "Dark Voodoo Magic." I have a friend, Tyler Stowe, who says that his job is to work on 6½ layers of the OSI model and the trainers and software support people take care of the other half layer. From a network administrator's point of view, that's accurate. As administrators, I and many others have to see that everything functions, and half of the Application Layer is making sure that an application, such as a database, is configured correctly. Everything else is up to the user. So long as the application runs, communicates with a printer, and gets its data properly, the user is the last thing standing in the way of a perfect system. Unfortunately, that last half of a layer seems to create more problems than any of the others combined.

Keep in mind that the OSI model is a method to describe network functionality. Often, a particular service or process of the network overlaps several layers of the model, or doesn't completely cover one layer. I'll describe the order of the layers from a real-world perspective.

Application Layer

A user, sitting at a workstation on the network, issues a copy command from the interface, be it DOS, OS/2, Windows, Windows NT, or any other interface. The command is to copy a file from the workstation to a network server. The application program, in this case the command interpreter, retrieves the location of the file and prepares to copy the file.

Presentation Layer

The Presentation Layer begins translating the raw data from the file that is being sent into a format that the network can understand. If the network employs security encryption, the Presentation Layer encrypts the file data so that it cannot be easily read as it travels down the wire to the destination computer, which in this case is the server.

Session Layer

The Session Layer does not work with the data to be sent, specifically. It works to establish a "session" with the receiving computer, setting up the parameters by which the two computers will communicate.

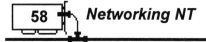

How long one machine will transmit, when to transmit, and how much has already been transmitted are all functions of the Session Layer. The "how much" function is achieved by the session layer placing markers in the data transmission which indicate the progress of the transmission. The information that the Session Layer needs to send to the other computer about the transmission itself is tacked on to the data being sent.

Transport Layer

The Transport Layer takes the data that is being sent and breaks it down into smaller, more manageable pieces called frames. Think of it this way: If you're sending a 100 KB file to another machine and the file is sent whole, if something happens to the transfer—like a collision of data on the network—the whole thing has to be sent again. By breaking up the file into smaller pieces, if a failure occurs, the retransmission can continue where it left off using the markers placed in the data transmission by the Session Layer. The Transport Layer also takes care of the "return receipt" function, which tells the sending computer that the data was received at the destination. If errors have occurred during transmission, the Transport Layer determines that there has been an error and attempts to correct the error by means of parity checking or other methods.

Network Layer

The Network Layer takes the data to be sent and addresses it. Every point of communication on the network has an address. With an Ethernet-based network, a workstation address is a 12-character alphanumeric code which is hard-coded into the network card when it is manufactured. No two network addresses can be the same. At one point a few years ago, Western Digital accidentally manufactured network cards whose addresses were the same as previously manufactured cards, this caused many problems.

The Network Layer also determines the route that the data should take in order to arrive at its destination based on the level of traffic on the network and the priority of the data being sent. Depending on the size of the frames that the Transport Layer sends to the Network Layer, the Network Layer either assembles the smaller frames into larger packets or makes smaller packets from a large frame. The data is now "right-sized" for transmission.

Data Link Layer

The Data Link Layer takes all of the information from the layers above it and packages the data into "data frames." The layer also adds error-correcting code to the frame so that on the receiving end, the network layer can assume that all transmissions are nearly error-free and retry if the data is not error-free.

Physical Layer

The Physical Layer carries the data over the network to its destination. Specifications such as medium, connectors, pin assignments, and the transmission technique to use are part of the Physical Layer. It's the hardware end of the network.

On the receiving end of the transmission, everything is done in reverse. As each layer on the sending end of the transmission place its own information into the data stream with the actual data to be sent, so the receiving machines' layers will strip away the added information, guaranteeing that the data the application layer on the receiving end gets is error-free, complete, and in the right place.

Each layer of the OSI model is designed to communicate only with the layer above it. The Session Layer of the model "thinks" that it is communicating with the Session Layer of the other computer. It simply wraps that data received from the Presentation Layer with its own information and is then pushed down to the Transport Layer. The information it is sending is important only to the Session Layer on the receiving computer.

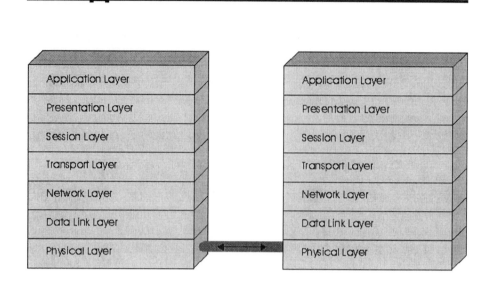

Figure 4-2
OSI Communication

That's the OSI model in a nutshell. In the early fifties, IBM and DEC had to resolve every aspect of the communications. With the OSI model, services of the network can be broken down into layers, allowing standardization. The application layer doesn't have to know anything about the network in order to run properly.

Remember that this a conceptual model. Networking services do not conform to this model strictly. It is easier to design a service with the OSI model in mind and then go back after the service is designed and describe the service in terms of the model. Sometimes a service overlaps several layers of the model, providing services from more than one layer. Conversely, sometimes a network service defines only a portion of one layer of the model.

In an ideal world, uniformity exists among communications standards. But since this isn't a world in a vacuum, Windows NT has focused on a networking model that is as close to ideal as one can get at this point in time. Let's start at the bottom.

At the bottom of the pile, there is the network card. The card is generic. Certainly, each card has different methods of interaction with other network services, but it is generic from the standpoint that, with the right software, most any method of communication is possible. The key here is that software is the enabling technology to functioning on the network. You could, in theory, design a software driver that would inter-pret keystrokes from the keyboard and make a network card issue Morse code for each keystroke. It's all in the drivers.

Microsoft wanted Windows NT to get as close to the OSI model as possible, with each layer doing its own job, and being entirely modular. With protocols today, we are getting closer to that vision, but we're not there yet. To facilitate modularity and uniformity, Microsoft has imple-mented two boundary layers in the OSI model. They are the NDIS and Transport Device Interface or TDI layers.

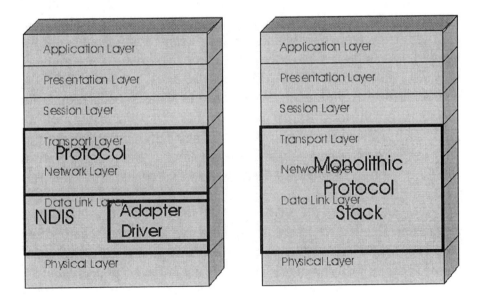

Figure 4-3
File System Options Based on Operating System

NDIS

There are two different approaches to designing a network driver. The first and least flexible is the "Monolithic Protocol Stack" method, to quote a phrase from the NT Resource Kit manual. This method combines the network adapter driver with the protocol. The whole driver is only for a specific protocol. This is similar to the IPX.COM that Novell uses as a driver for DOS machines connecting to a Novell LAN. It combines the network adapter card driver, hardware settings for the card, and protocol, which in this case is IPX/SPX, into one driver. None of the individual parts that make up the monolithic driver work with anything else.

The second approach to network drivers is the modular approach. If you are a network installer or administrator who has come across NDIS drivers, they are modular drivers for Microsoft networks. Just as the HAL in Chapter 1 set a standard for how NT would communicate with the underlying architecture of a computer, the NDIS API sets forth a standard set of commands by which a protocol can communicate with the network. When designing a network card device driver, a programmer writes the driver to the NDIS API. Any time a network uses NDIS, the network card driver plugs in. Writing to the NDIS specification is far easier than having to write a driver that defines everything in the protocol stack, such as in the monolithic example. The NDIS interface, combined with an NDIS driver for a network card, becomes a generic service which can run any protocol. Figure 4-3 shows how the two approaches look.

By developing to the NDIS standard, the card driver and protocol are separate items. An NDIS-compatible network can accept almost any protocol because the way in which it talks to the network card is standardized by the NDIS interface. The driver is a universal point of contact. Put any protocol you like on top. This concept is very similar to the ODI drivers that are used in NetWare servers and workstations. And, like the ODI drivers, multiple protocols can be used with one network card. Unlike the monolithic approach which requires one driver for each protocol/ network card, the NDIS structure allows two or more protocols to rest upon one NDIS interface.

The three protocols that ship with Windows NT that use the NDIS interface are NetBEUI, Streams-TCP/IP, and DLC. We'll get into each of these shortly. All of the adapter drivers that ship with NT are NDIS drivers.

You should know that there are some protocols that cannot work with the NDIS design. Unfortunately, Novell's IPX/SPX protocol is one of them. Novell uses a design called ODI, or Open Data Interface. Protocols in the ODI design are bound to the network card in much the same way as NDIS drivers are bound. The NDIS spec is a great method for new protocols and retrofitting older ones, but some protocols do not fit neatly into it, such as IPX/SPX. An ODI driver has to be loaded in order to run the IPX/SPX protocol. The NDIS interface cannot run it. Since all the drivers provided by Microsoft are NDIS, the NetWare requester software must replace the NDIS driver with an ODI driver. It is a hardware driver, specific to the type of network card in the machine just like the NDIS driver. Once it is loaded, the IPX/SPX protocol can be bound to the network card driver. An additional driver is loaded to give the ODI hardware driver NDIS support. Through bindings, the driver eventually ties into the other services and protocols in NT. From a user's point of view, operation is no different, but underneath, the OS is doing some very different things in order to reach the "seamless" integration with Novell LANs.

In reality, ODI and NDIS are very similar, but from two different companies who each have their own way of doing things and are trying to establish a standard. When Microsoft Windows for Workgroups was released, NetWare compatibility was achieved by an MSIPX.COM file that emulated the Novell IPX protocol. Now that NT is out, Novell has modified Microsoft's NDIS driver for their use. Tit for tat.

TDI

Beyond the transport layer, above the protocols, there is another Microsoft mechanism at work. Despite the incongruence of the Novell and Microsoft drivers for protocols and transport, which seemingly are at odds with one another, there is another layer which seeks to bring things together and present the applications and services of the network with a common method of communication. This is known as the TDI or Transport Device Interface. Upper-level networking services such as Sockets, NetBIOS, and the server and redirector of NT can still operate seamlessly with different protocols, protocol stacks, and transport methods, regardless of how they are set up, as long as they stop at the transport layer. Anything in the Transport Layer or below is covered by the TDI. If a monolithic protocol stack extends beyond the transport layer, defining functions in the session layer or above, the TDI cannot communicate with it.

The TDI rests in the session layer of the ODI model and, once again, presents the layers above it with a generic interface. An application using a NetBIOS function to communicate with another machine doesn't need to know that it is running through an ODI or NDIS protocol stack. The NetBIOS call is made to the TDI layer. The TDI then sends the call to a specific protocol stack.

The bottom line here is, for the best level of integration and modularity, write drivers for NDIS, but if you can't, write the upper level or top-end of the protocol stack to receive TDI calls. To a NetBIOS, Sockets, or server/redirector function, it doesn't matter. Now we take a closer look at the NDIS protocols that come with Windows NT.

NetBEUI

You should understand that, contrary to popular pronouncement, NetBIOS is not a protocol. It is an API; a set of commands and functions for communication over a network, but it is not a protocol. A protocol can be NetBIOS-compatible, which means that the functions and commands are derived from the NetBIOS API. Think of NetBIOS as a manual that tells programmers how to talk to the network. NetBIOS is a de facto standard within Microsoft's networking products. In Windows NT, NetBEUI and NetBIOS are two different pieces. NetBIOS is a loadable service API that allows programs that were written to communicate using NetBIOS calls to do so. NetBEUI is a protocol. NetBIOS depends on the NetBEUI protocol to transfer its calls across the network. You can have a NetBEUI network without NetBIOS running, but you can't have NetBIOS without NetBEUI.

NetBEUI, which stands for NetBIOS Extended User Interface was created by IBM in the mid-eighties as a protocol for LANs serving no more than 200 clients. NetBEUI is a very fast protocol for the smaller networks. One of the reasons it is so fast is because it is not routable. This means that you cannot install a router on your NetBEUI network to reduce traffic on one segment of the LAN.

Without a routable protocol, when a packet is sent from a workstation or server to anywhere else on the network, the packet is just "broadcast" to the network. Every station on the network must glimpse at the packet as it passes down the wire and determine whether the packet was meant for it by looking at the destination address of the packet. Every packet that is sent on the LAN has an address for the destination but without routing, the workstation sending the packet doesn't know where that destination is. The packet is addressed with a destination address and sent. Because it isn't routable, the packets that are transmitted go everywhere on the network so that all workstations can determine if the packet was meant for them. Think of it this way: If you sent a letter without a zip code, the letter would have to be passed around to each post office in the city you sent the letter to, so that each postmaster could determine if the address was in that particular postal zone. If that's all the post office did, or only had to deal with a few of these "letters," it wouldn't be too bad. As the number of letters without zip codes increases, the more work the post offices have to do to get the mail out.

The packets being sent go faster because they aren't bogged down with routing information, thus allowing a greater quantity of data to be sent with each packet. The obvious disadvantage to this protocol is that, once the number of stations climbs and network traffic climbs, the speed decreases because the packets cannot be routed to less-congested parts of the LAN.

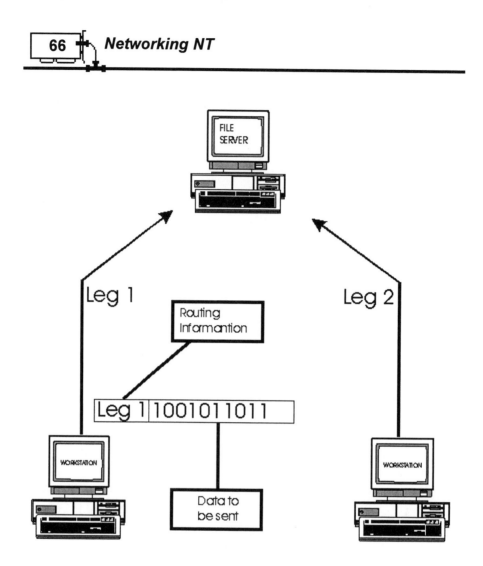

Figure 4-4
Network Routing to Reduce Traffic

In a NetWare environment, if traffic on the network is getting heavy, thus slowing performance, another network card can be added to the server and the network can be split into two "legs." The IPX/SPX protocol is routable and therefore, traffic on one leg that does not need to communicate with a machine on the other leg doesn't clog up the other leg. It stays on it's side of the router. With NetBEUI you can't do that.

Though NetBEUI is derived from NetBIOS, the version that ships with Windows NT, which is NetBEUI 3.0, is written to the TDI. Older versions of NetBEUI were written directly to NetBIOS, using NetBIOS as the interface that NetBEUI passed it commands to. Due to the new structure of Windows NT and the TDI, NetBEUI has become a full-fledged protocol. In its current version and format, NetBEUI 3.0 is occasionally referred to as NBF, or NetBIOS Frame.

Although NetBEUI is very fast on the workgroup or departmental LAN, its performance in a WAN (Wide Area Network) or campus-wide network is relatively slow. Again, this is due to its lack of routing ability. In order to hook NetBEUI into a much larger network, you have to establish a gateway. A gateway is piece of hardware that connects two different types of networks together. The *gateway* can package the NetBEUI packets into another packet structure and add routing information to it but this makes the packet larger and thus is slower to transmit. Using TCP/IP in conjunction with NetBEUI is the best solution. More on that when we get to TCP/IP.

When you install Windows NT, NetBEUI and the NetBIOS service will be installed for you automatically. It is the quickest way in which to get a couple of NT machines up and talking to one another. The Windows for Workgroups product also speaks NetBEUI and that makes connecting Windows NT into an existing WFW network very easy and vice versa.

TCP/IP

When the United States Department of Defense realized the benefits of networking one of its agencies, the Defense Advanced Research Projects Agency developed TCP/IP as a standard method of communication among networks having different hardware and operating systems. TCP/IP stands for Transmission Control Protocol/Internet Protocol and was created in the late seventies.

TCP/IP is routable, unlike NetBEUI, and is the only way to implement Small Network Management Protocol or SNMP. Because TCP/IP was developed for communication among different types of machines and operating systems such as UNIX, mainframes, Windows NT, and

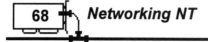

connection to the Internet, its obvious advantage is the ability to connect many different systems together, using the same protocol. TCP/IP is not very fast on small LANs because it carries so much overhead for inter-connection with other systems. If your LAN has 20 workstations and no need to interconnect with other systems, don't use TCP/IP.

Fortunately, with the structure of Windows NT, you don't have to run one or the other (NetBEUI or TCP/IP). You can run them both. Machines that need to connect to another TCP/IP source, over a Wide Area Network or WAN, for example, can run TCP/IP as the second pro-tocol and NetBEUI as the first protocol. The fast NetBEUI protocol will be used for local connections with other NetBEUI machines, and when you use or connect to a TCP/IP resource, the TCP/IP protocol kicks in to provide that connection.

As mentioned above, you have to use TCP/IP if you wish to imple-ment SNMP. SNMP stands for Simple Network Management Protocol. It is used by an administrator to monitor machines on the network. Pro-grams that, for instance, can run across a network and inventory every machine on the network, the station address, and other information about the machine, are examples of SNMP functionality.

TCP/IP is implemented in Windows NT as a STREAMS protocol. STREAMS is an environment developed for UNIX System V which makes it easier for developers to port protocols to different platforms. This is another layer of the networking model that seeks to modularize the pro-tocols. In much the same way that NDIS is a "wrapper" for a network card driver, STREAMS is a wrapper for TCP/IP. The upper level of STREAMS is bound to the TDI and the lower level is bound to NDIS. Inside this wrapper, the TCP/IP protocol exists. Unlike the NetBEUI protocol which extends from NDIS to TDI, the TCP/IP protocol is "smaller" and is combined with STREAMS to reach from NDIS to TDI.

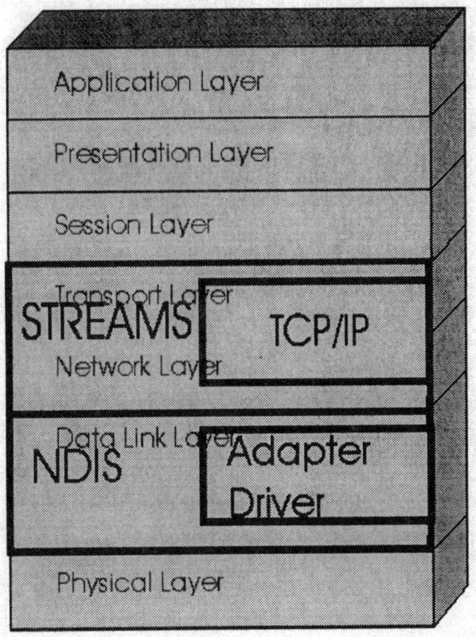

Figure 4-5
Streams Wrapper for TCP/IP

Other protocols that have been developed in the STREAMS environment for UNIX can easily be implemented in Windows NT with little or no modification. The STREAMS environment in Windows NT is very close to STREAMS from UNIX. It is not source-code compatible, but is nearly an exact duplicate with the addition of hooks for the NDIS and TDI interfaces. As protocols are ported to Windows NT, most of them will come as STREAMS protocols.

DLC

Data Link Control is a different kind of protocol. Unlike the first two protocols, DLC is not used to connect Windows NT machines or other networked PCs together. DLC serves only two functions:

- Connection to an IBM mainframe
- Connection to DLC-enabled printers like the Hewlett-Packard Laserjet IIIsi and 4si

Only machines needing to perform one or both of these services need to have the DLC protocol loaded. If a Windows NT machine will be a print server for a DLC printer, then only the print server needs to have the DLC protocol loaded. All other machines can send print jobs to the print server via NetBEUI, TCP/IP, or other protocol.

RPC

The final topic in NT Protocols and Services is RPC, which stands for Remote Procedure Call. Developers can write applications that are spread out over several machines.

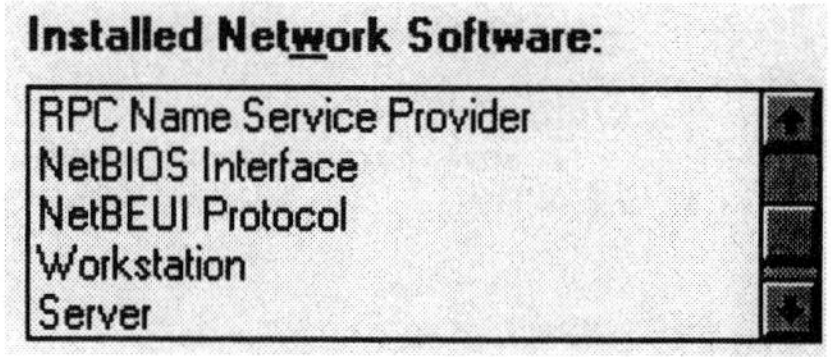

Installed Network Software:

```
RPC Name Service Provider
NetBIOS Interface
NetBEUI Protocol
Workstation
Server
```

Figure 4-6
Installed Protocols and Services Including RPC

Just as NT is multiprocessing internally, an application can process in different machines. One machine may do database access and query work, another for number crunching, and a third for graphic design. All these functions can be part of the same application. These functions are part of the program itself. When you run an application, you cannot identify it as an RPC application but the application is designed to make different types of requests to different machines like in the example above. As you can imagine, an RPC application will run faster than a stand-alone application because it asks other machines to do the work. The RPC is combined with a name service provider which identifies other computers in the environment that can service the application.

Part Three

Step-by-Step
Windows NT
as a Workstation

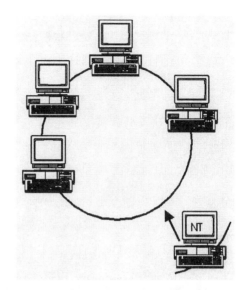

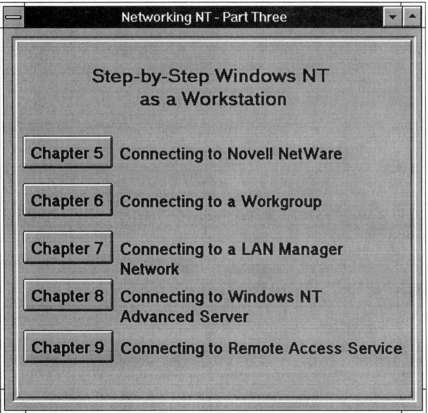

Networking NT - Part Three

Step-by-Step Windows NT
as a Workstation

Chapter 5	**Connecting to Novell NetWare**
Chapter 6	**Connecting to a Workgroup**
Chapter 7	**Connecting to a LAN Manager Network**
Chapter 8	**Connecting to Windows NT Advanced Server**
Chapter 9	**Connecting to Remote Access Service**

Chapter 5

Connecting to Novell NetWare

Novell NetWare is the most popular LAN on the market, with, as some estimate, a 60% – 70% market share. It stands to reason that the number one connectivity question on CompuServe and in the trade magazines is "How do I connect Windows NT to Novell?" We're going to answer that question. Other questions like "What can I do with NT on a Novell LAN?" and "How does it work?" will also be answered. First, we need to lay some groundwork for the project.

What You Need

- Novell NetWare v3.11 Server
  - ◇ NetWare Volume such as SYS must be mounted
  - ◇ One Network Card bound to IPX protocol

- Windows NT v3.1
  - ◇ Network Card supported by NetWare ODI for NT

- Novell NetWare Redirector Software for Windows NT

The first part is relatively easy since you are likely to already have a functioning server for your LAN. Make sure that at least one volume is mounted. This should be the SYS volume. Next, load your network adapter card. If the network is already established, lines similar to the ones shown on the next page will be in your **AUTOEXEC.NCF** file, which is located in the **SYS:SYSTEM** directory of your file server volume.

```
load C:HP386A16 port=300 int=3 frame=ETHERNET_802.3
bind IPX to HP386A16 net=F001
```

Make certain you know the frame type that your network card is using on the Novell LAN. When the Novell software is installed on NT it will use the 802.3 frame type, but that can be changed in the Windows NT registry after installation. This is necessary if you are communicating with NetWare 4.x or 3.12 both of which default to 802.2. To verify that all is well on the LAN, go to a station on the LAN and attempt to log on. If everything goes as expected, you're ready for the Windows NT side of the project.

There are two different reasons for and methods to connect Windows NT to a Novell LAN. The first and most obvious reason is to get a Windows NT user running on the LAN to user Novell resources such as printers and disks. The second purpose is to use Windows NT as an application server for other clients on the Novell LAN. This application-serving ability is limited to NetBIOS and IPX/SPX applications. This capability is provided by the NWLink protocol that is shipped with NT. NWLink does not make your NT machine a workstation on the LAN, but does allow other workstations on the LAN to connect to the Windows NT machine for tasks such as SQL server communication. We'll be focusing on the first method of connectivity.

Installation of Windows NT

There are several considerations to make when installing Windows NT, depending on the kind of connectivity services you want. There is one method for connecting one Windows NT machine to a Novell LAN, one method for connecting to a Novell LAN that will have other NT machines and Windows for Workgroups machines present as well. Finally, there are considerations for whether or not Windows NT supports the type of card you are using, which is not mandatory so long as the NetWare Requestor for Windows NT supports the card you have.

Sole NT Machine on a Novell LAN

If you are installing Windows NT into a Novell LAN and do not need any other connectivity, use the custom install option when you start to install NT. This is the "C" option from Disk 1 of the install disks. When you reboot the machine after Disk 9 and the graphical phase of the setup begins, you will be asked if you want to install networking, set up printers, search for applications, and so on. Ask the setup program not to install networks. Allowing NT to take this step only loads the NDIS drivers and Microsoft network protocols, which you don't need in a NetWare-only environment.

NT with Windows for Workgroups and Other NT Machines

If you are installing NT into a Novell LAN that has Windows for Workgroups or other NT machines on it, you may want to install the Microsoft network protocols and services so that your NT and WFW machines can communicate on a workgroup level while still maintaining a connection to the Novell LAN. If this scenario is the appropriate one, then install Windows NT as you normally would, selecting the appropriate driver for the network card that is in your Windows NT machine. The driver that is loaded will be an NDIS driver, but the NetWare redirector will replace it with and ODI driver during the redirector installation.

No NT Support for a Card but the Novell Redirector Supports It

If NT does not support the card you are using with an NDIS driver but there is an ODI driver for your card in the NetWare redirector software, use the custom install option when you start to install NT. This is the "C" option from Disk 1 of the install disks. When you reboot the machine after Disk 9 and the graphical phase of the setup begins, you will be asked if you want to install networking, set up printers, search for applications, and so on. Ask the setup program to install networks. Because NT doesn't support your card, the network card detector won't find it, but with the custom setup, you can tell it what card to use. Select any card, and ignore the warnings about NT not being able to verify that

the settings you gave it are correct. At the final stage of installation, you will also get a warning about the network not being able to start. Ignore this as well. The idea here is to force Windows NT to load the proper protocols and services for Microsoft networks anyway. Whether or not the networks operate is of no consequence. During the redirector install, we'll remove the bogus card driver and install the correct one.

If you didn't install the networking software during initial software installation, open the control panel and double-click on the "Network" icon. Windows NT will display a dialog box like the one shown in Figure 5-1, notifying you that Windows NT networking is not installed and asking you whether or not you want to install it now.

Figure 5-1
Loading Network Software after Installing NT

You should elect to install the software. You can't operate the NetWare redirector without Microsoft's protocols and drivers.

A note about the redirector software: You can't install the redirector software at the same time that you are installing Windows NT because the install program does not offer you the opportunity to install other network software and protocols before you select a hardware driver. That order makes it impossible to set up the redirector during installation. You can install other network adapters during the installation, but you must install network protocols and services at the very end.

Installing the NetWare Redirector for Windows NT

The first step, regardless of the method of your install is to log onto the NT machine with Administrator rights. See Figure 5-2.

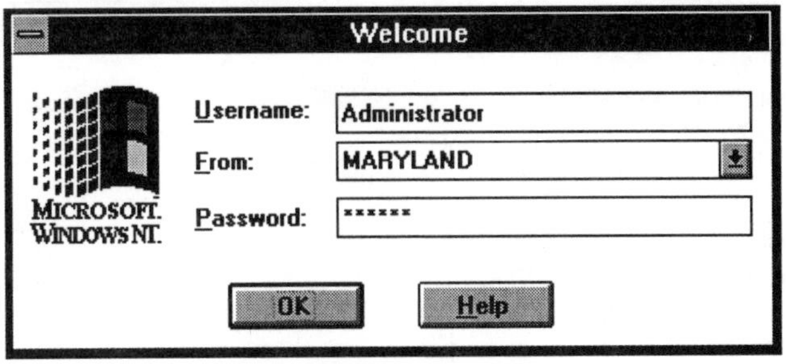

Figure 5-2
Administrator Logon

Next, locate the control panel icon in the program manager. It is located in the Main program group. Double-click on it and then locate the Network icon in the control panel. Double-click on that. Now, depending on how you chose to install NT, i.e., with or without networking, you get a different dialog box. See Figure 5-4 and Figure 5-5.

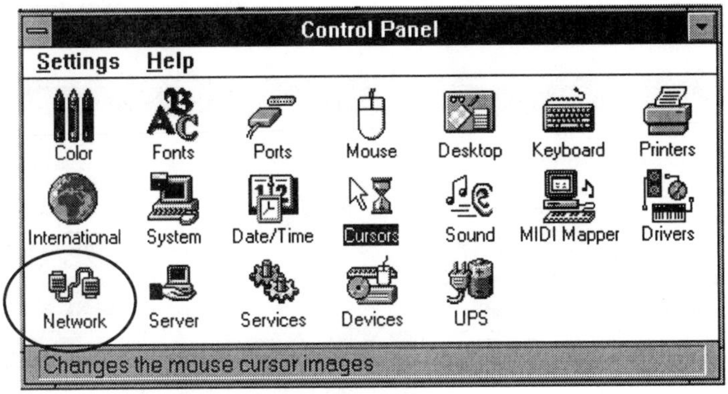

Figure 5-3
Network Icon in the Control Panel

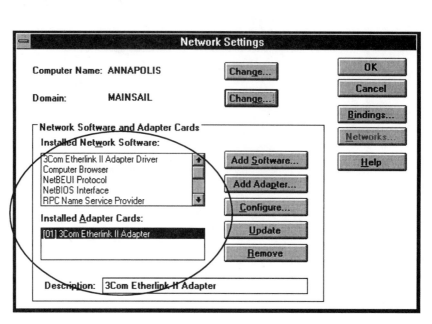

Figure 5-4
Microsoft Network Protocols and Services Installed

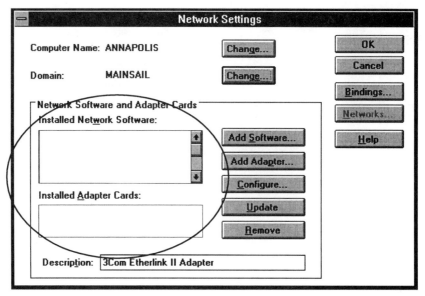

Figure 5-5
No Network Protocols or Services Installed

If you are installing for a sole NT machine or, if for any other reason you have chosen not to install NT networking, there will not be any network software or adapters installed. For either install method, select the **Add Software** button.

Add Software...

You'll get a dialog box like the one shown in Figure 5-6.

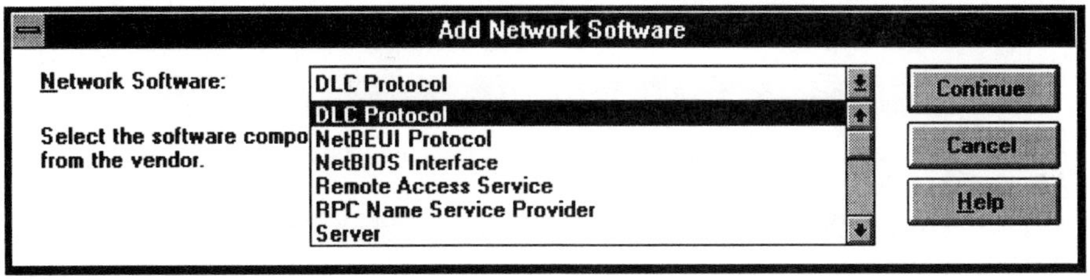

Add Network Software		
Network Software:	DLC Protocol	Continue
Select the software compo	DLC Protocol	Cancel
from the vendor.	NetBEUI Protocol	
	NetBIOS Interface	Help
	Remote Access Service	
	RPC Name Service Provider	
	Server	

Figure 5-6
Add Network Software Dialog Box

You have to add the software drivers first, before hardware drivers. Insert the NetWare Redirector for Windows NT disk into one of your floppy drives. Scroll down the list of available software options and select the **<Other>...** option to load from a floppy disk.

TCP/IP Protocol
Workstation
<Other> Requires disk from manufacturer

As soon as you select that, you get a dialog box that requests the location of the driver disk.

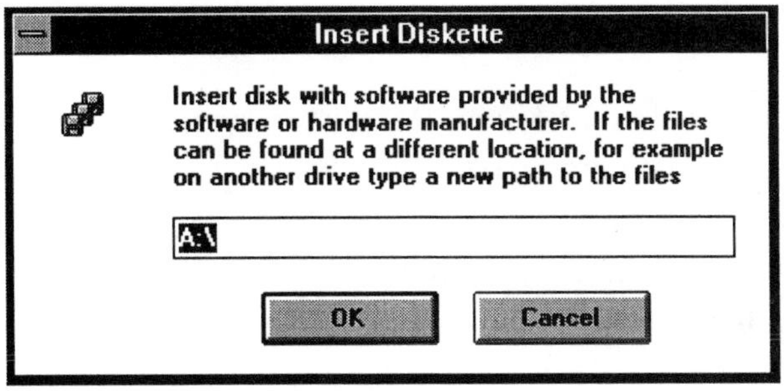

Insert Diskette
Insert disk with software provided by the software or hardware manufacturer. If the files can be found at a different location, for example on another drive type a new path to the files
A:\
OK   Cancel

Figure 5-7
Select Drive to Install From

After inserting the driver disk in the floppy drive and selecting the appropriate disk drive, you get a dialog box requesting confirmation of the driver you want to install. Windows NT goes out to the disk drive to locate a file called **OEMSETUP.INF**, which contains, among other things, the names of the drivers that are present on the disk. Since one driver disk or driver set may contain many individual drivers, you need to select and confirm the one that you want to install. In this case there's only one driver set on the disk, as shown in Figure 5-8.

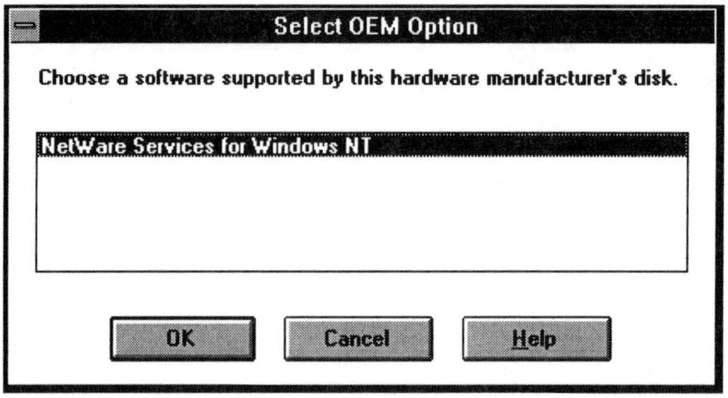

Figure 5-8
Select Driver to Load

Click on OK and Windows NT will read the disk and begin copying files from the requestor disk to your NT system. After about a minute of disk reading, Windows NT is finished adding drivers to your system. When complete, Windows NT notifies you by displaying the dialog box shown in Figure 5-9.

Bear in mind that the Novel Requestor screen shots and procedures are based on the beta version of the requestor using a production version of Windows NT. Some minor dialog box changes and procedure changes may accompany the actual commercial release of the requestor, when it becomes available.

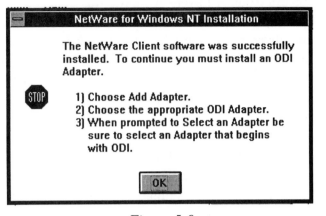

Figure 5-9
Network Software Install Complete

As the dialog box indicates, you're only halfway to the finish. The network software drivers are installed, but the Windows NT NDIS driver is still present if you chose to install Microsoft networking software. As we noted in Chapter 4, Novell uses ODI, and NDIS and ODI cannot coexist. You'll notice that the **Installed Network Software** list box contains three new drivers as shown in Figure 5-10.

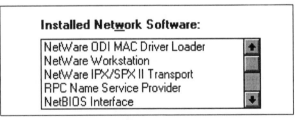

Figure 5-10
NetWare Drivers Installed

If you did not install the Microsoft network software, the top three protocols and services will be the only three in the list box. The first driver may interest some of you. The **"...ODI MAC..."** does not mean Apple Macintosh. It is a reference to a sublayer of the Data Link Layer of the OSI model, as discussed in Chapter 4. This sublayer, called the Media Access Control Layer, or MAC, was conceptualized by the IEEE. IEEE, which stands for Institute of Electrical and Electronics Engineers, standardized a division of the Data Link Layer into two parts, known as the Logical Link Control (LLC) and the MAC as part of project 802. From this specification we get the common 802.3 for Ethernet and 802.5 for Token Ring. There are several other specifications in the 802 project as well.

Microsoft addresses the LLC layer in the 802 project as NDIS which Novell addresses as ODI. Beneath them are the network drivers. The ODI MAC driver loader shown in Figure 5-10 is to control the loading of ODI network card drivers and how they interface with the LLC layer (ODI).

The next step is to install the ODI network adapter. Select the **Add Adapter...** button from the Network Settings dialog box.

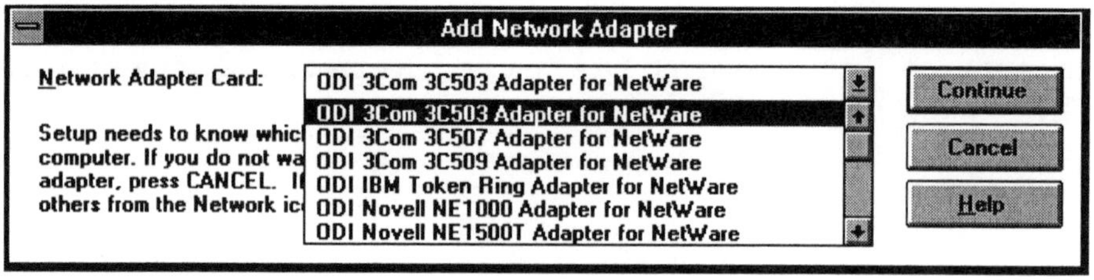

Figure 5-11
NetWare ODI Drivers Added to Available Adapters

You'll notice that several new network drivers have been added since we last saw this dialog box. All the drivers were added when you installed the NetWare Services disk. The above screen shot was taken from a beta version of the NetWare redirector so adapters may have been added or removed since then. You should select the appropriate driver from the list or select the **<Other>...** option if you have an additional NT ODI driver from a manufacturer. It must be a Windows NT ODI driver in order to work properly.

After you select the appropriate driver, click on **Continue** to install the driver. You will then be prompted, depending on the network card you chose, with the hardware configuration for the network card. You should know these settings before installing.

Be aware that sometimes the ODI drivers and the NDIS drivers vary in their hardware configuration approach. Such is the case with the 3Com 3C503 driver. The two different configuration dialog boxes are shown in Figures 5-12 and 5-13.

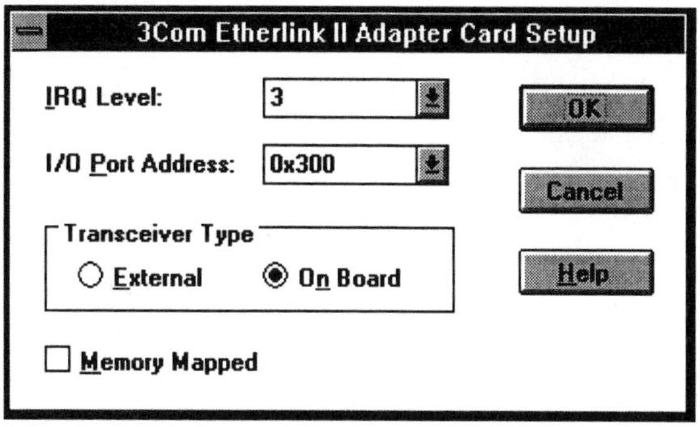

Figure 5-12
Windows NT NDIS Driver for 3Com 3C503

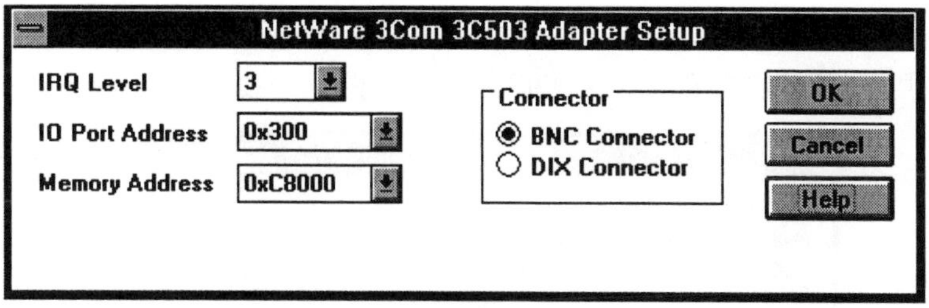

Figure 5-13
Windows NT NetWare ODI Driver for 3Com 3C503

From the dialog boxes, you can't really tell that the first setup is different from second, other than the different dialog box design. The difference is that memory mapping, in which you select a memory address for the card is optional on the NDIS driver. The 3Com 3C503 card

does allow you to disable the memory mapping, which, on an 8-bit card, really isn't needed. The ODI driver does not allow you to set the Memory Address to a disabled state. You must select a memory address. If you are using the 3C503 NDIS driver with no memory mapping and you want to install the ODI drivers, you'll have to open up your machine and change the settings. Other cards with more current technology may require you to run an adapter configuration program to change the EEPROM on the card. You can't run that adapter configuration program from the Windows NT command prompt because no program is allowed to talk directly with hardware in the machine. This is an example of the protection of Windows NT getting in the way. Your best bet is to boot with a DOS disk and run the config program from a floppy or from a FAT partition in your Windows NT system. If you must take these steps at any time, use the **Configure...** option in the Network Settings dialog box to tell Windows NT what settings to use to talk to the card. As you can see, it is wise to find out beforehand what the driver requires.

Once you have installed the ODI driver for your card and configured it for the correct hardware settings, the driver is installed and almost ready for use. If you're only working in a Novell LAN environment with no Microsoft networking, the next step is to close the Network Settings dialog box, and Windows NT will ask if it is okay to restart your system, so that the changes in drivers can take effect.

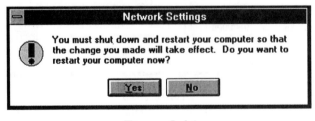

Figure 5-14
Time to Reboot

You can select **No** and the changes will not be lost, so that you can continue to work. The next time NT is restarted, the changes will take effect and you will have connectivity with the Novell LAN.

If you are going to use Microsoft networking services in addition to Novell, you still have a few more steps to take. First, you have to remove the NDIS driver, since both cannot operate at the same time for the same card. If your system does have two cards, you can have the NDIS software running on one and the ODI software on the other. To remove the NDIS driver, select the non-ODI driver from the list of **Installed Adapter Cards** in the Network Settings dialog box and click on **Remove**. As with everything in Windows NT, you'll be asked to confirm that you want the driver removed.

Now that the NDIS driver is gone, you have one last step. Since the NetBEUI protocol, as well as the other Microsoft network services requires NDIS, you need to add NDIS support to your ODI drivers. Novell has included a generic driver for NDIS support which plugs into the ODI driver suite. Select **Add Adapter...** from the Network Settings dialog box to pull up a list of available adapters.

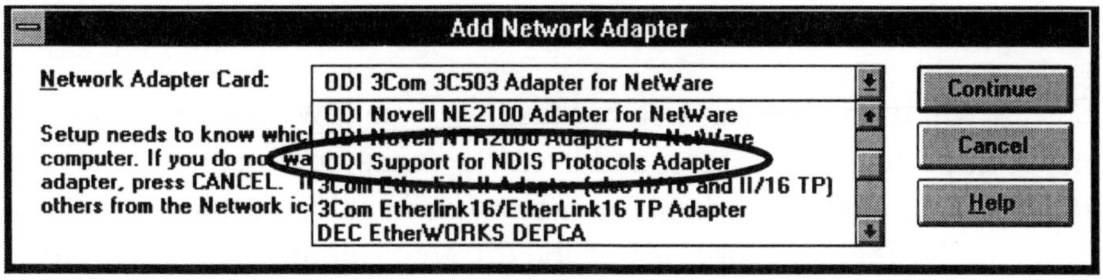

Add Network Adapter		
Network Adapter Card:	ODI 3Com 3C503 Adapter for NetWare	**Continue**
Setup needs to know whic	ODI Novell NE2100 Adapter for NetWare	**Cancel**
computer. If you do no wa	ODI Support for NDIS Protocols Adapter	
adapter, press CANCEL.	3Com Etherlink16/EtherLink16 TP Adapter	**Help**
others from the Network ic	DEC EtherWORKS DEPCA	

Figure 5-15
NDIS compatibility driver for ODI

Novell has implemented the ODI-to-NDIS compatibility as a pseudo hardware driver. Windows NT treats the driver as if it were another network adapter card in the system. In point of fact, it is directly linked to the true ODI hardware driver for your network card. Select **ODI Support for NDIS Protocols Adapter** and click on **Continue**.

Once the adapter has been added, your work is complete . . . almost. You will still have to reboot the machine in order for the changes to take effect. Now that you have two networks installed, the **Networks...**

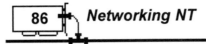

option is available in the Network Settings dialog box. This option, if you recall from Chapter 3, allows you to select the search order for multiple networks. By placing one above another, you are telling Windows NT to search one network before it searches another. This applies only to NT machines that have two or more different types of networks installed, not to the search order of servers in one type of network. When Windows NT goes out to search for a particular server, directory, file, or other resource, this dialog box tells Windows NT what order to search in.

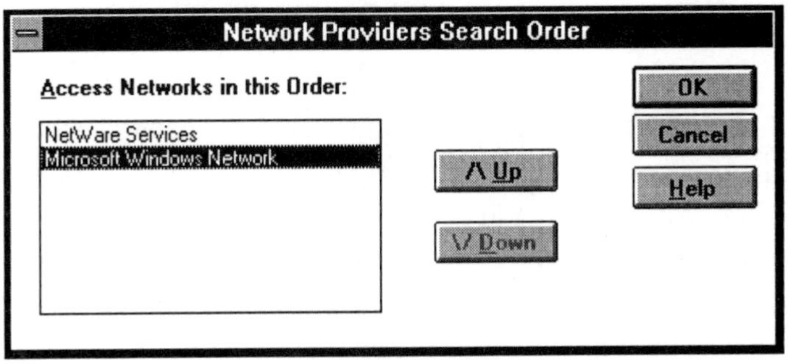

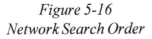

Figure 5-16
Network Search Order

If you wish, you can also review how Windows NT has bound the network protocols, services, and hardware adapters together. Knowing this information helps when you are trying to solve problems, because you can see the dependencies of the different modules of the network services.

REBOOT!

Now that all your software is installed, you can browse and connect to Novell servers on the same wire as your NT workstation. However, in order to gain access to NetWare services and resources, you must synchronize Windows NT and the NetWare bindery. With the Novell redirector software, the NetWare server you wish to gain access to will assume that the user name with which you logged on to the NT machine is the name that you wish to use to connect to the NetWare server. Whatever name you log onto Windows NT with should also be a user in the Novell bindery for the server you want to attach to. If you are using the name "IVY" as the NT logon, then there must be a user "IVY" in the NetWare bindery. If there isn't, you or your LAN administrator must run SYSCON and create a new user with the same name as your NT logon ID.

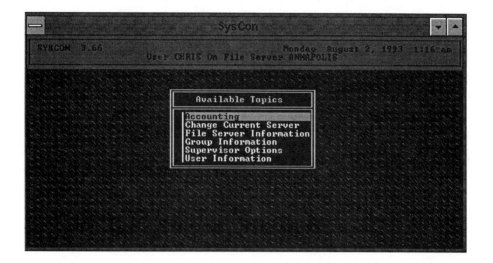

Figure 5-17
Novell NetWare SysCon Utility

Don't worry about the uppercase and lowercase letters; the NetWare redirector will convert all user IDs and passwords to uppercase before validation. The password for your NT machine logon should also be the same as the NetWare password for your user account. When you try to access any NetWare services, Windows NT will pass the user ID and password to the NetWare server and if both match, you're in. No need to log on twice.

Accessing NetWare Services

Now that you have everything set up, you should expect that you can connect to any Novell LAN that is on the wire. If, at any time during the start-up process, NT dies, you have a hardware-related configuration problem. You can restart your machine and hold down the space bar during boot up. This will tell Windows NT that you may want to use what is

called the "Last Known Good" configuration. You'll get a menu and one of the options is to boot up using the last known good configuration. This function backs out all changes since the last time you had a successful start. It may be due to the fact that you told Windows NT to talk to the network card with settings that conflict with another device in your computer. If all goes well and you get the chance to log on, then any problems are not critical to the system's functions. After you log on, you may get a dialog box like the one shown below.

If you see this dialog box, something isn't correct, and you need to review the event log in the Event Viewer utility. This utility is located in the Administrative Tools group of the Program Manager. You should review all recent entries in order from first to last. The first errors in the log are generally the most critical and can cause most of the other errors that are listed in the log. If, for instance, your network card was not set correctly, Windows NT cannot load the driver. As a result, almost all other network-related services will fail to load and each of those failures will be listed in the log.

When the start-up is completed successfully, it's time to start using the Novell server. There are two ways in which you can interact with a Novell server using the current redirector software. Those two methods are File services and Print services.

You can run applications that reside on the Novell server's volumes and you can print to NetWare queues.

File Services

To gain access to Novell files and directories, use the File Manager in the Main program group of the Program Manager.

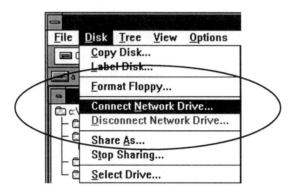

Figure 5-18
Adding a Network Drive

By default you'll see the drive that you are running Windows NT on. From the **Disk** menu select **Connect to Network Disk**. This puts the network browser into action and sometimes it will take a few seconds in order for the dialog box to open, while Windows NT searches the network for resources it can connect to.

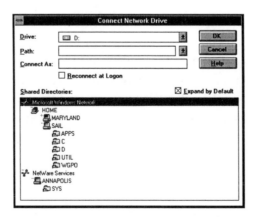

Figure 5-19
Making a Connection with a Novell Server in the File Manager

The dialog box shown in Figure 5-19 lists the available resources in a hierarchical structure, just as the network is laid out. The Microsoft network resources are listed in order of workgroup name, computer name, and finally, share name, which represents the names a user has given to the directories and drives on his or her machine that are shareable. The NetWare services are laid out in similar order. First is server name, then volume name, and finally directory names. The directories of the server are not shown here. The last level visible is the volume name: **SYS**. You can double-click on the volume name to show the available directories. If you, as a user, are not permitted access to the **SYSTEM** directory, then it will not appear in the list.

Remember when I told you about synchronizing with the Novell bindery? Well, if you haven't yet done that and attempt to access or browse any resource below the volume level of the hierarchy, and your user ID or password or both don't match the NetWare server, you'll get a dialog box like the one shown in Figure 5-20.

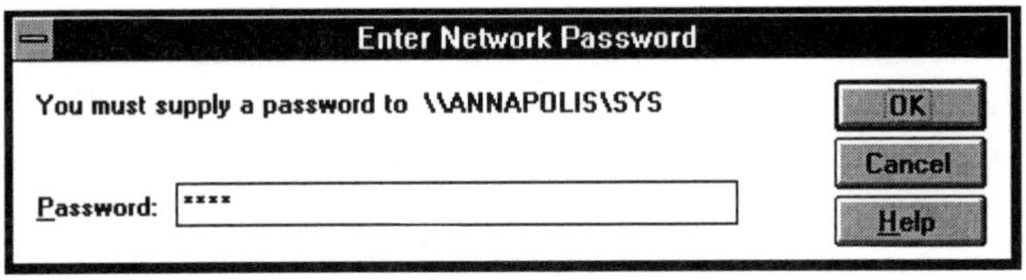

Enter Network Password	
You must supply a password to \\ANNAPOLIS\SYS	OK
	Cancel
Password: ****	Help

Figure 5-20
The Novell Server Doesn't Know Who You Are.

Be sure to synchronize them. Before we move on to printing, you should know that it is not currently possible to run NetWare utilities like SYSCON, FCONSOLE, PCONSOLE, or RCONSOLE on a Windows NT machine. This functionality will be available at a later time, along with 32bit Windows NT graphical utilities for managing the Novell LAN.

Printing Services

Windows NT machines can print directly to Novell print queues using regular printer drivers, which are provided with Windows NT or by third-party vendors. Unlike printing from one NT machine to another, an NT machine that prints to a Novell queue must have the printer driver for the network printer loaded on the machine, similar to Windows v3.1. If you didn't install any printer drivers during the installation of Windows NT, fear not, because you can add them as you go.

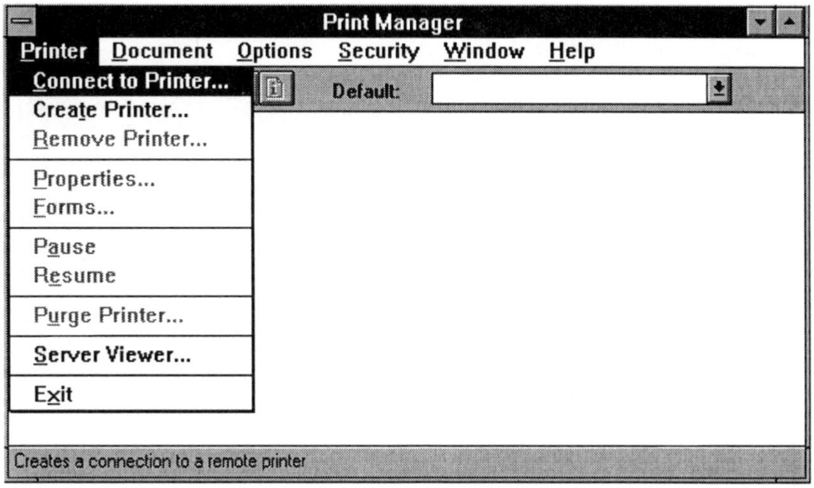

Figure 5-21
Starting the Process of Connecting to a NetWare Queue

To begin the process of connecting to a Novell queue, locate the Print Manager icon in the Main group of the Program Manager. You can access the same utility with the Printers icon in the Windows NT control panel. Unlike Windows 3.1, you don't have a choice in using or disabling the Print Manager. In Windows NT it's always on.

Once the Print Manager is open, select **Connect to Printer...** from the Printer menu. Before we get to that though, I want to tell you about another feature in this menu. The **Server Viewer** option allows your Windows NT machine to monitor the shared printers on other Windows NT and Windows for Workgroups machines. It's very handy if you have multiple places that you can send a print job to and want to know which is the least congested at the moment. This capability is only for Microsoft-networked computers.

You'll notice that, like the File Manager browser, the listing is in hierarchical order, from server name down to queue name. The Microsoft networks list the domain or workgroup name first, then the computer name and finally the shared printer name. Select the printer queue from the Novell server queues and click on **OK**. If your system already includes a printer driver then you're fine, but in the event that you have not installed a printer driver on your NT machine, you'll get a warning about that condition as shown in Figure 5-23.

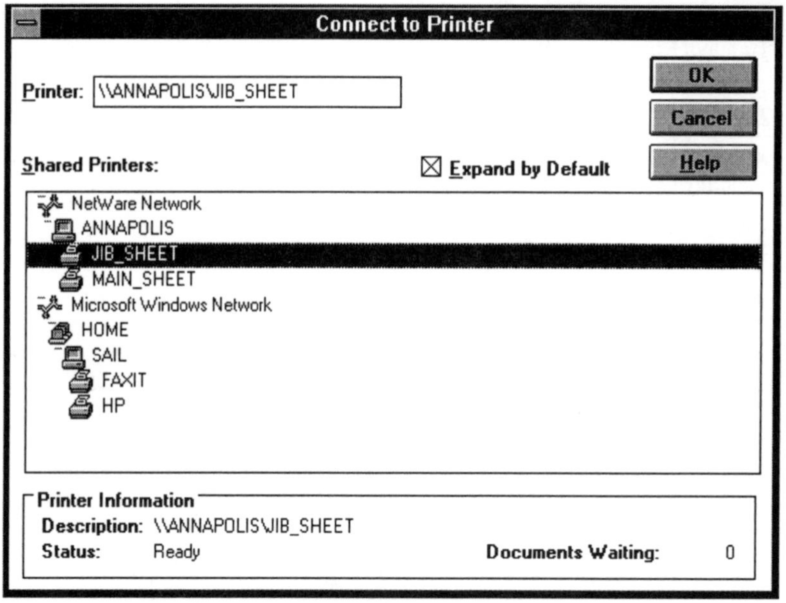

Figure 5-22
Locate the NetWare Queue You Want to Attach To

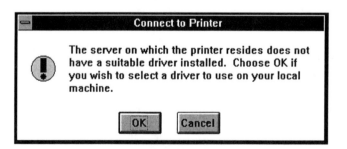

Figure 5-23
No Printer Driver Installed

If you don't have a printer installed, just click on **OK** and you'll get the opportunity to add one. Select the appropriate printer driver from the list box and click on **OK**.

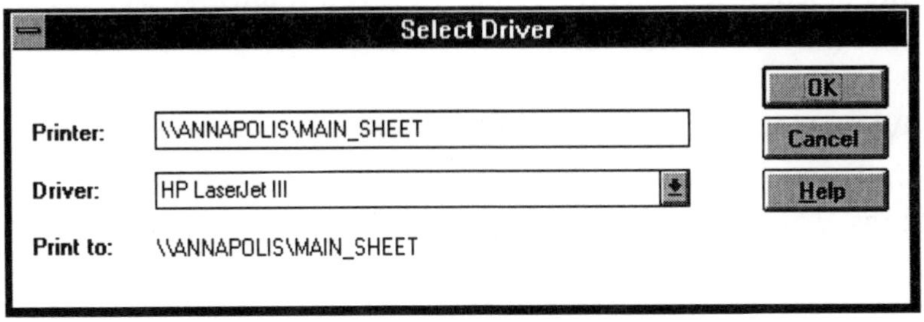

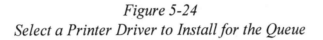

Figure 5-24
Select a Printer Driver to Install for the Queue

Once the printer driver is installed, you can begin printing to the network queue as LPT1. The defaults for the printer are:

$$/NFF \ /NB \ /TI=45 \ /L=1$$

The locations of many of these settings are all over the place. The main place to start is the `Print Properties` option of the Printers menu. You really should check out all the options by looking at them. Some of the adjustments, such as halftone printing with a LaserJet III are very new and quite interesting.

The `/NB` option listed above is really a misnomer. In Windows NT, they are called separator pages, and you can send a preformatted page to the printer for each print job. Though it is similar to a banner page, the obvious flexibility of creating your own banner pages with custom information, may be of great interest to administrators who use banner pages. For network printing you can use separator pages to delineate between one person's print job an the next one so that when the print jobs are sitting in the output tray of the printer, you know where on job ends and another begins. The separator pages are printer language codes in text form. Although Windows NT does not associate them with `NOTEPAD.EXE`, they are fully editable by Notepad, using the language

of your printer. One use, as shown from the sample separator pages included with Windows NT in the **SYSTEM32** directory is to effect mode
switching on a printer from PCL to PostScript and vice versa. The separator file is sent just before the actual print you want, and is encapsulated
as part of the same print job.

When you are up and running (printing) you can view your print
jobs in the queue alongside other print jobs. You can remove and add
print jobs as well as increase or decrease the priority of print jobs in the
queue.

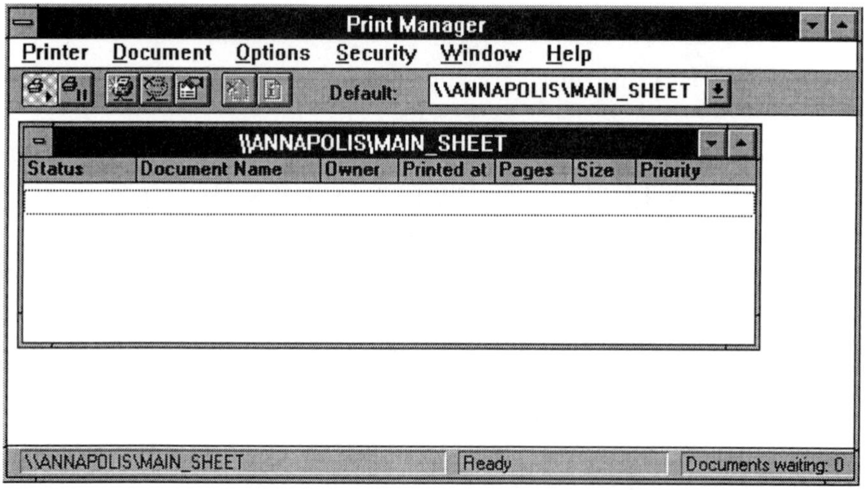

Figure 5-25
Monitoring the NetWare Queues with Print Manager

The ability to control network print jobs is, of course, dependent
upon your security authorization on the Novell server. You can now print
to the server just like you can in Windows 3.1.

That's about all there is to NetWare connectivity. It's relatively easy to implement and very easy to operate in. Using broadcast messages to users on Windows NT machines works the same as on DOS and Windows machines. There isn't any CASTOFF function in the redirector software as yet.

If you open the control panel after you have installed the redirector software, you'll notice that an icon has been added. See Figure 5-26.

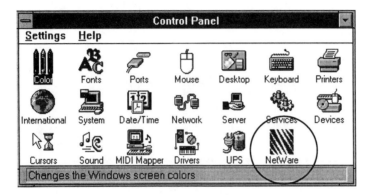

Figure 5-26
New Control Panel Icon for NetWare

Selecting the NetWare icon opens this dialog box:

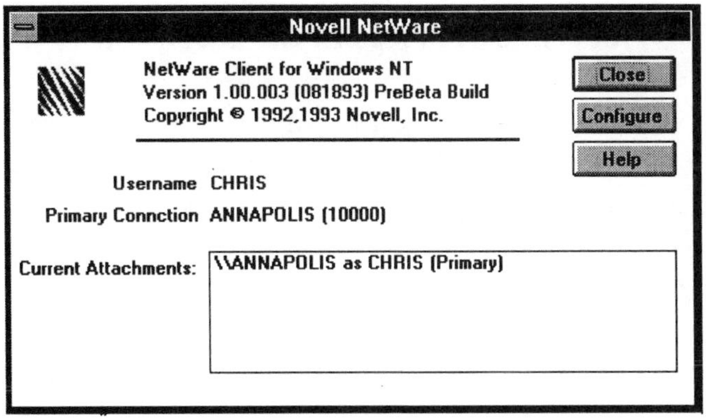

Figure 5-27
Tracking Connections from NT to the Novell Server

Figure 5-27 illustrates a beta requestor designed to run on the production version of Windows NT. Subsequent versions may change in appearance.

If you double-click on a current attachment listed in the dialog box, you'll get information about the user name, connection number and login time. The fact that the list of current attachments is capable of holding more than one entry causes one to speculate that it may be possible to connect as more than one user at a time. The dialog box is shown in Figure 5-28.

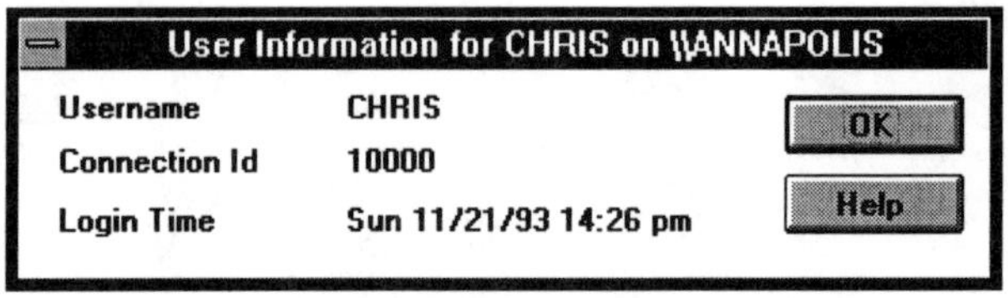

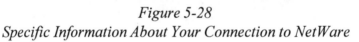

Figure 5-28
Specific Information About Your Connection to NetWare

If you think that you have a handle on the subject and you ready to start working with it, don't forget Part Four which covers many of the management tasks for a Windows NT machine.

Modifying NetWare Services in the Registry

After you have installed the NetWare requestor software for Windows NT, there will be some new entries in your registry. The registry is a database that holds all configuration information for Windows NT. If the terms and concepts in the next paragraph make no sense to you, read Chapter 11 first.

In the key handle **HKEY_LOCAL_MACHINE**, locate the following key:

```
HKEY_LOCAL_MACHINE\SYSTEM\CurrentControlSet...
\Services\IpxSpxII\Parameters
```

Next, locate the **FrameType** value. The value determines the frame type that your network card sends and receives. The valid values for Ethernet are:

> **ETHERNET_802.3**
> **ETHERNET_802.2**
> **ETHERNET_II**
> **ETHERNET_SNAP**

By adding a value called Preferred Server in the following path:

```
HKEY_LOCAL_MACHINE\SYSTEM\CurrentControlSet...
\Services\IpxSpxII\Parameters
```

and entering a **REG_SZ** value with the name of your preferred server, you will connect to that server when NT boots each time, just like the entry in your DOS-based **SHELL.CFG** or **NET.CFG**. Novell has not made public all the parameters that can be set through the registry at the time of this printing.

Chapter 6

Connecting to a Workgroup

The easiest possible connection that Windows NT can make is to another NT machine or a Windows for Workgroups network. Workgroup-based computing is the default configuration of Windows NT. When you install NT and install networking services during the installation, you wind up with a workgroup machine.

From a functional point of view, Windows for Workgroups and Windows NT are very similar. Obviously the underlying structure of Windows NT is much different, although gaining access to shared resources is pretty much the same. Windows NT does have far more extensive security features than Windows for Workgroups machines do, but given NT's design, that's to be expected. Let's get started.

What You Need

⌨ Windows for Workgroups machine v3.1 or higher
   ✧ A shared network resource, such as a directory
   ✧ Network card with NetBEUI running

⌨ Windows NT v3.1
   ✧ Network Card supported by NT NDIS or
   ✧ Network Card supported by NetWare ODI for NT
      running NDIS compatibility driver

In order to establish a workgroup, you need only one machine. Either a Windows for Workgroups or Windows NT machine can establish a workgroup. As discussed in Chapter 3, a workgroup is a logical grouping of machines. Any machine can be part of a particular workgroup. Once a workgroup is established by a single machine, other machines join the workgroup. If all the machines of a particular workgroup are turned off, then the workgroup doesn't exist. As soon as a single machine powers on and declares membership in the workgroup, the workgroup is established and other machines join it.

As a member of a workgroup, you can share resources with other members of the workgroup such as hard disk directories, files and printers. Here is how Windows NT fits into the workgroup and how NT machines can share their resources and get access to WFW shared resources.

Joining a Workgroup

In order to connect a Windows for Workgroups network and an NT machine together, you only need to know what the workgroup name is so that they both are on the same workgroup.

Determining the Workgroup Name

For this discussion, a functioning network of Windows for Workgroup machines must exist. The workgroup, called HOME, has two WFW machines on it and we are going to add a Windows NT machine.

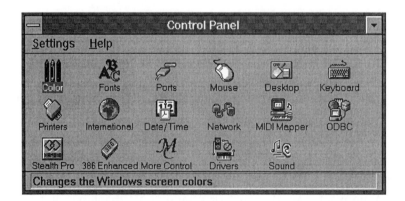

Figure 6-1
Windows for Workgroups Control Panel

Before beginning the installation of the Windows NT machine, it is wise to check and verify the name of the workgroup that you want to join. Locate a WFW machine that is in the workgroup you want to join and open the control panel. Locate the Network icon in the control panel and double-click.

The information we need is on the first dialog box when you open the network control panel. As shown in Figure 6-2, the computer name and workgroup name are displayed. Once you are certain of the spelling, you can close the control panel. That's all we need from WFW for now.

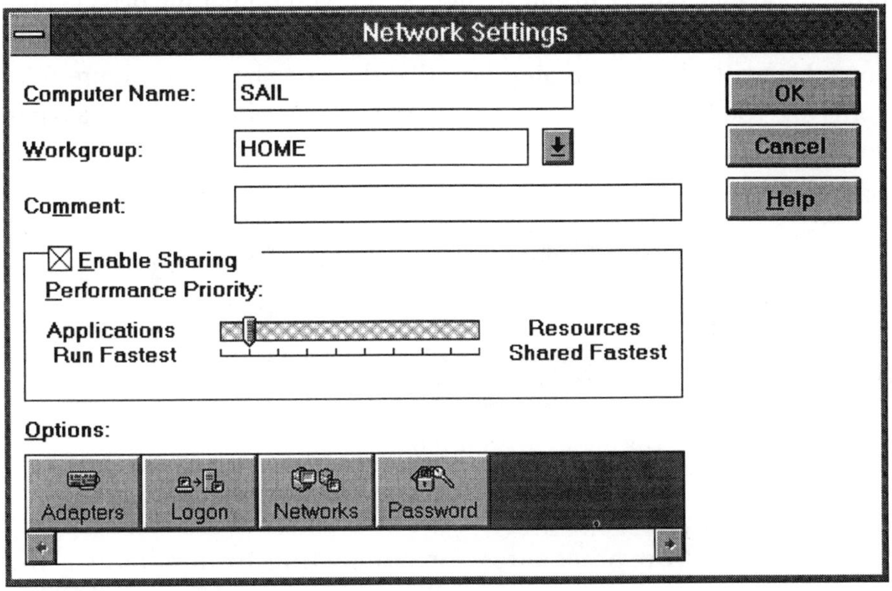

Figure 6-2
Windows for Workgroups Network Control

Configuring Windows NT for the Workgroup

If you are installing Windows NT from scratch, proceed through the entire installation and be sure that you install networking services. You must have a Windows NT NDIS-compatible driver for your network card, or in the case that Windows NT is running on a machine that will also have NetWare connectivity services, you'll need a Windows NT NetWare

ODI driver for your card and you must have the ODI-to-NDIS compatibility driver installed. Without NDIS, Windows NT will not be able to send NetBEUI, the native protocol of Windows for Workgroups, and without NetBEUI the machines will not see one another. For information on NetWare connectivity, refer to Chapter 5.

If your card is not one of the cards that Windows NT supports out of the box, you can install the networking option and use a third-party driver disk for your card during the installation. If you don't have a network card at the moment, then you can avoid the networking software installation and simply install it later. When you do get the drivers and card, open the control panel and double-click on the Network icon. Windows NT will display a dialog box like the one shown in Figure 6-3, notifying you that Windows NT networking is not installed and asking you whether or not you want to install it now.

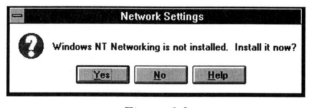

Figure 6-3
Networking Not Installed

There are two procedures for connecting to a Windows for Workgroups network, depending on the status of your NT machine: one method for new NT machines, where you will be installing the NT software from scratch, and another for previously installed NT machines that you want to add to a workgroup after the machine is already running NT.

New NT Machine

During the installation, you will be asked for a computer name. This name should uniquely identify your machine, and cannot be the same as the workgroup name or another computer name on the network.

Toward the end of the installation a dialog box appears that allows you to specify a workgroup or domain for the NT machine to join. You should enter the name that you got from the WFW machine in the dialog box as a workgroup name. The dialog box appears regardless of the installation method: Express or Custom. This makes you a member of the specified workgroup.

If you chose the custom install method, the next dialog box will list the installed protocols, services, and adapters. This is the same dialog box that you get when you double-click on the network icon in the control panel of an NT machine. If you didn't use the custom install, just wait until NT is up and running and then go to the control panel and select the Network icon.

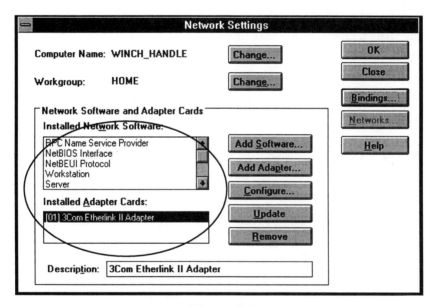

Figure 6-4
Windows NT Network Control Panel

You want to verify that the necessary protocols are installed and that the network card driver is installed and configured properly.

The default services installed for Microsoft networking are:

- 🖳 Computer browser service
- 🖳 NetBEUI protocol
- 🖳 NetBIOS interface
- 🖳 RPC name service provider
- 🖳 Workstation service
- 🖳 Server service
- 🖳 Network card driver

All of these drivers should be loaded in order to connect to a workgroup resource. The only one that is really optional is the NetBIOS interface which can be removed using the **Remove** button in the **Network Settings** dialog box or by deactivating the NetBIOS binding using the **Bindings** dialog box. To deactivate the binding, press the **Bindings...** button. You get a dialog box that looks like the one shown at the top of the next page. Either double-click on the light bulb next to the NetBIOS binding or select the binding and click **Disable**.

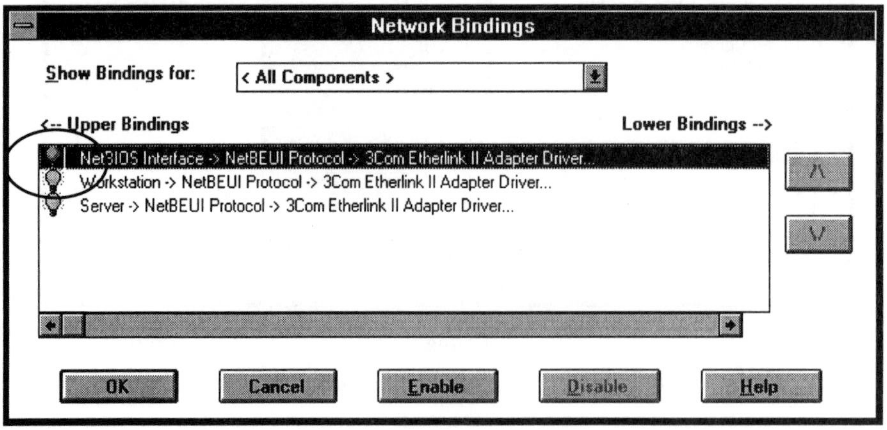

Figure 6-5
Workgroup Bindings

Be aware that any application that you have that needs a NetBIOS interface will not function including MS-Mail and Schedule+, and doing this you will receive a message during start-up of NT that something failed to load.

Figure 6-6
Something Didn't Work

This error in loading is caused by Windows NT attempting to install the NetBIOS DLL even though the binding for the service has been disabled. There really isn't any reason to disable the NetBIOS binding or remove the service, but it can be done. The reason it is still trying to load the DLL is because the NetBIOS network software is still installed.

Existing NT Machine

If you already have an existing NT machine, everything up to this point should have already been completed. You jump in where we verify the workgroup name.

After confirming all the settings for the network services, protocols, and cards, you need to verify the workgroup name that you entered. The workgroup name is prominently displayed at the top of the Network Settings dialog box, below the Computer Name.

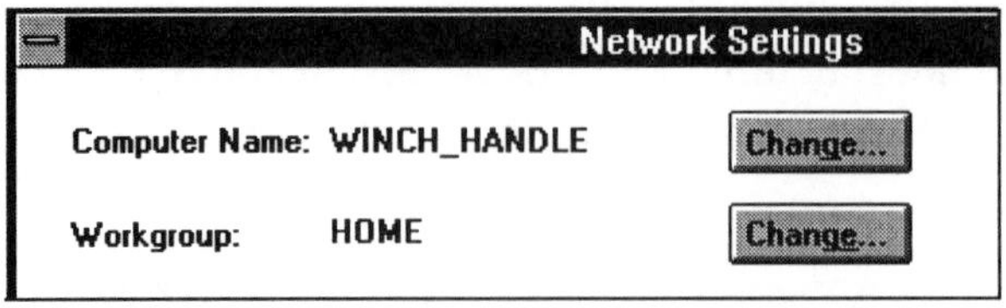

Figure 6-7
Checking the Workgroup Name

As you can see, the name has been entered properly. If you do need to change the name, in the case of an existing NT machine, just click on the **Change...** button. Make certain that the Workgroup option is entered and type or retype the workgroup name you want to join as shown in Figure 6-8. When entering a workgroup name for the first time or changing a workgroup name, you'll have to reboot your Windows NT machine just as you would for a Windows v3.1 installation, so that the machine can start up declaring itself as a member of the specified workgroup.

Once you have confirmed all the settings to your satisfaction and rebooted if necessary, you can verify your membership in the workgroup by opening the Windows NT File Manager and selecting **Connect Network Drive** from the Disk menu.

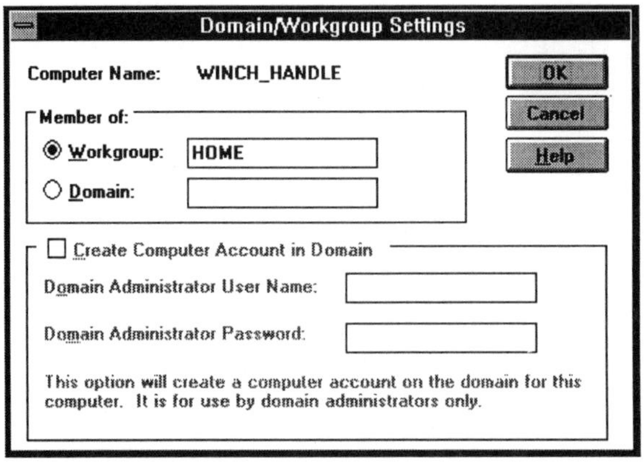

Figure 6-8
Modifying the Windows NT Workgroup Name

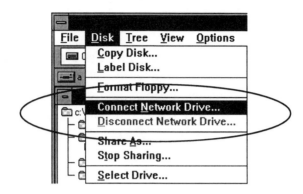

Figure 6-9
NT File Manager Disk Menu

This menu choice starts the Computer Browser service that you saw in the Network Settings dialog box. The browser is responsible for searching the network for valid connections. These connections appear in a hierarchical order with the network type displayed as the highest order. Workgroups are the next level. Below that are individual machines in the workgroup, and finally, share names round out the hierarchy.

Windows NT reads the valid names and displays them. Sometimes, when a machine has been removed from the workgroup, the machine name will linger in the browser list for quite some time. The information is stored in the Windows NT registry, which we'll cover later on in the book.

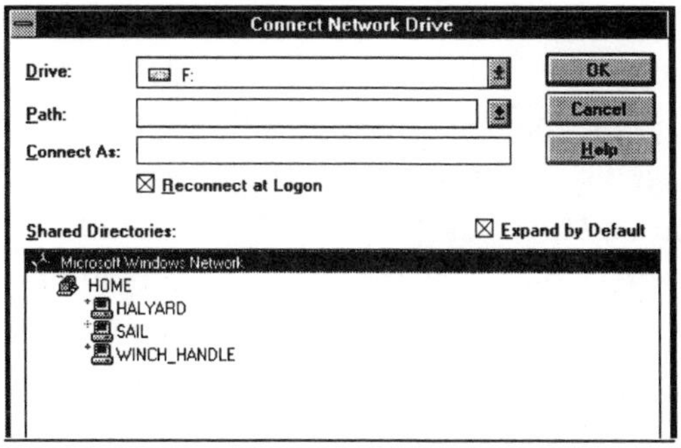

Figure 6-10
Browsing Network Resources

File Services

If your computer name appears in the list with the other computers in the workgroup, NT is configured correctly. You are now a member of the workgroup and can participate in workgroup sharing. In a workgroup there are two categories of file services: resources you access which are offered by another machine in the workgroup, and resources that you offer or share with others in the workgroup.

Accessing Remote Shares

You can select a share from one of the network machines and connect. Depending on the share you choose, you may or may not encounter a password validation check before gaining access. Select the share you want to connect to. In Figure 6-11, I want to connect to the VIRUS share on a WFW \\SAIL machine.

```
┌────────────────────────────────────────────────────────────┐
│ ─          Enter Network Password                           │
├────────────────────────────────────────────────────────────┤
│  You must supply a password to  \\SAIL\VIRUS    ┌────────┐  │
│                                                 │   OK   │  │
│                                                 ├────────┤  │
│                                                 │ Cancel │  │
│  Password:  [*******        ]                   ├────────┤  │
│                                                 │  Help  │  │
│                                                 └────────┘  │
└────────────────────────────────────────────────────────────┘
```

Figure 6-11
Password-Protected Resource

Double-click on the share and Windows NT displays a password dialog box, meaning that the share in the **SAIL** machine has been password-protected by the user of **SAIL**. Whenever you get this dialog box, you can be sure that it is a WFW machine because only WFW has password-protection for shares. If this were an NT share, the share would be granted or not based on your user name and membership in groups. You would never get a password dialog box for an NT share. There is no way to tell from the browser what type of machine you are connecting to unless the name or comment for the share indicates it. These are both user-selectable parameters, so you may not know by the name.

Offering Resources to the Workgroup

Selecting shares on a WFW/NT workgroup is pretty much the same, but whether you get access to a share is based on how the owner of the share decided to implement the resource. Remember that in a workgroup, every user is responsible for managing their own shared resources and determining how to make them available to other users in the workgroup.

With a WFW machine, where user names and groups are don't exist, the options for how you share a resource are very limited. Take a look at the dialog box shown in Figure 6-12. You cannot specify certain users or groups, or specify which rights a person has. You can implement a password for a particular right.

```
┌─────────────────────────────────────────────────────────────┐
│ ─                    Share Directory                          │
├─────────────────────────────────────────────────────────────┤
│  Share Name:   ┌─────────────────────┐      ┌──────────┐     │
│                │ VIRUS               │      │    OK    │     │
│                └─────────────────────┘      └──────────┘     │
│  Path:         ┌─────────────────────┐      ┌──────────┐     │
│                │ D:\UTIL\VIRUS       │      │  Cancel  │     │
│                └─────────────────────┘      └──────────┘     │
│  Comment:      ┌─────────────────────┐      ┌──────────┐     │
│                │                     │      │   Help   │     │
│                └─────────────────────┘      └──────────┘     │
│                ☒ Re-share at Startup                          │
│  ┌─Access Type:──────────────────────────────────────┐      │
│  │  ○ Read-Only                                       │      │
│  │  ○ Full                                            │      │
│  │  ● Depends on Password                             │      │
│  └────────────────────────────────────────────────────┘      │
│  ┌─Passwords:────────────────────────────────────────┐      │
│  │  Read-Only Password:   ┌──────────────┐           │      │
│  │                        │ CREW         │           │      │
│  │                        └──────────────┘           │      │
│  │  Full Access Password: ┌──────────────┐           │      │
│  │                        │ SKIPPER      │           │      │
│  │                        └──────────────┘           │      │
│  └────────────────────────────────────────────────────┘      │
└─────────────────────────────────────────────────────────────┘
```

Figure 6-12
Windows for Workgroups Share Implementation

If you want to let somebody use a password-protected resource, you have to tell them what the password is. This is much like LAN Manager servers and the "Share Level Security" method. It isn't very flexible, but for small groups of people, it works.

NT machines are much more flexible in how shares are administered. Unfortunately, most of the flexibility extends only to other NT machine. To start the process of sharing a disk directory with a workgroup member, select a directory you want to share. Next, select **Share As...** from the Disk menu in the NT File Manager.

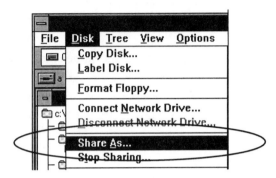

Figure 6-13
Creating an NT Share

This brings up a dialog box for specifying settings for the new share, shown in Figure 6-14.

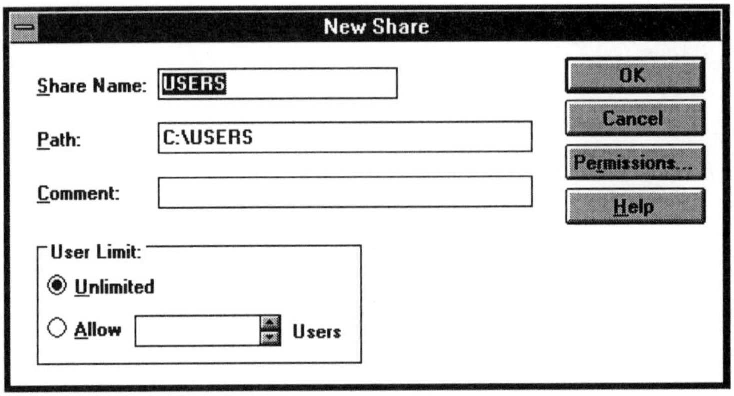

Figure 6-14
Windows NT New Share dialog box

Notice that you can set the maximum number of users that have access to the share. You can use this setting in two ways. First and most common is to limit the number of machines so that the NT machine does not spend most of its time serving other machines in the workgroup and thus slowing performance on the host. The other use of this setting is to limit the number of users to a particular application, based on the number of user licenses that you have. If you have a five-user license for Excel, then you can install Excel into a shared directory and set the limit to five. Be aware that just because a user is connected to the share does not mean he or she is running the application, so users should be instructed to disconnect from the share when not using the application. You could also set up a batch file to connect to the application, run it, and then disconnect when the application is closed.

You can specify what name you would like to represent the share, so that when users are browsing the network for resources to attach to, your share has a unique identifier. Bear in mind that it isn't necessary for the share name to be unique, but should be descriptive so that browsing users know what is inside the directory that they may need access to. The comment text will also appear next to the share name, so that additional information may be specified. You could, for instance, type in the people who might need a particular share, or specify a share as an NT-only share if the applications within the directory are 32-bit Windows NT applications.

By default, any new share is implemented with full access for the Windows NT group "Everyone." If you go no further than specifying a share name and the number of users, and click on **OK** then the share will be established, and anyone can use it. As mentioned earlier, Windows for Workgroups does not have users and groups for security management. If you want WFW machines to access an NT-hosted share, you have to make certain the permissions list contains at least one of four possible groups.

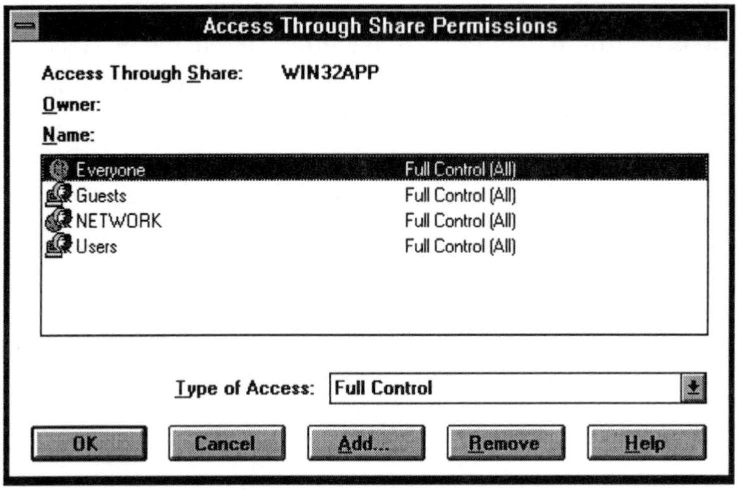

Figure 6-15
Valid Groups for WFW Access

Windows for Workgroups machines can access any share in which one of the four groups shown above is part of the permissions list. Including any one of the above listed permissions in a share will give a WFW user access to the share. If the group **Everyone** has the **Read** permission and the group **Guests** has the **Full** permission, then the WFW machine using the share will have **Read** permission. This is called pessimistic trust, where the lowest specified permission is the one that is granted. To adjust the rights for a share, you can change the **Type of Access** for a group listed in the permissions box. The available choices are:

🖳 **No Access**   (No access to files)
🖳 **Read**   (Read-only on files)
🖳 **Change**   (Write changes to, read, delete, execute)
🖳 **Full Control** (All privileges)

You may be wondering why you would have a **No Access** permission. The reason for it is to exclude a specific user who would normally be included in a group that has permission for the share. For instance, you have the group **Everyone** listed in the permissions list for a share, but you don't want one of the users in the group **Everyone** to have access. By placing the user in the permission list with the **No Access** permission, the individual user will be excluded from the share while all other users who are part of the group **Everyone** will have access. You can add additional groups and users to the share by clicking on **Add**. Doing so will bring up a list of all groups, and optionally, all users for the machine.

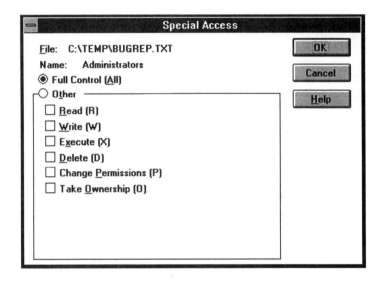

Figure 6-16
Granting Special Access Rights

Up to this point, we have only addressed security at the directory level. Windows NT can also control access at the file level. If your Windows NT installation is on an NTFS volume, you can specify access to a file with six attributes as shown in Figure 6-16.

Since granting of rights is pessimistic, a file in a shared directory that has fewer permissions than the directory it resides in will be available with the lower permissions. You can use this to ensure that certain files in a directory cannot be deleted or changed while other files in the directory can be accessed with higher permissions. These capabilities are available only for files on a volume that is formatted as NTFS, the Windows NT New Technology File System. HPFS and FAT volumes cannot protect files this way. For complete information about security, see Chapter 10.

That's pretty much it for disk shares. As you can see, most of the real security capabilities of NT are reserved for other NT machines, but with careful implementation, you can protect your files and operate efficiently with WFW machines as well.

Printing Services

Windows NT machines and Windows for Workgroups machines can share printers using regular printer drivers, which are provided with Windows NT, Windows 3.1, or by third-party vendors. There are three divisions of functionality when printing in a workgroup. NT to WFW, NT to NT, and WFW to NT.

Windows NT to Windows for Workgroups and Windows NT to Windows NT

Unlike printing from one NT machine to another, an NT machine that prints to a Windows for Workgroups hosted printer must have the printer driver for the network printer loaded on the machine. Windows 3.1/WFW printer drivers don't have the ability to process remote print jobs. The processing of the print job must occur at the remote computer and then be sent in complete form to the printer on the WFW machine. If you didn't install any printer drivers during the installation of Windows NT, fear not, because you can add them as you go.

Windows NT machines that wish to print to a printer that is connected to another NT machine do not have to have a printer driver loaded. Windows NT machines can share a printer driver where the NT machine that hosts the shared printer is the only one that must have a printer driver loaded. All other NT machines in the network can use the printer driver on the host computer.

To begin the process of connecting to a Windows for Workgroups printer, locate the Print Manager icon in the Main group of the Program Manager. You can access the same utility with the Printers icon in the Windows NT control panel. Unlike Windows 3.1, you don't have the choice of using or disabling the Print Manager.

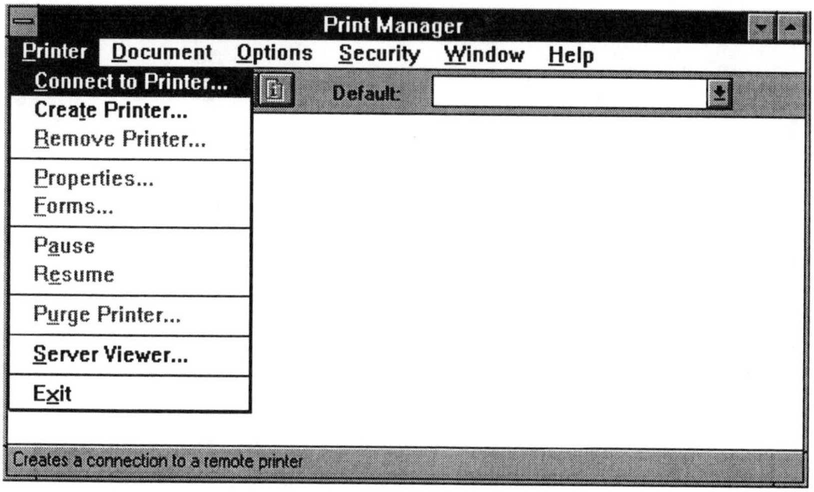

Figure 6-17
Connecting to a Remote Printer

Once the Print Manager is open, select the **Connect to Printer...** option from the Printer menu. You'll notice that, like the File Manager browser, the listing is in hierarchical order, from Server Name down to queue name. The Microsoft networks list the domain or workgroup name first, then the computer name, and finally the shared printer name. Select the printer share name from the machine you want and click on **OK**.

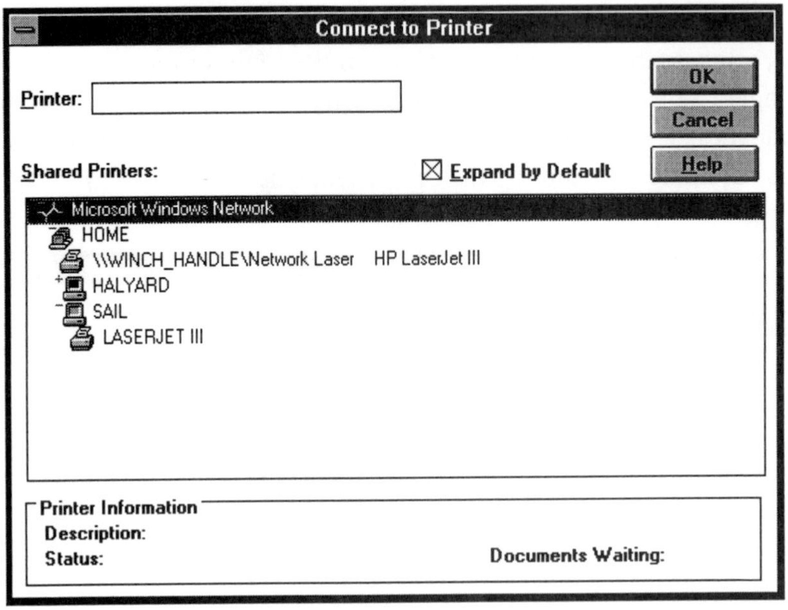

Connect to Printer

Printer: [   ]

OK

Cancel

Help

Shared Printers: ☒ Expand by Default

⌐ Microsoft Windows Network
  HOME
    \\WINCH_HANDLE\Network Laser   HP LaserJet III
  HALYARD
  SAIL
    LASERJET III

Printer Information
Description:
Status: Documents Waiting:

Figure 6-18
Browsing Remote Printers

If your system already has a printer driver installed, you're fine. In the event that you have not installed a printer driver on your NT machine, you'll get a warning about that condition, as shown in Fingure 6-19.

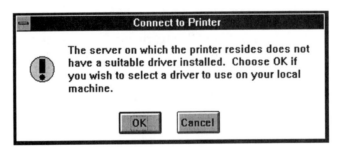

Connect to Printer

The server on which the printer resides does not have a suitable driver installed. Choose OK if you wish to select a driver to use on your local machine.

OK   Cancel

Figure 6-19
No Printer Drivers Installed

If you don't have a printer installed, just click on **OK** and you'll get the opportunity to add one. Select the appropriate printer driver from the list box and click on **OK**. You may have to load a Windows NT installation disk if the driver is not already on your system.

```
┌──────────────────────────────────────────────────────────────┐
│ ─    │            Select Driver                                │
├──────────────────────────────────────────────────────────────┤
│                                             ┌──────────┐       │
│                                             │    OK    │       │
│  Printer:    \\ANNAPOLIS\MAIN_SHEET         ├──────────┤       │
│                                             │  Cancel  │       │
│  Driver:     HP LaserJet III            ▼   ├──────────┤       │
│                                             │   Help   │       │
│  Print to:   \\ANNAPOLIS\MAIN_SHEET         └──────────┘       │
│                                                                │
└──────────────────────────────────────────────────────────────┘
```

Figure 6-20
Selecting a Printer Driver to Use for Printing to WFW

Once the printer driver is installed, you can begin printing to the network printer as LPT1. Windows NT printer drivers are different and have many different settings. The locations of these settings are all over the place. The main place to start is the **Print Properties** option of the Printer menu. You really should check out all the options by looking at them. Some of the adjustments, such as halftone printing with a LaserJet III are quite amazing.

For network printing you can use separator pages to delineate between one person's print job and the next one so that when the print jobs are sitting in the output tray of the printer, you know where one job ends and another begins. In the NetWare world this is known as a banner page, but with Windows NT, banner pages (separator pages) can send a preformatted page to the printer for each print job. The obvious flexibility of creating your own banner pages with custom information may be of great interest to administrators who use banner pages. The separator pages are printer language codes in text form. Although Windows NT does not associate them with **NOTEPAD.EXE**, they are fully editable by Notepad, using the language of your printer. One use, as shown from the sample separator pages included with Windows NT in the **SYSTEM32** directory is to effect mode switching on a printer from PCL to PostScript and vice versa. The separator file is sent just before the actual print you want, and is encapsulated as part of the same print job.

When you're up and running (printing) you can view your print jobs in the queue alongside other print jobs. You can remove and add print jobs as well as increase or decrease priority of print jobs in the queue. By increasing the priority, a print job will be printed before other jobs of lesser priority, regardless of how many other jobs are in the queue.

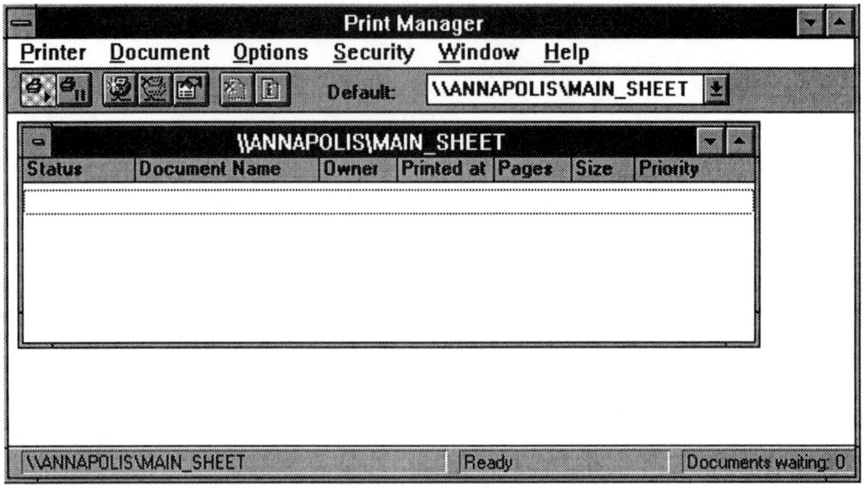

Figure 6-21
Viewing the Status of a Printer Queue You Are Connected To

If your Windows NT machine will be the host to a printer that other workgroup users will attach to, then there is another process to discuss.

Windows for Workgroups to Windows NT

When a Windows NT machine will host a printer, WFW machines can connect to the printer using any printer driver. You would, of course, want to print using a driver compatible with the destination printer but from a WFW machine, you can choose any printer driver. The sending machine doesn't know anything about the destination—except that the printer exists—so in theory, you could print from a WFW machine using a PostScript printer driver even though the destination printer is a non-PostScript printer. Your first indication that something was wrong would come when the destination printer started churning out 300 pages of garbage for a single-page graphic.

Establishing a printer from an NT machine that users can share is very easy. From the Printer menu select **Create Printer**. From this dialog box, as shown in Figure 6-22, you tell Windows NT what the printer should be called locally (within the NT machine), what driver to use for the printer, what printer port to use, and whether or not you want to share the printer on the network. One note about the printer port: If you are connected to a printer on a WFW machines, you can select that printer as the printer port for a shared printer. This means that a user could send a job to an NT machine and the NT machine will send the print job to another machine. This is not a standard configuration and can result in some serious lockup problems if the machine that originated the print job is also the host of the printer that the NT machine directs its print jobs to. You wind up with a circular reference, where the WFW machine uses its printer driver to format the print job and send it out. At the same time, the Windows NT machine receives the print job and sends it back out to the WFW machine. The printer driver doesn't know what to do because it is still send the job out using the printer driver and cannot also use it for receiving a print job.

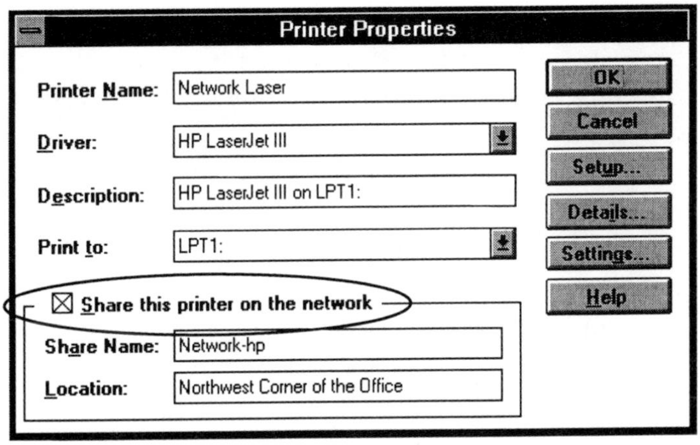

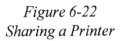

Figure 6-22
Sharing a Printer

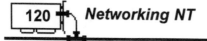

As you can see from the dialog box, you can also define the settings for the printer, and for print job specifics. The **Settings...** button currently brings up a retry time-out setting which you can adjust. The **Location** text at the bottom is more or less like a comment line and simply lets you define where the printer is physically located.

You can also operate your printer with security, preventing or allowing users of the workgroup to access your printer with different types of rights. Just as a file or directory can be shared with different levels of access depending on users and groups, so too can printers. On the next page is shown the default share permission list for a new printer share.

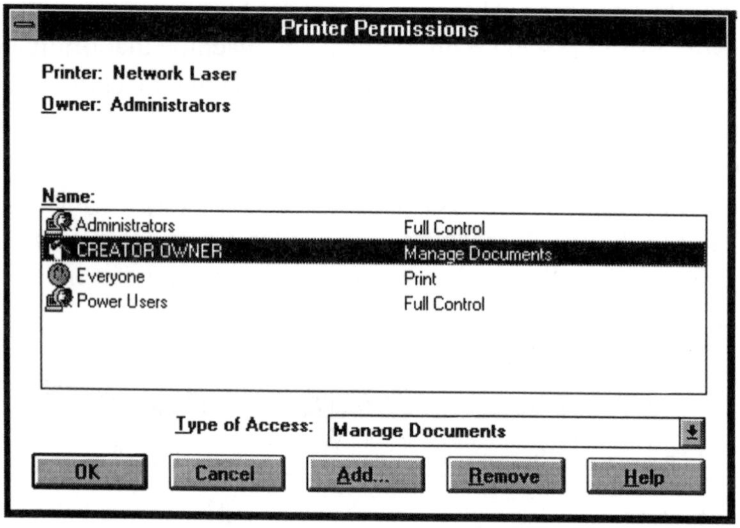

Printer Permissions	
Printer: Network Laser	
Owner: Administrators	
Name:	
Administrators	Full Control
CREATOR OWNER	Manage Documents
Everyone	Print
Power Users	Full Control
Type of Access:	Manage Documents
OK Cancel Add... Remove Help	

Figure 6-23
Printer Permissions List

The available rights for any user or group in the local user accounts database is shown in Figure 6-24.

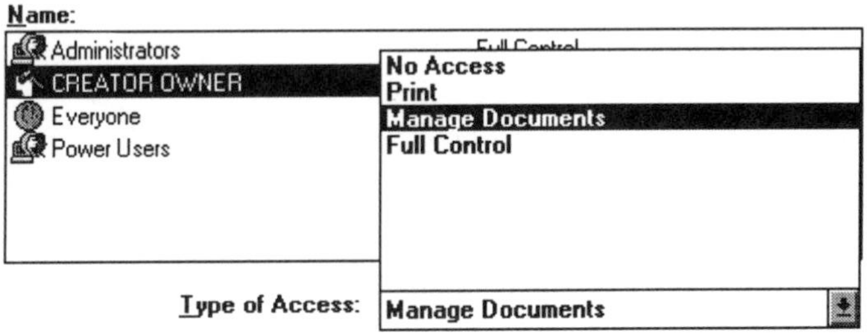

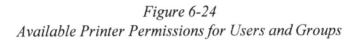

Figure 6-24
Available Printer Permissions for Users and Groups

The **Manage Documents** option lets a user delete, modify, and promote or demote a print job in a particular queue.

Remember that when you want a WFW machine to access and print to a printer, the permissions list must include one of the four groups shown in Figure 6-15.

Server Viewer

Another great feature of the NT Print Manager is the ability to view the status of other shared printers in the network. The **Server Viewer** option in the Printers menu allows your Windows NT machine to monitor the shared printers on other Windows NT and Windows for Workgroups machines. It's very handy if you have multiple locations that you can send a print job to and want to know which is the least congested at the moment. The view will display the status of the printer, number of jobs to be printed, and which printer driver the printer is using.

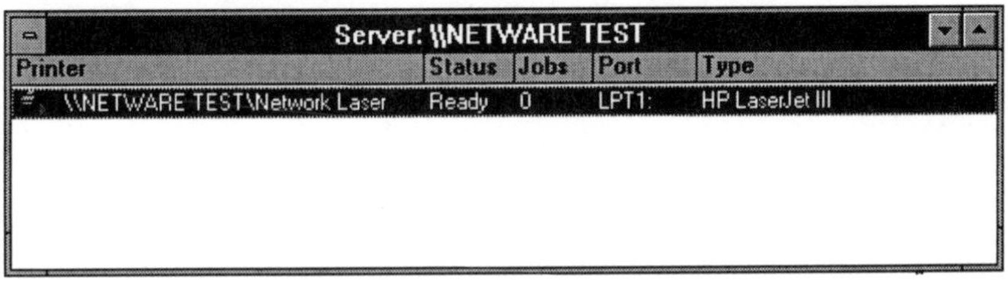

Server: \\NETWARE TEST				
Printer	Status	Jobs	Port	Type
\\NETWARE TEST\Network Laser	Ready	0	LPT1:	HP LaserJet III

Figure 6-25
Status of Viewed Printer Queues

Chapter 7

Connecting to a LAN Manager Network

LAN Manager has been upgraded into the new Windows NT Advanced Server product and while the upgrade is stable and dependable, many LAN Manager networks still exist. Fortunately, it's easy to connect to LAN Manager with Windows NT.

The first rule of LAN Manager to Windows NT connectivity is that to Windows NT, LAN Manager domains are not domains. Windows NT only recognizes a domain as a domain if the domain controller is a Windows NT Advanced Server. To Windows NT, LAN Manager domains look like workgroup names. Let's start from the beginning, connecting NT to LAN Manager.

What You Need

- LAN Manager network with at least one server
  - ✧ A user account on the LAN Manager domain
  - ✧ One shared network resource, such as a directory
  - ✧ One network card with NetBEUI running

- Windows NT v3.1
  - ✧ Network card supported by NT NDIS or
  - ✧ Network card supported by NetWare ODI for NT running NDIS compatibility driver

This procedure assumes that you already have a functional LAN Manager network operating, with one stand-alone server or domain controller and, at your option, backup domain controllers and member servers in addition to the requisite workstations.

The first step is to verify the domain name of the LAN Manager domain. As an administrator, you can run the command **NET ADMIN** from the LAN Manager domain server to determine this information. Generally speaking, if you are a network administrator, you probably already know the domain name. For my example, the domain name is just "HOME."

Configuring Windows NT for LAN Manager Access

If you are installing Windows NT from scratch, proceed through the entire installation and be sure that you install networking services. You must have a Windows NT NDIS-compatible driver for your network card. In case you are running on a machine that will also have NetWare connectivity services, you'll need a Windows NT NetWare ODI driver for your card and you must have the ODI-to-NDIS compatibility driver installed. For more information on NetWare connectivity, see Chapter 5.

If your card is not one of the cards that Windows NT supports out of the box, you can install the networking option and use a third-party driver disk for your card during the installation. If you don't have a network card at the moment, then you can avoid the networking software installation and simply go back and install it later. When you do get the drivers and card, open the control panel and double-click on the Network icon. Windows NT will display a dialog box like the one shown in Figure 7-1, notifying you that Windows NT Networking is not installed and asking you whether or not you want to install it now.

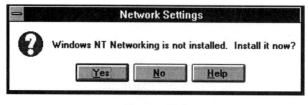

Figure 7-1
Networking Not Installed

There are two procedures for connecting to a LAN Manager network, depending on the status of your NT machine. There is one procedure for new NT machines, where you will be installing the NT software from scratch, and another for existing NT machines.

New Windows NT Machine

During the installation, you will be asked for a computer name. This name should uniquely identify your machine, and cannot be the same as the domain name or another computer name on the network.

Toward the end of the installation a dialog box appears that allows you to specify a workgroup or domain name for the NT machine to join. You should enter the name that you got from the domain controller in the dialog box as a workgroup name. The dialog box appears regardless of the installation method: Express or Custom. This makes you a member of the specified domain. Remember that this entry must be made in the workgroup entry box, not the domain entry, because Windows NT sees LAN Manager domains as workgroups.

If you chose the custom installation method, the next dialog box will list the installed protocols, services, and adapters. This is the same dialog box that you get when you double-click on the Network icon in the control panel of an NT machine. If you didn't use the custom installation, just wait until NT is up and running and then go to the control panel and select the Network icon.

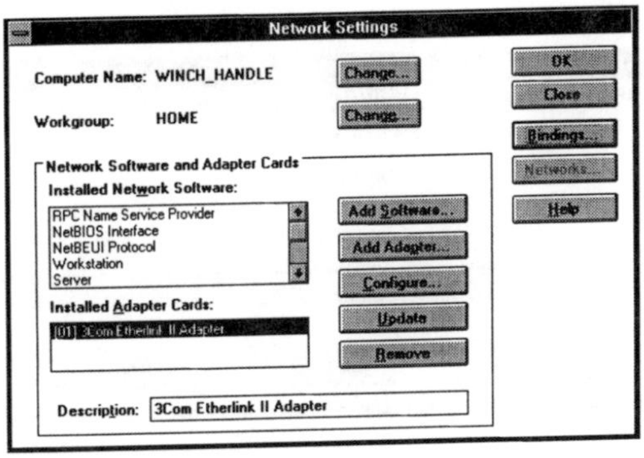

Figure 7-2
Windows NT Network Control Panel

You want to verify that the necessary protocols are installed and that the network card driver is installed and configured properly. The default services installed for Microsoft networking are:

- Computer browser service
- NetBEUI protocol
- NetBIOS interface
- RPC name service provider
- Workstation service
- Server service
- Network card driver

All of these drivers should be loaded in order to connect to a LAN Manager resource. The only one that is really optional is the NetBIOS interface which can be removed using the **Remove** button in the Network Settings dialog box or by deactivating the NetBIOS binding using the Network Bindings dialog box. To deactivate the binding, press the **Bindings...** button. You get a dialog box that looks like the one shown in Figure 7-3. Either double-click on the light bulb next to the NetBIOS binding or select the binding and click on **Disable**.

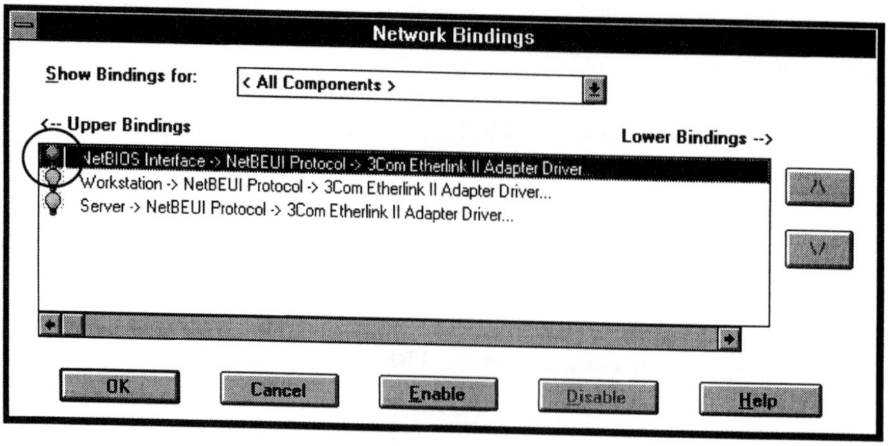

Figure 7-3
Domain Bindings

Be aware that any application that you have that needs a NetBIOS interface will not function. This includes MS Mail and Schedule+. By doing this you will receive a message during start-up of NT that something didn't load.

This error in loading is caused by Windows NT attempting to install the NetBIOS DLL even though the binding has been disabled. There really isn't any reason to disable the NetBIOS binding or remove the service, but it can be done. The reason it is still trying to load the DLL is because the NetBIOS network software is still installed.

Figure 7-4
Something Didn't Work

Keep going; this is where the existing NT machine comes in. Everything after this point applies to both methods.

Existing NT Machine

If you already have an existing NT machine, everything up to this point should have already been completed. You jump in where we verify the domain name.

After confirming all the settings for the network services, protocols and cards, you need to verify the workgroup name that you entered. The workgroup name is prominently displayed at the top of the Network Settings dialog box, below the Computer Name.

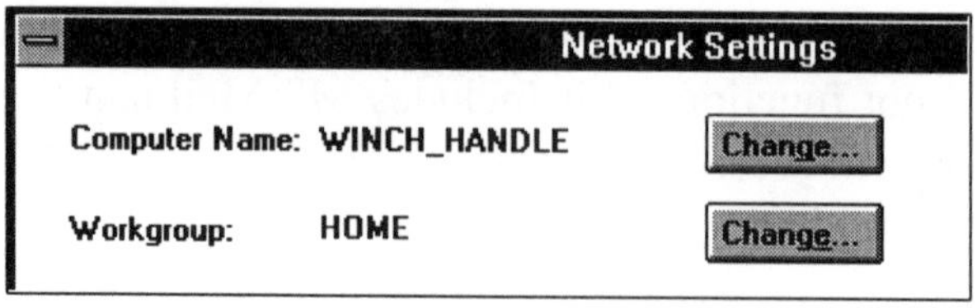

Figure 7-5
Checking Workgroup Name

As you can see, the name has been entered properly. If you do need to change the name, in the case of an existing NT machine, just click on the **Change...** button. Make certain that the Workgroup option is enabled and type the domain name you want to join as shown in Figure 7-6. When entering a workgroup name for the first time or changing a workgroup name, you'll have to reboot your Windows NT machine just as you would for a Windows v3.1 installation, so that the machine can start up declaring itself as a member of the specified domain or workgroup.

Once you have confirmed all the settings to your satisfaction, and rebooted if necessary, you can verify your membership in the domain by opening the Windows NT File Manager and selecting **Connect to Network Drive** from the Disk menu.

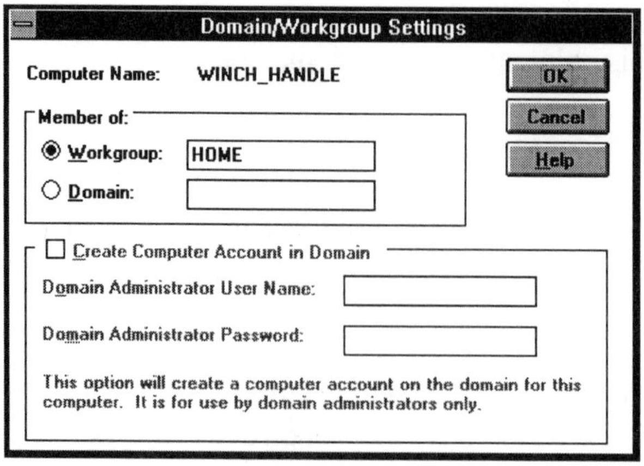

Figure 7-6
Modifying Windows NT Workgroup Name

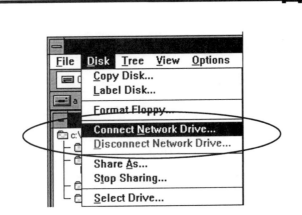

Figure 7-7
Windows NT File Manager Menu

This menu choice runs the Computer Browser service that you saw in the Network Settings dialog box. The browser is responsible for searching the network for valid connections. These connections appear in a hierarchical order with the network type displayed as the highest order. Workgroups and Domains are the next level. Below that are individual machines in the domain, and finally, share names round out the hierarchy.

I want to point out the layout of the image shown in Figure 7-8. Both **DOMAIN** and **HOME** are on the second level of the hierarchy, but **HOME** is a Windows for Workgroups workgroup and **DOMAIN** is a LAN Manager domain. In a domain, servers are the only objects on the network that can share resources and all servers that are part of a domain are listed in the hierarchy. Some may not have any resources to offer the network but are listed because they make up the domain. Unlike WFW, where every machine is listed, in a LAN Manager or Windows NT Advanced Server domain, the only listed resources are the servers of the domain. The LAN Manager Server in Figure 7-8 is the **ANNAPOLIS** listing. The **SPINNAKER** entry is my Windows NT machine. Although we identified the NT machine as part of a workgroup, the NT machine is seen as part of the LAN Manager domain. It's kind of weird, but it works. Workstations connected to the LAN Manager server from DOS or OS/2 will see the NT machine. It also appears in the browser hierarchy of NT and WFW machines and LAN Manager 2.x servers, if you configure it to do so. This is discussed at the end of this chapter.

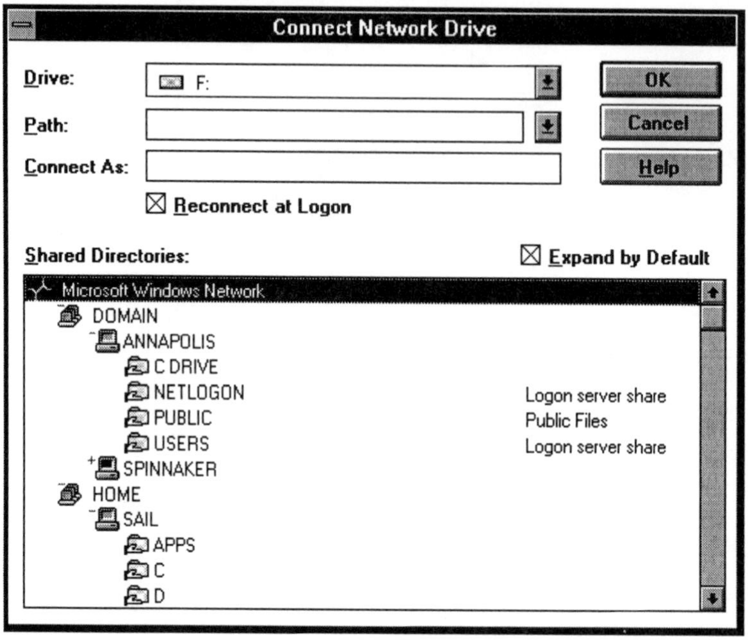

Figure 7-8
Browsing Network Resources

Windows NT reads the valid names and displays them. Sometimes, when a machine has been removed from the domain, the machine name will linger in the browser list for quite some time.

File Services

If your computer's name appears in the list with the other servers in the domain, you can be assured that you have configured your machine correctly. One obstacle remains in the way of connecting to LAN Manager resources, depending on the type of LAN Manager server you are connecting to.

User Level Security

There are two ways to implement security in a LAN Manager network. One is by user-level security, which is the most effective and secure method. It requires having specific user accounts and logging into a domain in order to gain access to network resources. What each user is allowed to access is governed by his or her user account, administered by the network administrator. In order to access resources on a LAN Manager server with user-level security, the domain user accounts database must have a user account that is identical in name and password to the Windows NT logon name that you entered. If your NT user name varies from a LAN Manager account, you will not have access to the domain resources. You can do one of two things: create a Windows NT user and password that matches a user account on the LAN Manager server, or create a LAN Manager account that matches the NT user name and password that you are using. For more information on creating and modifying user accounts in Windows NT, see Chapter 10.

Share Level Security

The other option for LAN Manager resource allocation is by share level security. This level of security offers no validation of users and simply places a password on each share offered by a server in the domain. In order for a Windows NT machine to access shares from a LAN Manager server that is using share level security, you must know the password associated with that individual share. Depending on the share you choose, you may or may not encounter a password validation check before gaining access. Select the share you want to connect to. In the case below, I want to connect to the **VIRUS** share on a LAN Manager server called **\\SAIL**.

```
┌─────────────────────────────────────────────────────┐
│ ━     Enter Network Password                         │
├─────────────────────────────────────────────────────┤
│ You must supply a password to  \\SAIL\VIRUS    ┌──────┐│
│                                                │  OK  ││
│                                                └──────┘│
│                                                ┌──────┐│
│ Password: ┌────────────────────────────┐      │Cancel││
│           │*******│                     │      └──────┘│
│           └────────────────────────────┘      ┌──────┐│
│                                                │ Help ││
│                                                └──────┘│
└─────────────────────────────────────────────────────┘
```

Figure 7-9
Password-Protected Resources

NOTE: There is a problem with Windows NT browsing valid shares on a server that is using share-level security. The server name will appear, but upon double-clicking on the server name to get a list of shares, you will receive error number 2141. Do not be alarmed. You should just type the share name that you want to access in the Path text box above the hierarchy using standard UNC. UNC, which stands for Universal Naming Convention, is a way of notating shareable resources on a LAN. If the server you want to connect to is called **ANCHOR** and the share name you want is **EXCEL** then you simply enter **ANCHOR****EXCEL** in the path entry box. If the share has a password, you'll be asked for it; if not, you'll be connected. You can browse the available share names for a LAN Manager server by running the NET ADMIN utility from the LAN Manager server.

Double-click on the share and Windows NT displays a password dialog box, meaning that the share in the **SAIL** machine has been password-protected by the user of **SAIL**.

Making NT Resources Available to LAN Manager Clients

In addition to accessing LAN Manager resources, Windows NT can offer shares to other users on a LAN Manager network. Remember that Windows NT "thinks" that it is running in a workgroup and therefore, all workgroup functionality still exists. To servers and clients on a LAN Manager 2.x network, Windows NT looks like a server. If you decide to share resources of your NT machine with clients on the network, you can do so while still maintaining a link to the LAN Manager servers. To start the process of sharing a disk directory with the network, select a directory you want to share from the File Manager. Next, select **Share As...** from the Disk menu.

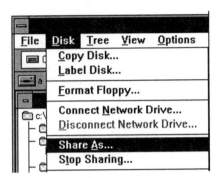

Figure 7-10
Windows NT File Manager Disk Menu

This brings up a dialog box for specifying settings for the new share.

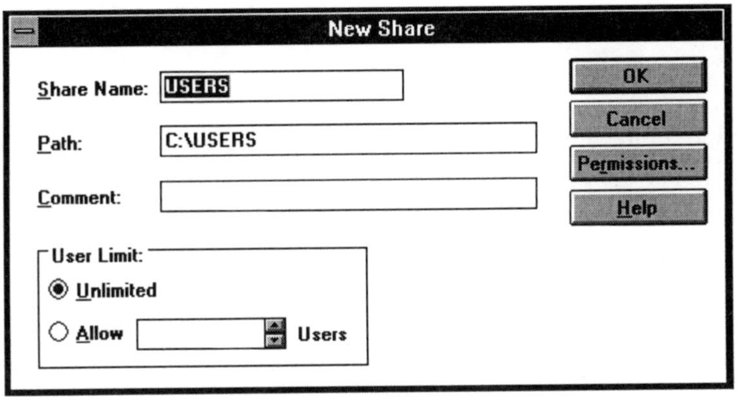

Figure 7-11
Setting Up a New Share for LAN Manager Clients

Notice that you can set the maximum number of users that have access to the share. You can use this setting in two ways. First and most common is to limit the number of machines so that the NT machine does not spend most of its time serving other machines in the workgroup and thus slowing performance on the host. The other use of this setting is to limit the number of users to a particular application, based on the number of user licenses that you have. If you have a five-user license for Excel, then you can install the Excel into a shared directory and set the limit to five. Be aware that just because a user is connected to the share does not mean he or she is running the application, so users should be instructed to disconnect from the share when not using the application. You could also set up a batch file to connect to the application, run it, and then disconnect when the application is closed.

You can specify what name you would like to represent the share, so that when users are browsing the network for resources to attach to, your share has a unique identifier. Bear in mind that it isn't necessary for the share name to be unique, but should be descriptive so that browsing users know what is inside the directory that they may need access to. The comment text will also appear next to the share name, so that additional information may be specified. You could for instance, type in the people who might need a particular share, or specify a share as an NT-only share if the applications within the directory are 32-bit Windows NT applications.

By default, any new share is implemented with full access for the Windows NT group **Everyone**. If you go no further than specifying a share name and the number of users, and click on **OK**, then the share will be established, and anyone can use it.

Clients on a LAN Manager network can access the shared resources of an NT machine just as they would any other LAN Manager-based resource. In the LAN Manager environment you have the choice of setting up share level security or user level security. With an NT machine, the only security scheme available is user level. The User Accounts Database on the NT machine must have a user account for any user that wishes to access an NT-offered resource. You can, using a LAN Manager 2.x server, use the NET ADMIN utility to administrate user accounts on the NT machine, but you cannot modify permissions for NT shares.

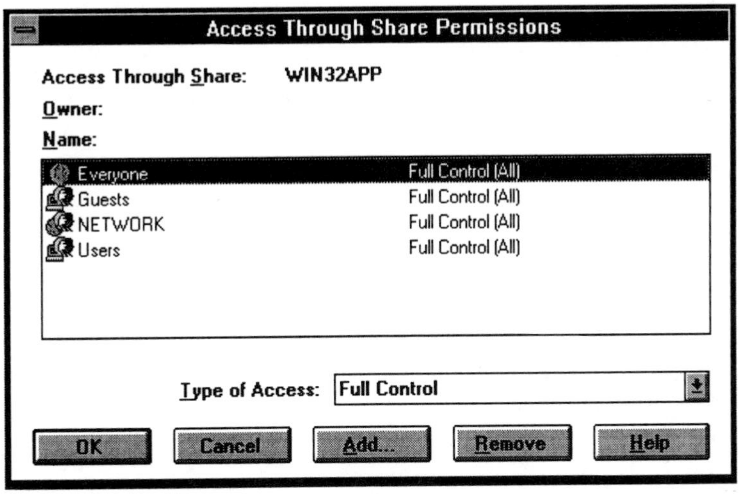

Figure 7-12
Granting Permissions

You grant permissions to LAN Manager clients either by user or with one of the four groups shown in Figure 7-12. If the group **Everyone** has the **Read** permission and the group **Guests** has the **Full** permission, then the WFW machine using the share will have **Read** permission. This is called pessimistic trust, where the lowest specified permission is the one that is granted. To adjust the rights for a share, you can change the **Type of Access** for a group listed in the permissions box. The available choices are:

- **No Access**   (No access to files)
- **Read**   (Read-only on files)
- **Change**   (Write changes to, read, delete, execute)
- **Full Control** (All privileges)

You may be wondering why you would have a **No Access** permission. The reason for it is to exclude a specific user who would normally be included in a group that has permission for the share. For instance, you have the group **Everyone** listed in the permissions list for a share, but you don't want one of the users in the group **Everyone** to have access. By placing the user in the permission list with the **No Access** permission, the individual user will be excluded from the share while all other users who are part of the group **Everyone** will have access. You can add additional groups and users to the share by clicking on **Add**. Doing so will bring up a list of all groups, and optionally, all users for the machine, as shown in Figure 7-13.

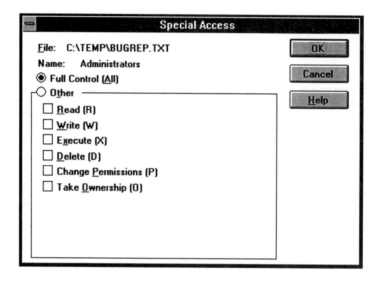

Figure 7-13
Setting File Level Permissions

Up to this point, we have only addressed security at the directory level. Windows NT can also control access at the file level. If your Windows NT installation is on an NTFS volume, you can specify access to a file with six attributes, as shown in Figure 7-13.

Since granting of rights is pessimistic, a file in a shared directory that has fewer permissions than the directory it resides in will be available with the lower permissions. You can use this to ensure that certain files in a directory cannot be deleted or changed while other files in the directory can be accessed with higher permissions. These capabilities are only available for files on a volume that is formatted as NTFS, the Windows NT New Technology File System. HPFS and FAT volumes cannot protect files in this way. For information about security, see Chapter 10.

Printing Services

Windows NT machines can utilize LAN Manager printer queues as network resources just the same as file resources, with one rather striking difference. Printer queues implemented in a LAN Manager network with share-level security cannot be located or attached to by Windows NT machines, even by typing the UNC name. Only printer shares implemented in a LAN Manager server with user-level security can be attached to by a Windows NT machine. This may change with subsequent releases of Windows NT.

Windows NT machines that wish to print to a printer that is connected to a LAN Manager server must have a printer driver loaded that closely mimics the printer driver on the LAN Manager server. Unlike printing from one Windows NT machine to another, a Windows NT machine that prints to a LAN Manager-hosted printer must have the printer driver for the network printer loaded on the machine. LAN Manager printer drivers don't have the ability to process raw remote print jobs. The processing of the print job must occur at the remote computer and then be sent in complete form to the printer queue on the LAN Manager server. If you didn't install any printer drivers during the installation of Windows NT, fear not, because you can add them as you go.

To begin the process of connecting to a LAN Manager printer, locate the Print Manager icon in the Main group of the Program Manager. You can access the same utility with the Printers icon in the Windows NT control panel. Unlike Windows 3.1, you don't have a choice in using or disabling the Print Manager. In Windows NT it's always on.

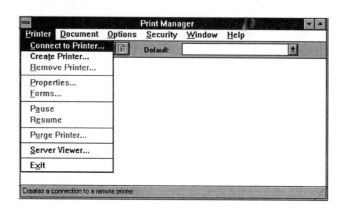

Figure 7-14
Connecting to a Remote Printer

Once the Print Manager is open, select the `Connect to Printer...` option from the Printer menu. You'll notice that, like the File Manager browser, the listing is in hierarchical order, from server name down to queue name. The Microsoft networks list the domain or workgroup name first, then the computer name and finally the shared printer name. Select the printer share name from the machine you want and click on **OK**.

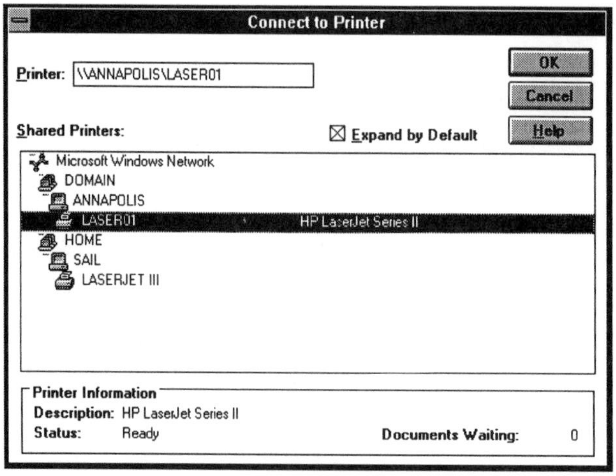

Figure 7-15
Browsing Remote Printers

Windows NT cannot utilize the printer driver of a LAN Manager server and will therefore notify you that a printer driver will be needed for the NT machine to print through.

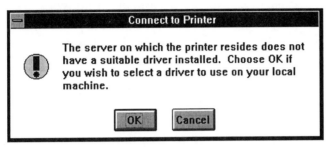

Figure 7-16
No Printer Drivers Installed

If you don't have a printer installed, just click on **OK** and you'll get the opportunity to add one. Select the appropriate printer driver and click on **OK**. You may have to load a Windows NT installation disk or third-party driver disk if the driver is not already on your system.

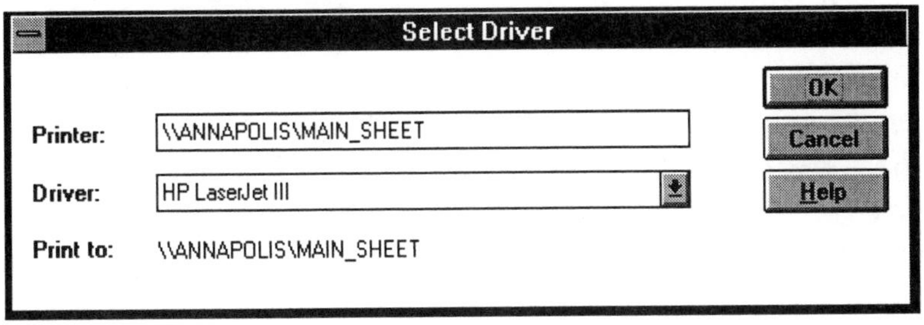

Figure 7-17
Selecting a Printer Driver To Use for Printing to LAN Manager

Once the printer driver is installed, you can begin printing to the network printer as LPT1. Windows NT printer drivers are different and have many different settings. The locations of these settings are all over the place. The main place to start is the **Print Properties** option of the Printers menu. You really should check out all the options by looking at them. Some of the adjustments, such as halftone printing with a LaserJet are very powerful.

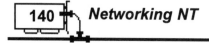

For network printing you can use separator pages to delineate between one person's print job and the next one so that when the print jobs are sitting in the output tray of the printer, you know where one job ends and another begins. In the NetWare world this is known as a banner page, but with Windows NT, banner pages (separator pages) can send a pre-formatted page to the printer for each print job. The obvious flexibility of creating your own banner pages with custom information may be of great interest to administrators who use banner pages. The separator pages are printer language codes in text form. Although Windows NT does not associate them with **NOTEPAD.EXE**, they are fully editable by Notepad, using the language of your printer. One use, as shown from the sample separator pages included with Windows NT in the **SYSTEM32** directory is to effect mode switching on a printer from PCL to PostScript and vice versa. The separator file is sent just before the actual print you want, and is encapsulated as part of the same print job.

When you're up and printing you can view your print jobs in the local queue alongside other print jobs. You can remove and add print jobs as well as increase or decrease priority of print jobs in the queue. By increasing the priority, a print job will be printed before other jobs of lesser priority, even though there may be ten other jobs waiting to be printed. One final note about NT printing to LAN Manager: You cannot use the **Server Viewer** option of the Print Manager to view LAN Manager printer queues and you cannot administer those queues from your machine like you can with other NT machines.

That's it! You should now be able to print and share resources of your LAN Manager network with ease. Remember the "gotchas" for the different types of security implementation in a LAN Manager domain. As for how LAN Manager sees your workstation: It sees it as a server with a user logged on, all messages sent to you will arrive just like always, in a pop-up dialog box.

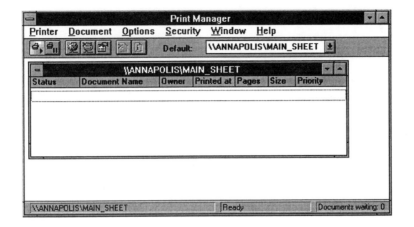

Figure 7-18
Viewing the Status of a Printer Queue You Are Connected To

NT Machines in a LAN Manager Network

Because NT machines appear as servers in a LAN Manager network, you probably want to configure NT so that it appears in the browse
lists of LAN Manager clients. To do this, locate and double-click on the
network icon in the NT control panel. Select the **Server** option from
the **Installed Network Software** list box. Then, click on **Configure...** The bottom item in the dialog box allows you to tell NT to
make its presence known to LAN Manager 2.x clients. This will allow
LAN Manager 2.x clients to browse through your shared resources, such
as directories and printers. If you don't do this, LAN Manager clients will
have to use manual UNC naming to connect to NT resources.

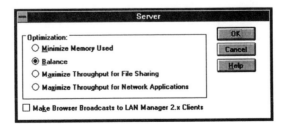

Figure 7-20
Making NT Machines Visible to LAN Manager Clients

Chapter 8

Connecting to Windows NT Advanced Server

Windows NT Advanced Server is the upgrade to LAN Manager 2.2. It is a 32-bit network operating system designed for the enterprise. With the same appearance and basic structure as Windows NT, Advanced Server possesses the ability to manage and control domains; whereas Windows NT may be a client on a domain, Advanced Server establishes and maintains the domain. For more information on what a domain is, see Chapter 3.

What You Need

⌨   Windows NT Advanced Server network
- ◇   A user account on the Advanced Server domain
- ◇   One shared network resource, such as a directory
- ◇   One network card with NetBEUI running

⌨   Windows NT v3.1
- ◇   Network card supported by NT NDIS or
- ◇   Network card supported by NetWare ODI for NT running NDIS-compatibility driver

This procedure assumes that you already have a functional Advanced Server network operating, with one server and, at your option, backup domain controllers in addition to the workstations.

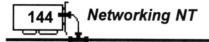

Configuring Windows NT for a Domain

When connecting to an Advanced Server domain, there is a paradigm shift in the management of users and machine. With all other methods of connectivity, the individual NT machine was responsible for management of users and computer. While connectivity with Novell and LAN Manager require that the NT machine have a user account that matches a user account on the network, connecting to Advanced Server requires a user account on the server only. No account on the local machine need be present. In addition, Windows NT Advanced Server needs to know about your machine in order to make it a member of the domain. We'll show you how all this is accomplished and how to interact with Advanced Server.

If you are installing Windows NT from scratch, proceed through the entire installation and be sure that you install networking services. You must have a Windows NT NDIS-compatible driver for your network card or, if you are running on a Windows NT machine that will also have NetWare connectivity services, you'll need a Windows NT NetWare ODI driver for your card and you must have the ODI-to-NDIS compatibility driver installed. For more information on NetWare connectivity, see Chapter 5.

If your card is not one of the cards that Windows NT supports out of the box, you can install the networking option and use a third-party driver disk for your card during the installation. If you don't have a network card at the moment, then you can avoid the networking software installation and simply go back and install it later. When you do get the drivers and card, open the control panel and double-click on the Network icon. Windows NT will display a dialog box like the one shown in Figure 8-1.

Figure 8-1
You Haven't Installed Networking

There are two methods for connecting to a domain, depending on the status of your NT machine: one method for new NT machines, where you will be installing the NT software from scratch, and another for previously installed NT machines that you want to add to a domain after the machine is already running NT.

New NT Machine

During the installation, you will be asked for a computer name. This name should uniquely identify your machine, and cannot be the same as the domain name or another computer name on the network.

Toward the end of the installation a dialog box appears that allows you to specify a workgroup or domain name for the NT machine to join. You should enter the name of the domain you are joining. If you don't know the domain name, you can obtain this information from your network administrator or by locating the domain controller you want to connect to and running the network control panel from the controller's control panel. One additional method is to browse the available networks using the File Manager or another application that lets you browse available network connections. If you are installing from scratch, however, you can't browse for names, so you must use one of the previous two methods. The dialog box appears regardless of the installation method: Express or Custom.

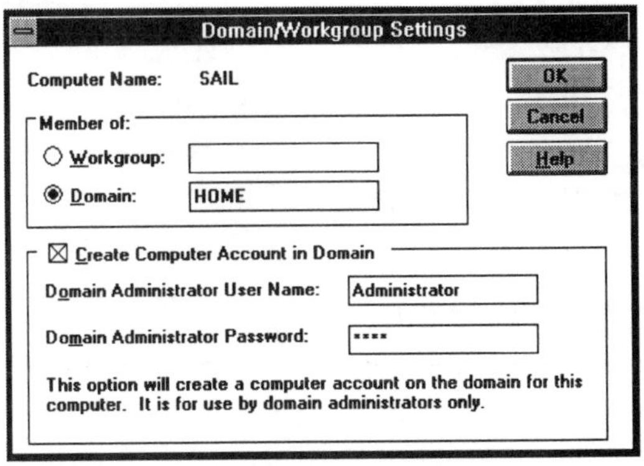

Figure 8-2
Setting Up Domain Membership

As you can see from Figure 8-2, when joining a domain you have the option of connecting using an account for the computer in the domain's accounts database. Windows NT Advanced Server must make you a member of the domain which involves making changes to the Advanced Server's configuration. In order to do that, you must have administrative privileges on the domain. Not just anyone can make changes to a domain configuration. Every Windows NT machine must register with the domain and be validated before joining. The reason for this is a rather simple one: Windows NT has some special privileges and abilities in an Advanced Server domain and the domain must know about the NT machine in order to allow those abilities. We'll get to those in a little while, but for now, enter an administrator logon name and password to join the domain.

If you chose the custom install method, the next dialog box will list the installed protocols, services, and adapters (Figure 8-3). This is the same dialog box that you get when you double-click on the Network icon in the control panel of an NT machine. If you didn't use the custom install, just wait until NT is up and running and then go to the Control Panel and select the Network icon.

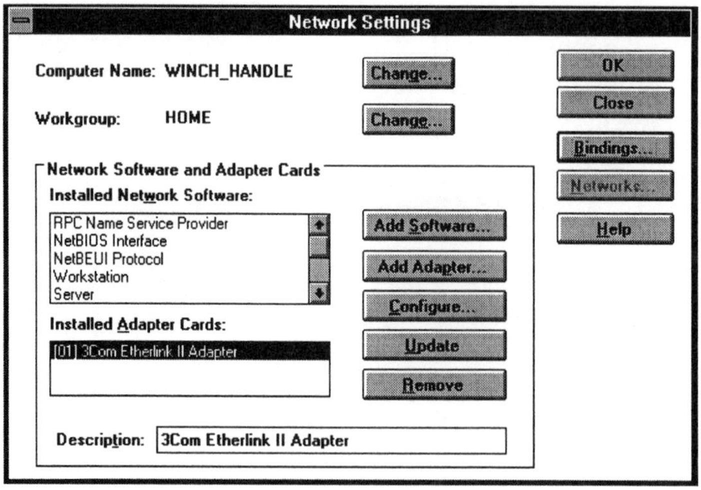

Figure 8-3
Checking Network Settings

You want to verify that the necessary protocols are installed and that the network card driver is installed and configured properly. Departing from the usual, Windows NT does not have a certain set of protocols that it must run on in order to connect to a domain. On the contrary, the only requirement is that the domain controller and the Windows NT machine are running the same protocol. If, for whatever reason, you decide to run your domain controller on TCP/IP, then the only protocol necessary for the Windows NT workstation to connect is TCP/IP. One other possible scenario is that the Windows NT workstation is bridged to the domain; in that case, the bridge must be running the same protocol as the domain controller and the workstation. Since it is unlikely that most networks will be configured in this way, the default is usually fine.

The default services installed for Microsoft networking are:

- Computer browser service
- NetBEUI protocol
- NetBIOS interface
- RPC name service provider
- Workstation service
- Server service
- Network card driver

All of these drivers should be loaded in order to connect to a domain resource. Remember, however, that this is for a default configuration and that the domain controller may be running a different protocol. The only one that is really optional is the NetBIOS interface, which can be removed using the **Remove** button in the Network Settings dialog box or by deactivating the NetBIOS binding in the Bindings dialog box. To deactivate the binding, press the **Bindings...** button. You get a dialog box that looks like the one shown at the top of the next page. Either double-click on the light bulb next to the NetBIOS binding or select the binding and click on **Disable**.

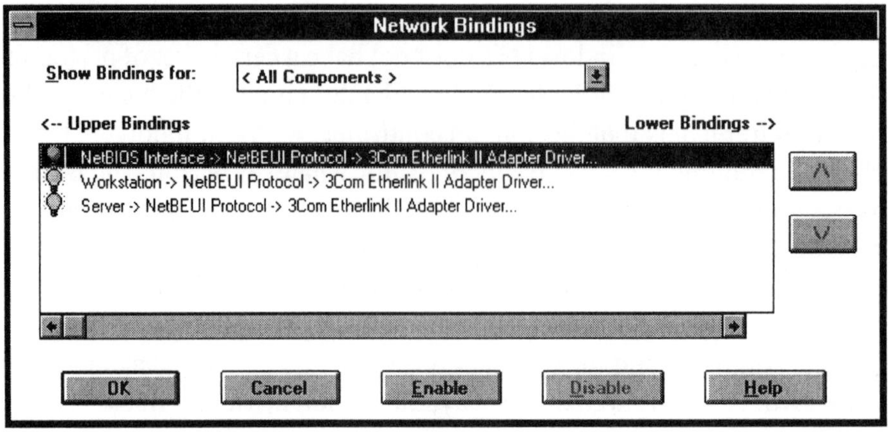

Figure 8-4
Checking Bindings

Be aware that any application that you have that needs a NetBIOS interface will not function. This includes MS-Mail and Schedule+. By doing this you will receive a message during start-up of Windows NT indicating that something failed to load.

Service Control Manager

At least one service or driver failed during system startup. Use Event Viewer to examine the event log for details.

OK

Figure 8-5
Something Didn't Work

This error in loading is caused by Windows NT attempting to install the NetBIOS DLL even though the binding has been disabled. There really isn't any reason to disable the NetBIOS binding or remove the service, but it can be done. The reason it is still trying to load the DLL is because the NetBIOS network software is still installed.

Existing NT Machine

If you already have an existing NT machine, everything up to this point should have already been completed. You jump in where we verify the domain name.

After confirming all the settings for the network services, protocols, and cards, you need to verify the domain name that you entered. The domain name is prominently displayed at the top of the Network Settings dialog box, below the computer name.

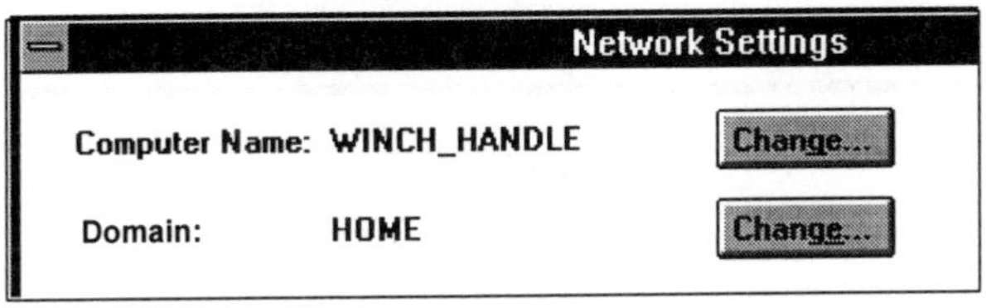

Figure 8-6
Checking the Domain Name

As you can see, the name has been entered properly. If you do need to change the name, in the case of an existing Windows NT machine, just click on the **Change...** button. Make certain that the Domain option is entered and type or retype the domain name you want to join, as shown in Figure 8-7. When entering a domain name for the first time on a Windows NT machine you must enter an administrator user name and password. Anytime you enter or change a domain name, you'll have to reboot your Windows NT machine just as you would for a Windows v3.1 installation, so that the machine can start up declaring itself as a member of the specified domain.

Once you have confirmed all the settings to your satisfaction, and rebooted if necessary, you can verify your membership in the domain by opening the Windows NT File Manager and selecting the **Connect to Network Drive** command from the Disk menu.

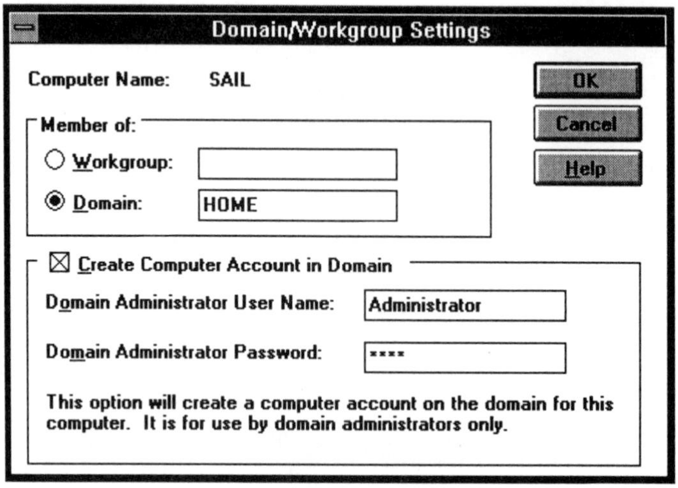

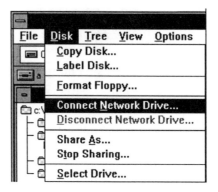

Figure 8-7
Setting Up Domain Membership

Figure 8-8
Connecting to a Network Resource

This menu choice starts the Computer Browser service that you saw in the Network Settings dialog box as a software service. The browser is responsible for searching the network for valid connections. These connections appear in a hierarchical order with the network type displayed as the highest order. Domains and workgroups are the next level. Below that are individual servers in the domain or workstations in the workgroup, and finally, share names for each computer round out the hierarchy.

I want to point out the layout of the image shown in Figure 8-9. Both **DOMAIN** and **HOME** are on the second level of the hierarchy, but **HOME** is a Windows for Workgroups workgroup and **DOMAIN** is an Advanced Server domain. In a domain, servers are the only objects on the network that can share resources, and all servers that are part of a domain are listed in the hierarchy. Windows NT machines appear as servers in the hierarchy for the domain because of the inherent workgroup capabilities in NT. An NT machine in a domain may offer its resources to the domain much as a server would. The rights to access the resources of an NT machine can be governed by an Advanced Server accounts database. When sharing the resources of an NT machine on a domain, the user establishing the share can access a user list from the domain controller.

Some listed servers may not have any resources to offer the network but are listed because they make up the domain. The Advanced Server in this image is the **ANNAPOLIS** entry. The **SPINNAKER** entry is my Windows NT machine.

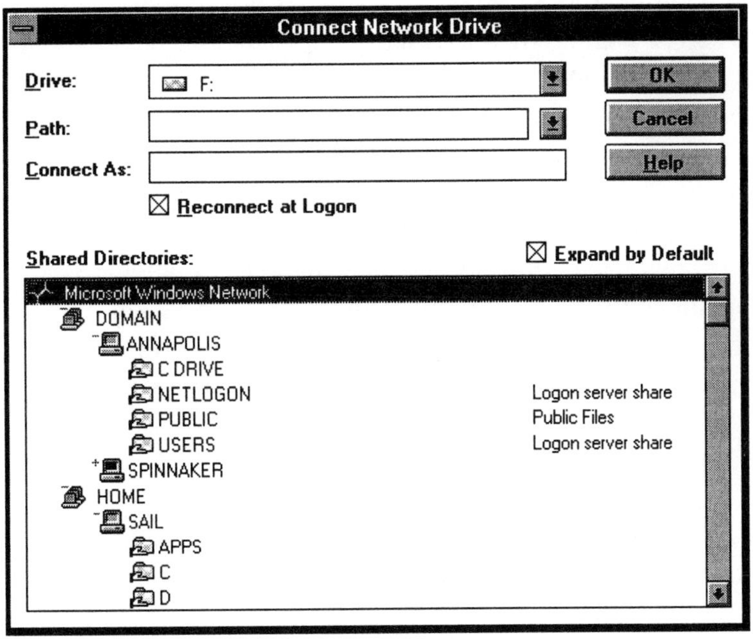

Figure 8-9
Browsing Network Resources

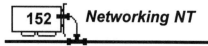

Windows NT reads the valid names and displays them. Sometimes, when a machine has been removed from the domain, the machine name will linger in the browser list for quite some time.

If your computer name appears in the list under the domain name and with other NT machines and Advanced Server controllers, you're connected properly. The most common reason why you may not see things in the browser correctly is having an improperly configured network card. This is usually indicated by Windows NT taking an exceptionally long time trying to retrieve the available resources in the domain. It is unlikely, however, that you specified an incorrect domain name because Windows NT will validate the domain name at the time you specify it. If the domain name does not exist or cannot be found, you'll know about it right away.

Domain Users

Once you have verified that you are connected correctly, it's time to learn something about users and Windows NT in a domain. You see, Windows NT has it's own user accounts database which is held in the registry of the NT machine; however, this database is not necessary for a user to connect to a domain. When any machine connects to a domain, access authentication takes place on the domain controller or other member Advanced Server machines. While you may have user names in the local NT user accounts database, if Windows NT is configured as a member of a domain, then the only accounts that really matter are the ones on the domain controller. A user account need not exist on the local user accounts database in order to log on to the domain. It must exist on the domain controller though.

Domain Users	Local Users
CHRIS	TAMMY
IVY	JAMAL
JEANNIE	BRIAN
RHONDA	GAIL

I have listed some sample names that may be found in their respective user accounts databases. If I sit down at this NT machine and log on as **CHRIS**, I'll have access to the domain because I have a user account on the domain. If I log on as **JAMAL**, I will have access only to local resources of the Windows NT machine where I am sitting because **JAMAL** does not have a user account on the domain.

All rights for network resources are governed by the domain user accounts database and managed from a server or workstation using the domain version of the User Manager. If the user logs on to a domain from a workstation that does not have his name in the local user accounts database, that user will have *guest* rights

User Manager for Domains

for the local machine along with all other granted rights in the domain. If a user logs onto an NT machine that has no domain account, but does have a local account, then the user will have whatever rights are granted to that account, but will not have any access to the domain.

For more information on users, groups, rights, and managing them, be sure to read Part Four.

File Services

As an NT client in a domain, users can share their disk resources and also gain access to other domain resources. The level of security that can be assigned to shareable resources depends on the type of hard disk partition that your NT machine runs on. For the highest level of security, you should always use the NTFS partition type as it allows the greatest number and type of attributes that can be assigned to a disk resource.

To start the process of sharing a disk directory with the domain, select a directory you want other users to be able to access. Next, select **Share As** from the Disk menu in the NT File Manager.

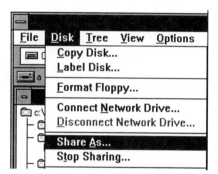

Figure 8-10
Establishing a Network Share

This brings up a dialog box for you to specify settings for the new share.

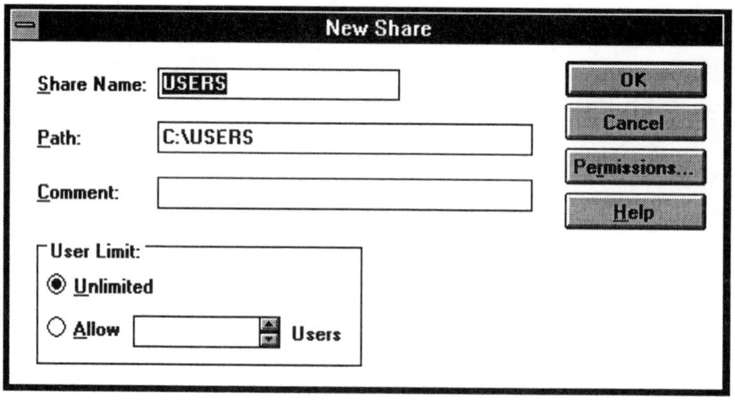

Figure 8-11
Specifying Settings for a New Share

Notice that you can set the maximum number of users that have access to the share. You can use this setting in two ways. First, and most common is to limit the number of machines so that the NT machine does not spend most of its time serving other machines in the workgroup. The other implementation of this setting is to limit the number of users to a particular application, based on the number of user licenses that you have. If you have a five-user license for Excel, then you can install the Excel into a shared directory and set the limit to five. Be aware that just because a user is connected to the share does not mean he or she is running the application, so users should be instructed to disconnect from the share when not using the application.

You can specify what name you would like to represent the share, so that when users are browsing the network for resources to attach to, your share has a unique identifier. Bear in mind that it isn't necessary for the share name to be unique, but should be descriptive so that browsing users know what is inside the directory that they may need access to. The comment text will also appear next to the share name, so that additional information may be specified. You could for instance, type in the people who might need a particular share, or specify a share as an NT-only share.

By default, any new share is implemented with full access for the Windows NT group Everyone. If you go no further than specifying a share name and the number of users and click on **OK**, then the share will be implemented, and anyone can use the share.

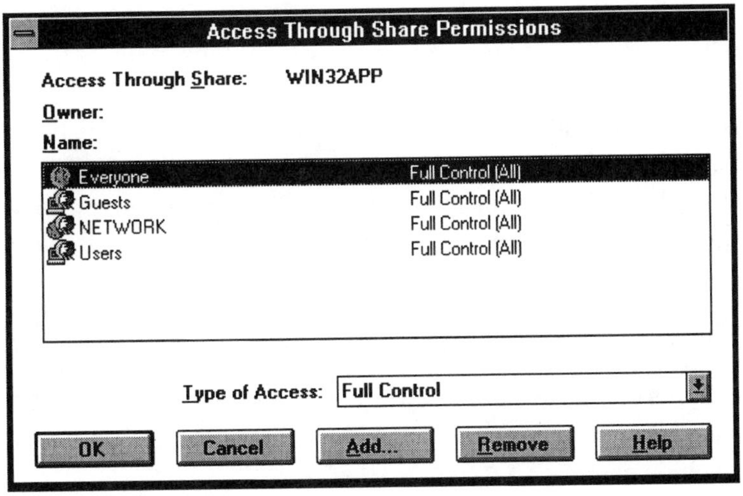

Figure 8-12
Changing Share Permissions

Windows NT grants access to shares by way of groups or users and has different levels of rights for shares. If the group **Everyone** has the right **Read** and the group **Guests** has the right **Full**, then the user using the share will have **Read** rights. This is called *pessimistic trust*, where the lowest specified right is the one that is granted. To adjust the rights for a share, you can change the **Type of Access** for a group listed in the permissions box. The available choices are:

⊟	**No Access**	(No access to files)
⊟	**Read**	(Read-only on files)
⊟	**Change**	(Write changes to, read, delete, execute)
⊟	**Full Control**	(All privileges)

You may be wondering why you would have a **No Access** permission. The reason for it is to exclude a specific user who would normally be included in a group that has permission for the share. For instance, you have the group **Everyone** listed in the permissions list for a share, but you don't want one of the users in the group **Everyone** to have access. By placing the user in the permission list with the **No Access** permission, the individual user will be excluded from the share while all other users who are part of the group **Everyone** will have access.

You can add additional groups and users to the share by clicking on **Add**. Doing so will bring up a list of all groups as shown in Figure 8-13, and optionally, all users for the machine. When connected to a domain, the default list of users and groups that appears is the list from the domain user accounts database like the one shown in Figure 8-13. Notice that the selected source for the names is the domain **HOME**. If you wish to grant access to other users from other domains, or from the Windows NT local user accounts database, simply click on the list box button to get a list of available sources as shown in Figure 8-14. The domain is **HOME** and the local machine name is **\\SAIL**.

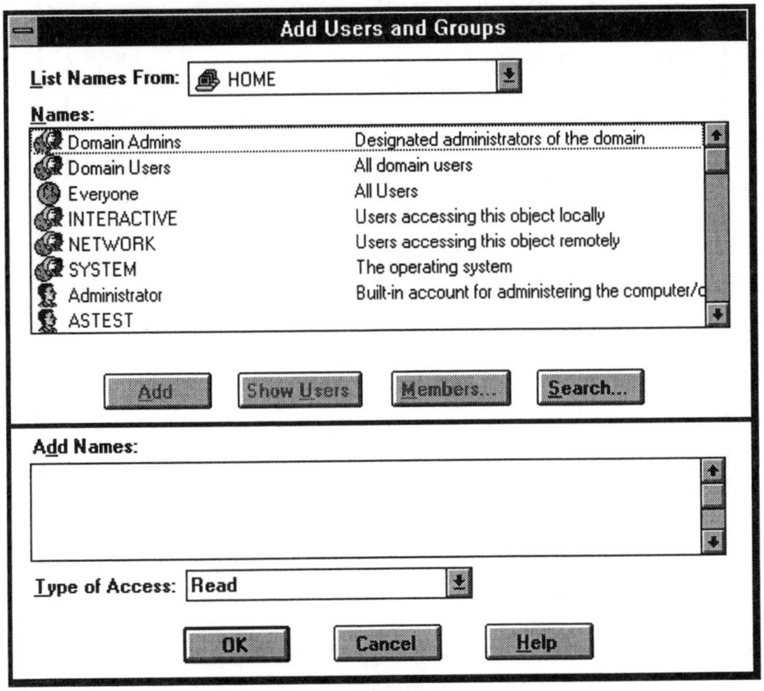

Figure 8-13
Managing Access to Shares

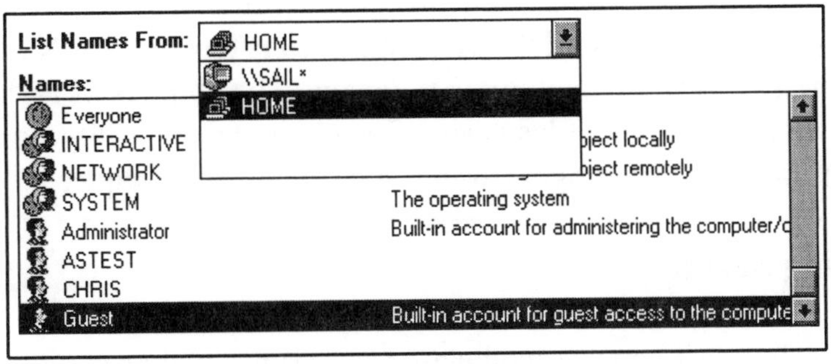

Figure 8-14
Selecting a Source for User Names

Up to this point, we have only addressed security at the directory level. Windows NT can also control access at the file level. If your Windows NT installation is on an NTFS volume, you can specify access to a file with six attributes.

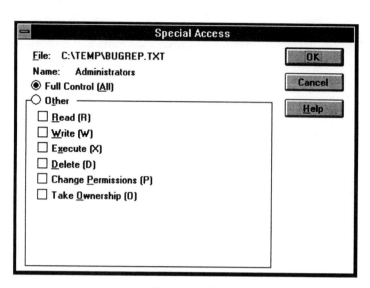

Figure 8-15
Special Access Permissions

Again following the pessimistic granting of rights, if a file in a shared directory has less rights than the directory, the user accessing will have the rights of the file, not the directory. You can use this to ensure that certain files in a directory cannot be deleted or changed while other files in the directory can be accessed with higher permissions. These capabilities are only available for files on a volume that is formatted as NTFS, the Windows NT New Technology File System. The abilities of HPFS and FAT volumes to protect files is significantly less than NTFS. For complete information about rights, users, and groups, see Chapter 10.

Printing Services

Windows NT can use and be used as a print server, accessing printers on other domain clients and servers, as well as offering a printer to other clients and servers.

Windows NT Printing to a Print Server

Windows NT machines that wish to print to a printer that is connected to another NT machine or to an Advanced Server do not have to have a printer driver loaded. You see, Windows NT machines can share a printer driver, where the NT machine that is a host to a printer and shares the printer on the LAN is the only one that has to have a printer driver loaded. All other NT machines in the network can use the printer driver on the host computer. As you may imagine, this cuts down on the processing needs of the client, since the job is sent raw to the print server, where page formatting and other print processing takes place at the host, thus freeing the client more quickly for another print job.

When you connect to a printer that is hosted by another type of machine, the NT workstation must have a printer driver loaded and print processing takes place on the NT machine before it is sent to the host machine.

To begin the process of connecting to a domain printer, locate the Print Manager icon in the Main group of the Program Manager. You can access the same utility with the Printers icon in the Windows NT control panel. Unlike Windows 3.1, you don't have a choice in using or disabling the Print Manager. In Windows NT it's always on. This is in keeping with the standards for NT; NT cannot talk directly to a hardware device. Everything must pass through the Print Manager before it is sent to the port.

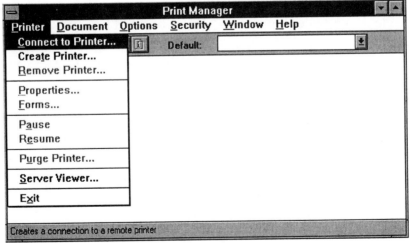

Figure 8-16
Setting Up Printing

Once the Print Manager is open, select the **Connect to Printer...** option from the Printer menu. Before we get to that, though, I want to tell you about another feature in this menu. The Server Viewer option allows your Windows NT machine to monitor the shared printers on other Windows NT, Windows for Workgroups, and Advanced Server machines. It's very handy if you have multiple places that you can send a print job to and want to know which is the least congested at the moment. The view will display the status of the printer, number of jobs to be printed and which printer driver the printer is using. This capability is only for Microsoft-networked computers but it's a great tool to have. You'll get a dialog box like the one shown in Figure 8-17.

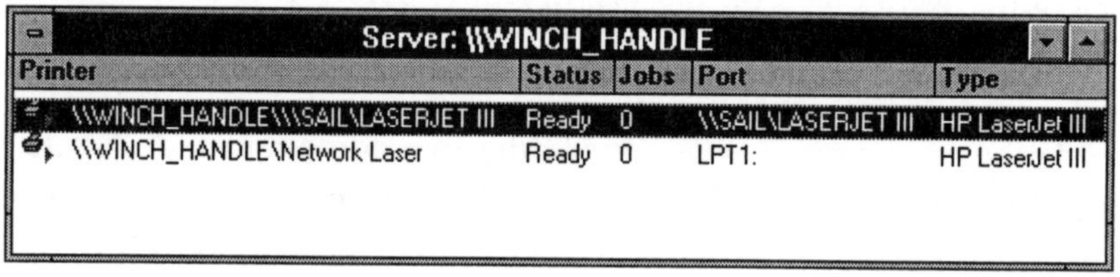

Server: \\WINCH_HANDLE				
Printer	**Status**	**Jobs**	**Port**	**Type**
\\WINCH_HANDLE\\\SAIL\LASERJET III	Ready	0	\\SAIL\LASERJET III	HP LaserJet III
\\WINCH_HANDLE\Network Laser	Ready	0	LPT1:	HP LaserJet III

Figure 8-17
Viewing Network Printers

When connecting to a remote printer, you'll notice that, like the File Manager browser, the listing is in hierarchical order, from server name down to queue name (Figure 8-18). The Microsoft networks list the domain or workgroup name first, then the computer name and finally, the shared printer name. Select the printer share name from the machine you want and click on **OK**.

If you are connecting to a printer that resides on another NT machine or on an Advanced Server machine you'll select the printer and that's it. When connecting to a printer that resides on a different type of client you'll get a warning about that condition as shown in Figure 8-19.

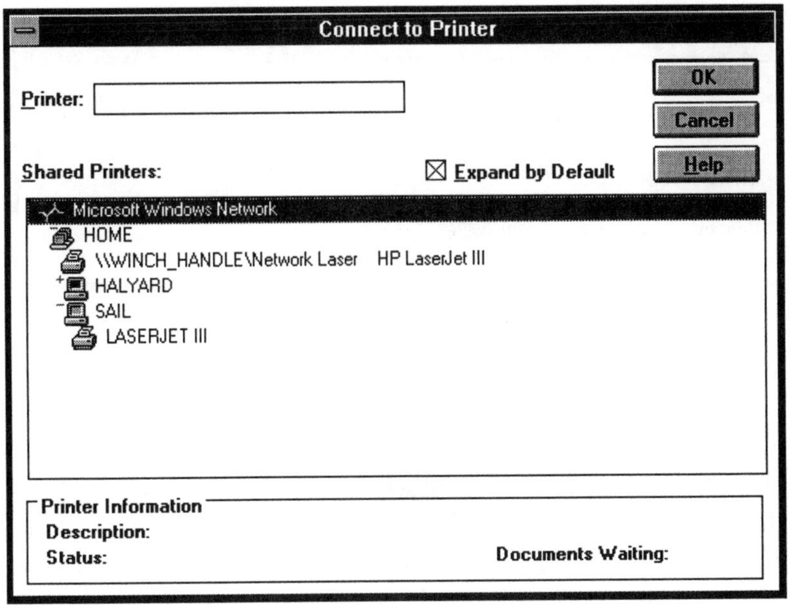

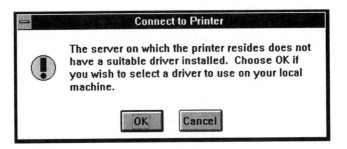

Figure 8-18
Connecting to a Remote Printer

Figure 8-19
No Printer Driver Installed

If you don't have a printer installed, just click on **OK** and you'll get the opportunity to add one. Select the appropriate printer driver from the list box and click on **OK**. You may have to load a Windows NT installation disk if the drivers are not already on your system.

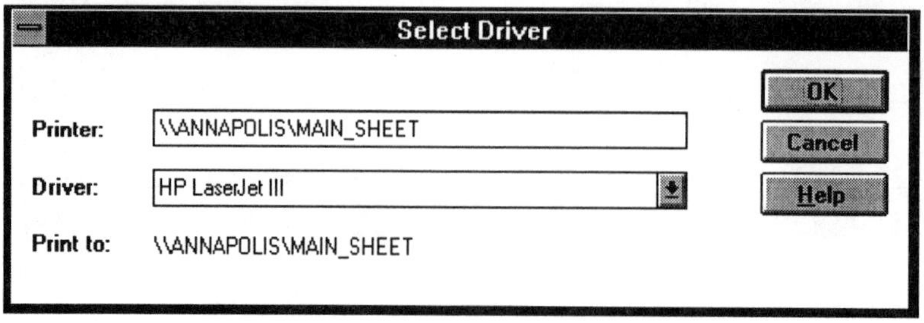

Select Driver		
Printer:	\\ANNAPOLIS\MAIN_SHEET	OK
Driver:	HP LaserJet III	Cancel
Print to:	\\ANNAPOLIS\MAIN_SHEET	Help

Figure 8-20
Selecting a Driver to Use when Printing to a Network Printer

Once the printer driver is installed, you can begin printing to the network printer as LPT1. Windows NT printer drivers are different and have many different settings. The locations of these settings are all over the place. The main place to start is the **Print Properties** option of the Printer menu. You really should check out all the options by looking at them. Some of the adjustments, such as halftone printing with a LaserJet III, are quite amazing.

For network printing you can use separator pages to delineate between one person's print job and the next one so that when the print jobs are sitting in the output tray of the printer, you know where one job ends and another begins. In the NetWare world this is known as a banner page, but with Windows NT, banner pages (separator pages) can send a preformatted page to the printer for each print job. The flexibility of creating your own banner pages with custom information may be of great interest to administrators who use banner pages. The separator pages are printer language codes in text form. Although Windows NT does not associate them with **NOTEPAD.EXE**, they are fully editable by Notepad, using the language of your printer. One use, as shown from the sample separator pages included with Windows NT in the **SYSTEM32** directory, is to effect mode switching on a printer from PCL to PostScript and vice versa. The separator file is sent just before the actual print you want, and is encapsulated as part of the same print job.

When you're up and running (printing) you can view your print jobs in the queue alongside other print jobs. You can remove and add print jobs as well as increase or decrease priority of print jobs in the queue. By increasing the priority, a print job will be printed before other jobs of lesser priority, even though there may be ten other jobs waiting to be printed.

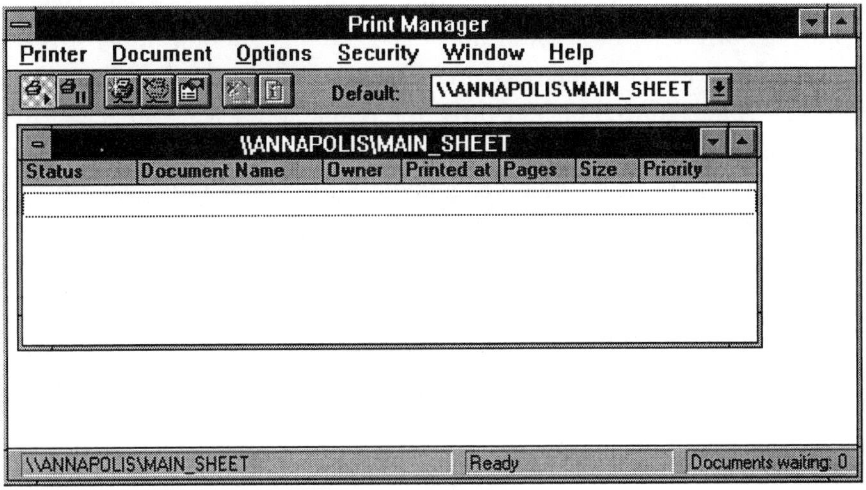

Figure 8-21
Windows NT Print Manager

If your Windows NT machine will be the host to a printer that other domain users will attach to, then there is another process to discuss.

Windows NT as a Print Server

When a Windows NT machine will host a printer, domain clients can connect to the printer using any printer driver. You would, of course, want to print using a driver compatible with the destination printer but from a Windows machine, you can choose any printer driver. The sending machine doesn't know anything about the destination except that the printer exists, so in theory, you could print from a Windows machine using a PostScript printer driver even though the destination printer is a non-PostScript printer. Your first indication that something was wrong

would come when the destination printer started churning out 300 pages of garbage for a single-page graphic.

Establishing a printer from an NT machine that users can share is very easy. From the Printer menu select `Create Printer...`. From this dialog box, as shown in Figure 8-22, you tell Windows NT what the printer should be called locally (within the NT machine), what driver to use for the printer, what printer port to use, and whether or not you want to share the printer on the network. One note about the printer port: If you are connected to a printer on a WFW machine, you can select that printer as the printer port for a shared printer. This means that a user could send a job to an NT machine and the NT machine will send the print job to another machine. This is not a standard configuration and can result in some serious lockup problems if the machine that originated the print job is also the host of the printer that the NT machine directs its print jobs to. You wind up with a circular reference, where WFW machine uses its printer driver to format the print job and send it out. At the same time, the Windows NT machine receives the print job and sends it back out to the WFW machine. The printer driver doesn't know what to do because it is still sending the job out using the printer driver and cannot also use it for receiving the same print job.

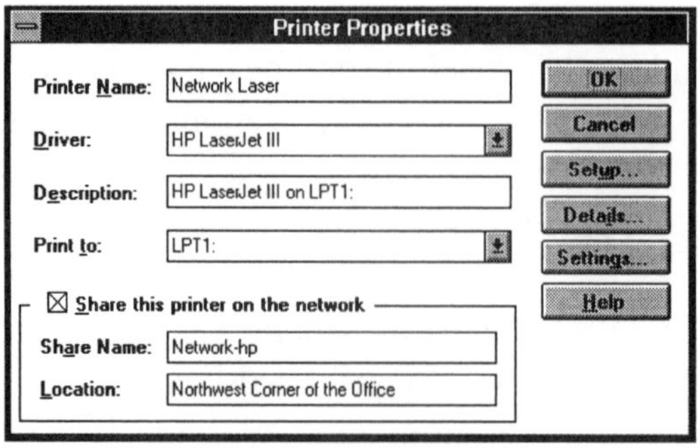

Printer Properties	
Printer **Name:** Network Laser	OK
Driver: HP LaserJet III ▼	Cancel
	Setup...
Description: HP LaserJet III on LPT1:	Details...
Print **to:** LPT1: ▼	Settings...
☒ **Share this printer on the network**	Help
Sh**are Name:** Network-hp	
Location: Northwest Corner of the Office	

Figure 8-22
Setting Print Properties

As you can see from the dialog box shown in Figure 8-22, you can also define the settings for the printer, and print job specifics. The `Set-`

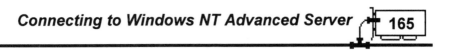

tings button currently brings up a retry time-out setting which you can adjust. The **Location** text box at the bottom is like a comment line and simply lets you define where the printer is physically located.

You can also operate your printer with security, preventing or allowing users of the domain to access your printer with different types of rights. Just as a file or directory can be shared with different levels of access depending on users and groups, so too can printers. Figure 8-23 shows the default share permission list for a new printer share.

```
┌──────────────────────────────────────────────────────────┐
│ ─                  Printer Permissions                    │
│                                                            │
│ Printer: Network Laser                                     │
│ Owner: Administrators                                      │
│                                                            │
│                                                            │
│ Name:                                                      │
│ ┌────────────────────────────────────────────────────┐   │
│ │ 🖳 Administrators            Full Control            │   │
│ │ 🖳 CREATOR OWNER             Manage Documents        │   │
│ │ 🖳 Everyone                  Print                   │   │
│ │ 🖳 Power Users               Full Control            │   │
│ │                                                     │   │
│ └────────────────────────────────────────────────────┘   │
│          Type of Access: │ Manage Documents        │▼│    │
│  ┌───────┐ ┌────────┐ ┌──────┐ ┌────────┐ ┌───────┐       │
│  │  OK   │ │ Cancel │ │ Add..│ │ Remove │ │ Help  │       │
│  └───────┘ └────────┘ └──────┘ └────────┘ └───────┘       │
└──────────────────────────────────────────────────────────┘
```

Figure 8-23
Default Permissions List

```
Name:
┌────────────────────────────────────────────────────┐
│ 🖳 Administrators            Full Control            │
│ 🖳 CREATOR OWNER     │ No Access              │      │
│ 🖳 Everyone          │ Print                  │      │
│ 🖳 Power Users       │ Manage Documents       │      │
│                     │ Full Control           │      │
│                     │                        │      │
└─────────────────────┴────────────────────────┘
        Type of Access: │ Manage Documents        │▼│
```

Figure 8-24
Available Rights

The available rights for any user or group in the domain or on the local user accounts database is shown in Figure 8-24. The **Manage Documents** option lets a user delete, modify, promote, or demote a print job.

Chapter 9

Connecting To Remote Access Service

RAS is roughly equivalent of Norton pcAnywhere for Windows in an NT environment. Of course, pcAnywhere for Windows will not run under NT. RAS is not a remote control package, however. The RAS service allows a remote NT or Advanced Server client to dial in to a Windows NT or Advanced Server machine and become a user in the workgroup or domain. You may wonder why that doesn't make RAS a remote control package. Remember that Windows NT is a multitasking, multithreading operating system. The RAS service runs in the background on a host and when a user connects, it's as if there are two or more machines in one. At the remote end, the connected user may access network resources, shares, printers, and everything else that any other NT machine can do as if it were running as a local workstation on the net.

What You Need

🖳　　Windows NT v3.1 or Advanced Server
　✧　　One shared network resource, such as a directory
　✧　　One communications adapter

🖳　　Windows NT v3.1
　✧　　One communications adapter

As you can see, the requirements for getting going with RAS are not very difficult to meet. How you begin to install RAS depends on the status of your Windows NT machines or Advanced Server machines. Additionally, the method of installation depends on whether or not you have a network card. This entire installation and configuration example fo-

cuses on a modem-to-modem connection, and we'll cover X.25 and ISDN connections at the end of this chapter. The first method deals with a new installation of Windows NT. Since there are so many different ways to arrive at a functional RAS installation, we'll approach it like this. There are four methods:

- Installing new Windows NT with no network card
- Installing new Windows NT with a network card
- Installing RAS on a machine with no network card
- Installing RAS on a machine with a network card

RAS can be used without a network, either on one end or on both. You can have a LAN and a remote computer at someone's house which can connect into the LAN. Additionally, you can connect two computers together, where neither is on a LAN and the connection is just from one remote machine to another. The obvious advantage of connecting into the LAN is that the remote user can operate as any other user with a local workstation on the LAN. Select your method of install from one of the four and then proceed to the section of this chapter titled "Installing RAS."

Installing New Windows NT with No Network Card

You should choose the Custom installation method when you start to install NT. After restarting Windows NT into the graphical part of the installation make certain that you install the network services.

When installing Windows NT and RAS without a network card, during the Custom installation method, Windows NT will prompt you with the dialog box illustrated in Figure 9-1.

Since you don't have a network card, you don't want Windows NT to attempt to detect the card, so click on the **Do** **Not** **Detect** button. Windows NT takes that answer as an indication that you may want to install RAS. As a result, the next dialog box will look like the one shown in Figure 9-2.

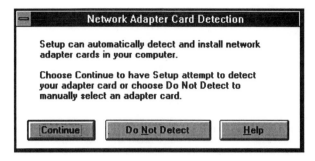

Figure 9-1
NT Can Attempt to Detect your Network Card

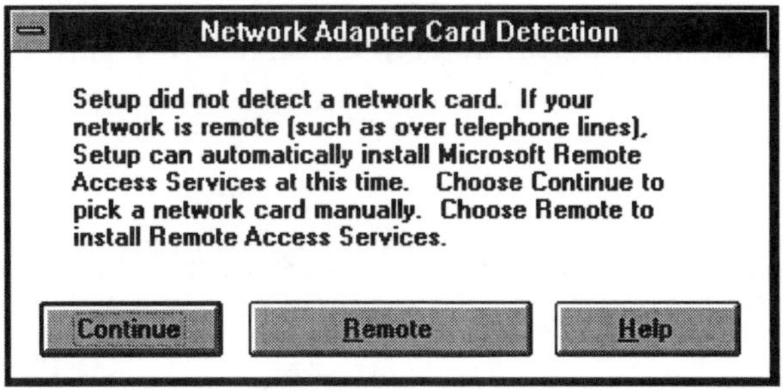

Figure 9-2
Do You Want to Install Remote Access Service?

At this point, your next option is pretty obvious. Click on **Remote**. Windows NT will automatically begin installing RAS. The next job for you to do is confirm the installation parameters for your communications adapter.

Installing New Windows NT with a Network Card

You should choose the Custom installation method when you start to install NT. After restarting Windows NT into the graphical part of the installation make certain that you install the network services.

When installing Windows NT and RAS without a network card, during the Custom installation method, Windows NT will prompt you with the dialog box shown in Figure 9-3.

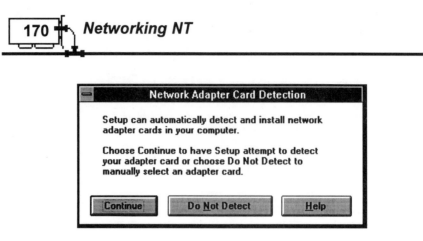

Figure 9-3
NT Can Attempt to Detect your Network Card

When the dialog box for detection of a network card comes up, ask NT to detect the card. Confirm the hardware settings of the card and proceed.

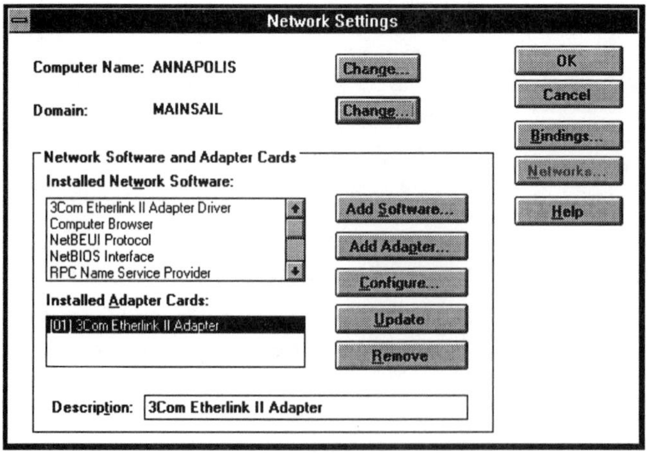

Figure 9-4
Reviewing Installed Network Options in a Custom Install

Once you get to this dialog box, you're ready to begin installing RAS. Click on the **Add Software** button and select **Remote Access Service**.

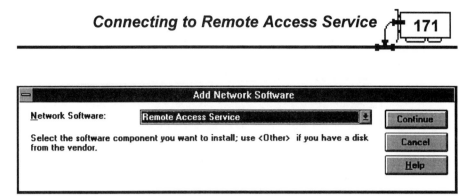

Figure 9-5
Select a Service to Install

Click on the **Continue** button and the RAS installation begins.

Installing RAS on a Machine with No Network Card

If you didn't install the networking software during initial software installation, open the Control Panel and double-click on the Network icon. Windows NT will display a dialog box like the one shown in Figure 9-6, notifying you that Windows NT networking is not installed and asking you whether or not you want to install it now.

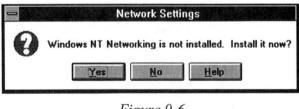

Figure 9-6
No Networking Services Installed

Select **Yes** and Windows NT will prompt you with a dialog box like the one shown in Figure 9-7.

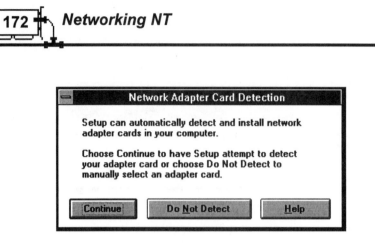

Figure 9-7
NT Can Attempt to Detect your Network Card

Since you don't have a network card, you don't want Windows NT to attempt to detect the card, so click on the **Do Not Detect** button. Windows NT takes that answer as an indication that you may want to install RAS. As a result, the next dialog box will look like Figure 9-8.

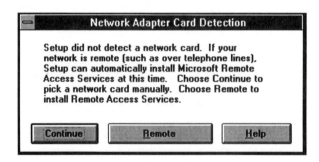

Figure 9-8
Do You Want to Install Remote Access Service?

At this point, your next option is pretty obvious. Click on **Remote**. Windows NT will automatically begin installing RAS. The next job for you to do is confirm the installation parameters for your communications adapter. Make sure you have either the CD-ROM or Disks 3, 7, 9, and 10 ready because NT will need them.

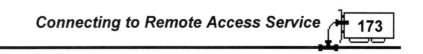

Installing RAS on a Machine with a Network Card

To install RAS, double-click on the Network icon. Windows NT will display a dialog box like the one shown in Figure 9-9.

```
┌──────────────────────── Network Settings ────────────────────────┐
│                                                                   │
│  Computer Name: ANNAPOLIS        [ Change... ]       [   OK   ]   │
│                                                                   │
│  Domain:        MAINSAIL         [ Change... ]       [ Cancel ]   │
│                                                                   │
│  ┌─ Network Software and Adapter Cards ─┐           [ Bindings...]│
│  │ Installed Network Software:          │           [ Networks...]│
│  │ ┌──────────────────────────────┐     │                        │
│  │ │3Com Etherlink II Adapter Driver▲│  [ Add Software...]        │
│  │ │Computer Browser              │     │              [ Help ]  │
│  │ │NetBEUI Protocol              │    [ Add Adapter... ]         │
│  │ │NetBIOS Interface             │     │                        │
│  │ │RPC Name Service Provider    ▼│    [ Configure... ]          │
│  │ └──────────────────────────────┘     │                        │
│  │ Installed Adapter Cards:             │    [ Update ]           │
│  │ ┌──────────────────────────────┐     │                        │
│  │ │[01] 3Com Etherlink II Adapter │    [ Remove ]                │
│  │ └──────────────────────────────┘     │                        │
│  │                                      │                        │
│  │ Description: [3Com Etherlink II Adapter    ]                   │
│  └──────────────────────────────────────┘                        │
└───────────────────────────────────────────────────────────────────┘
```

Figure 9-9
Reviewing Installed Network Options in a Custom Install

Once you get to this dialog box, you're ready to begin installing RAS. Click on the **Add Software** button and select **Remote Access Service**.

```
┌──────────────────── Add Network Software ────────────────────┐
│                                                              │
│ Network Software:  [Remote Access Service          ▼]  [Continue]│
│                                                              │
│ Select the software component you want to install; use <Other> if you have a disk │  [Cancel]│
│ from the vendor.                                             │
│                                                         [Help]│
└──────────────────────────────────────────────────────────────┘
```

Figure 9-10
Select a Service to Install

Click on **Continue** and the RAS installation begins. Make sure you have either the CD-ROM or Disks 3, 7, 9, and 10 ready because NT will need them.

Installing RAS

Now that you are at the same step as all other methods of installation, let's get started. After the installation of drivers and services Windows NT will begin asking you about the configuration of your communications hardware. In this case, I'm using a Hayes-compatible 2400-baud modem running on COM 1. Windows NT will usually detect the proper port that your modem is running on.

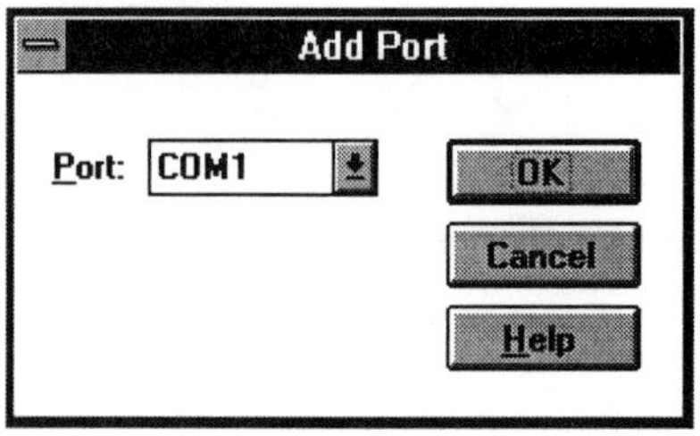

Figure 9-11
Select an Available Communications Port

Next, tell Windows NT what type of modem you have and specify the default configuration of the modem.

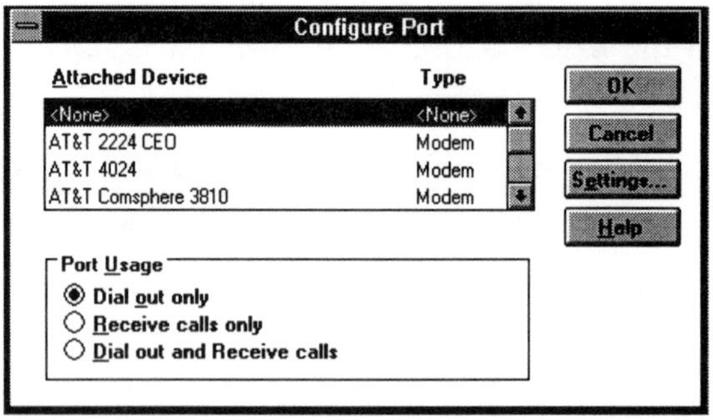

Figure 9-12
Setting the Modem Type and Options

Once RAS is installed, you should check out the RAS **README.TXT** file which does contain some specific information regarding the idiosyncrasies of certain modems. There are four points of configuration that you can set for the modem. Once you have selected the modem that you have, to check the advanced configuration of the modem click on the **Settings** button.

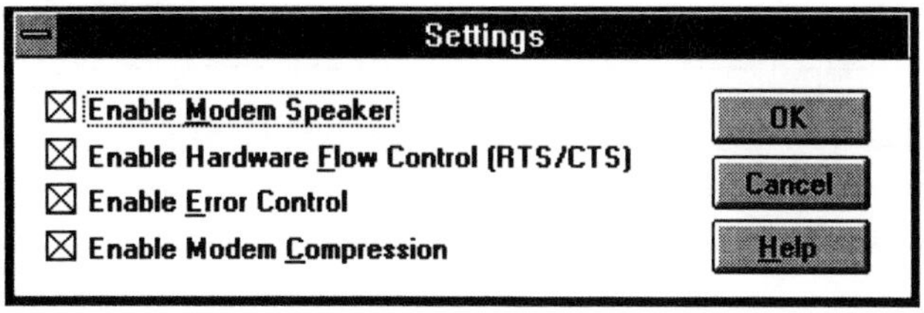

Figure 9-13
Modem Specific Settings

Again, I have to stress that you should read the **README.TXT** file for RAS, because the settings for the modem can be affected by the type of modem. There is no harm in setting all these options, even if they're wrong. You can always go back and reconfigure it later. After confirming the settings, select the mode of communications service that your machine will perform.

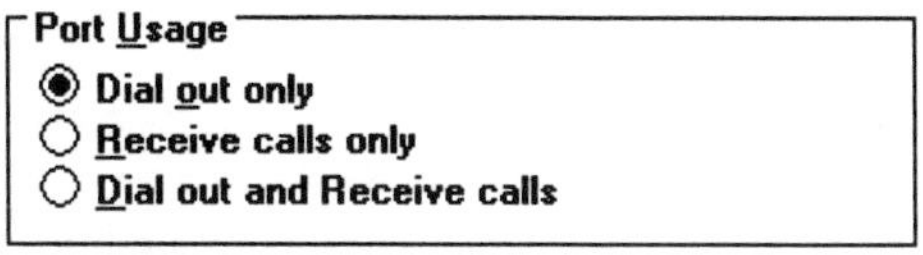

Figure 9-14
How Should RAS Run?

Once all of this is complete, you see the RAS Setup dialog box, showing the installed modem (Figure 9-15)

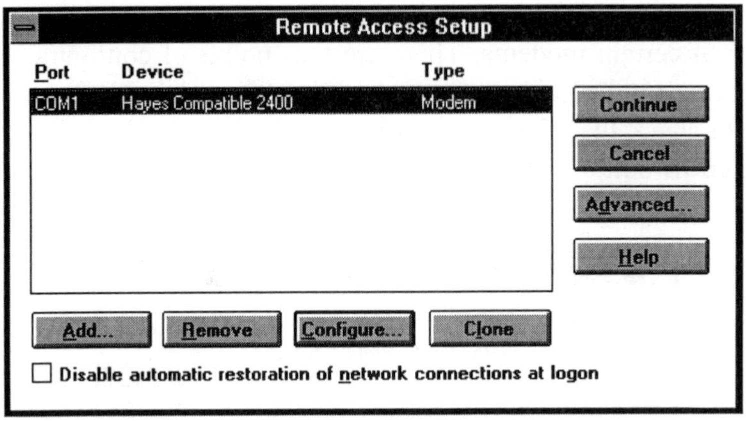

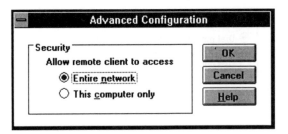

Figure 9-15
Reviewing Installed Modems

Selecting `Configure...` will take you back to the Modem Selection dialog box. The **Advanced** function is for defining the access
that a remote user will have once he or she is connected. If you did not
elect to allow the modem to receive incoming calls or you do not have a
network card installed, the **Advanced** button will do nothing but tell
you that you can't run the advanced setup. If you don't fall into one of
those two criteria, you get a dialog box like the one in Figure 9-16.

Figure 9-16
Setting Incoming User Access

Select the option appropriate to your installation and click on **OK**.
Once you get back to the Remote Access Setup dialog box, click on
`Continue`.

Now that the initial installation and configuration of RAS is complete, Windows NT will let you know (Figure 9-17).

> **Remote Access Service Setup**
>
> Remote Access Service has been installed successfully.
>
> Please use the Remote Access Admin program to assign Remote Access permissions to users. Start Remote Access Admin from the Program Manager by double-clicking the Remote Access Admin icon in the Remote Access Service program group.
>
> [OK]   [Help]

Figure 9-17
All Done . . . REBOOT

Clicking on **OK** will result in two different responses, depending on your installation. If you already have Windows NT installed, the operating system will notify you that a reboot is needed to cause the changes to take effect. If you're installing Windows NT from scratch, the installation program will continue.

After rebooting, or the completion of the installation and rebooting, Windows NT will have created a new program group in the Program Manager with the RAS application and utilities.

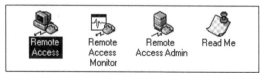

Figure 9-18
Program Manager Icons for RAS

Starting the RAS Server Service

If you have configured your RAS service to accept incoming calls, you must start the RAS server service. Starting the server service is initially a manual process.

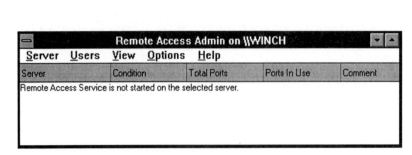

Figure 9-19
RAS Service Not Started

As you can see from the dialog, the Server service is not started. Select **Start Remote Access Service...** from the Server menu. RAS will ask you which server to start. Confirm that the name listed in the dialog box is the name of your machine and click on **OK**.

Although starting the service is manual, you can automate the process. The starting and stopping of RAS can be performed from the RAS administration utility, but it can also be controlled with the Service Control Panel. Locate the Control Panel icon in the Main group and double-click.

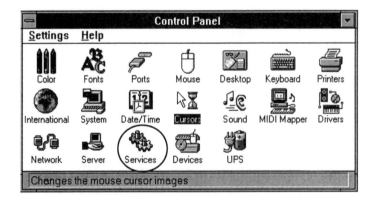

Figure 9-20
Services Control Panel for RAS Autostart

Locate the Services icon and double-click. This utility controls all services of Windows NT that can be started and stopped while running.

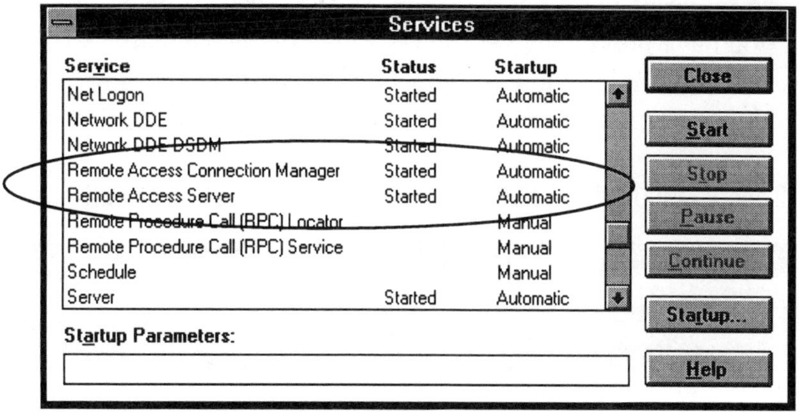

Figure 9-21
Configuring RAS Start-up Mode

The two services circled in Figure 9-21 are the ones you should be concerned with. Both services should be set to **Automatic** and should also be started. You can adjust the start-up mode of the services by selecting the service from the list and clicking on the **Start-up...** button.

You can also automate the process of selecting the server or domain to administer and the connection speed of the RAS server by placing the RASADMIN utility in a logon script or a Start-up group of the Program Manager. Simply starting RASADMIN does not set the parameters for the server service but several command-line parameters are available to make it automatic. The command-line structure and parameters are:

```
rasadmin [domainname | servername] [/l] [/h]
```

domainname	=	The domain you want to administer
servername	=	The server you want to administer
/l (L)	=	Low-speed connection
/h	=	High-speed connection

You can specify either a domain name or a server name, but not both.

The mode of operation (low- or high-speed) for each domain or server you have previously selected is saved in the Registry. So, if you need to change the previous setting from a low-speed to a high-speed connection, you must specify **/h** as a parameter to RASADMIN.

Locate and double-click on the Remote Access Admin utility.

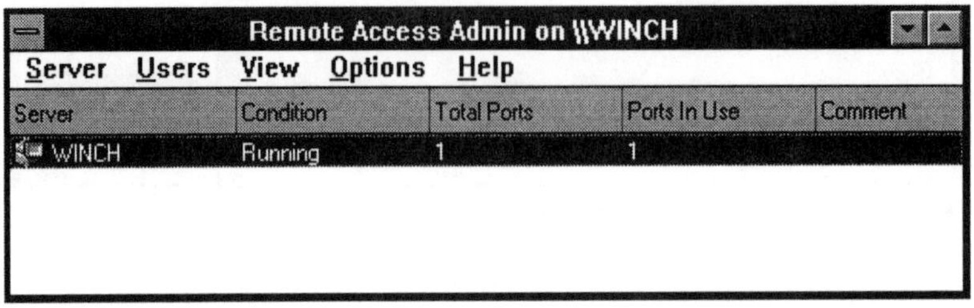

Remote Access Admin on \\\\WINCH				
Server	Users	View	Options	Help
Server	Condition	Total Ports	Ports In Use	Comment
WINCH	Running	1	1	

Figure 9-22
RAS Communications Status

After some fancy time dialog box procedure, your RAS admin utility will look like the one pictured in Figure 9-22, with the exception that the **Ports In Use** column will probably still read "0." The reason Windows NT requests the name of the server to start is because you can start the server service of another NT machine on the LAN.

Depending on the type of connection you will be receiving, you may wish to turn on **Low Speed Connection**. This option, found in the Options menu of the RAS Admin utility is for connections that will be made over a modem running at low speeds. What it does is discontinue the browsing of user names and domain names, which can take a lengthy period of time over a modem connection.

Once the server service is started, users may begin calling your RAS.

Monitoring Connections to Your RAS Service

When a user calls into your RAS service, you can monitor the status of the connection and the status of the communications taking place.

From the admin utility, you can double-click on one of your RAS services and you can get information on which ports are active, what user name is using a selected port, and what time the session started as shown in Figure 9-23.

```
┌─────────────────────────────────────────────────────────────┐
│ ─              Communication Ports                           │
│                                                              │
│   Server:  WINCH                        ┌──────────────────┐ │
│                                         │       OK         │ │
│   Port     User          Started        └──────────────────┘ │
│   COM1     Chris          8/28/93 8:08:46 PM  ┌────────────┐  │
│                                         │  Port Status   │ │
│                                         └──────────────────┘ │
│                                         ┌──────────────────┐ │
│                                         │ Disconnect User  │ │
│                                         └──────────────────┘ │
│                                         ┌──────────────────┐ │
│                                         │ Send Message...  │ │
│                                         └──────────────────┘ │
│                                         ┌──────────────────┐ │
│                                         │  Send To All...  │ │
│                                         └──────────────────┘ │
│                                         ┌──────────────────┐ │
│                                         │      Help        │ │
│                                         └──────────────────┘ │
│                                                              │
└─────────────────────────────────────────────────────────────┘
```

Figure 9-23
Viewing Communications Ports

You can disconnect users—thus clearing ports—and send messages to connected users. This is useful if you intend to shut down your machine and want everyone to disconnect after saving open files and closing open applications. Clicking on the **Port Status** button will give you a summary of the communication statistics for the active session as shown in Figure 9-24.

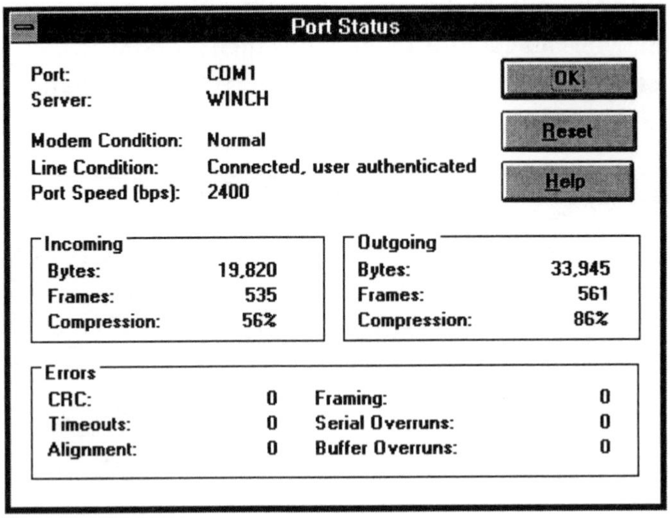

Figure 9-24
RAS Port Status

If you're more interested in the users that are using the RAS service, you can select the **Active Users** option from the Users menu.

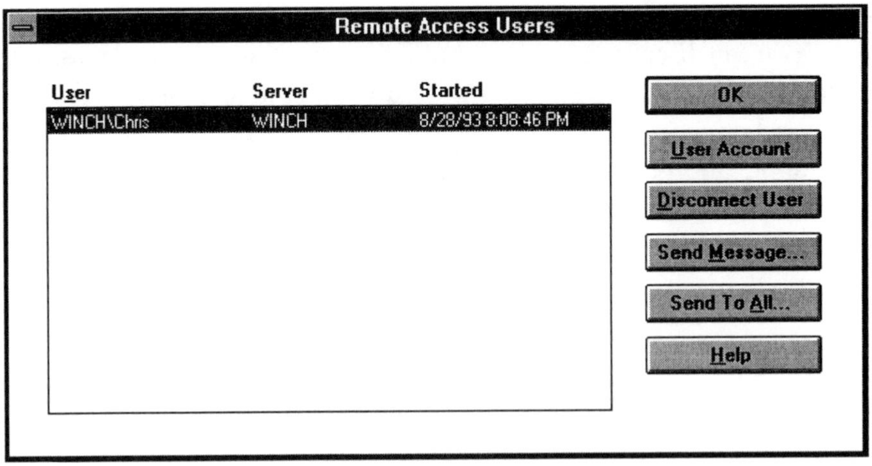

Figure 9-25
Checking Connected Users

As you can see from the dialog box, this is very much like the Communications Port dialog box shown in Figure 9-23, with the exception that you can view information about the user that is connected by clicking on the **User Account** button (Figure 9-26).

```
┌─────────────────────────────────────────────────────────────┐
│ ─                      User Account                          │
├─────────────────────────────────────────────────────────────┤
│                                                              │
│  User Name:             Chris                    ┌─────────┐ │
│  Full Name:             Christopher W. Monro     │   OK    │ │
│  Password Last Changed: 8/23/93 5:55:49 AM       └─────────┘ │
│  Password Expires:      Never                    ┌─────────┐ │
│  Privilege Level:       ADMIN                    │  Help   │ │
│  Call Back Privilege:   No callback              └─────────┘ │
│  Call Back Number:                                           │
│                                                              │
└─────────────────────────────────────────────────────────────┘
```

Figure 9-26
RAS User Account Information

Another utility in the Remote Access group is the Remote Access Monitor. The utility is a very small one, but allows you to keep tabs on the ongoing communications and performance of your RAS service.

```
┌──────────────────────────┐
│ ─ Remote Acce │ ▼ │ ▲ │
├──────────────────────────┤
│ Settings                 │
├──────────────────────────┤
│  ▢    ▬    ▢    ▢        │
│  TX   RX   ERR  CD       │
└──────────────────────────┘
```

Figure 9-27
RAS Monitor Utility

With this little utility, you can monitor the communications session of any active communications port running RAS on your system. From the settings menu you can select which port to monitor and whether or not to make sound for different events such as receive, transmit, errors, and connection/disconnect. By clicking on one of the four status indicators you can list the current communication statistics of the port shown in Figure 9-28.

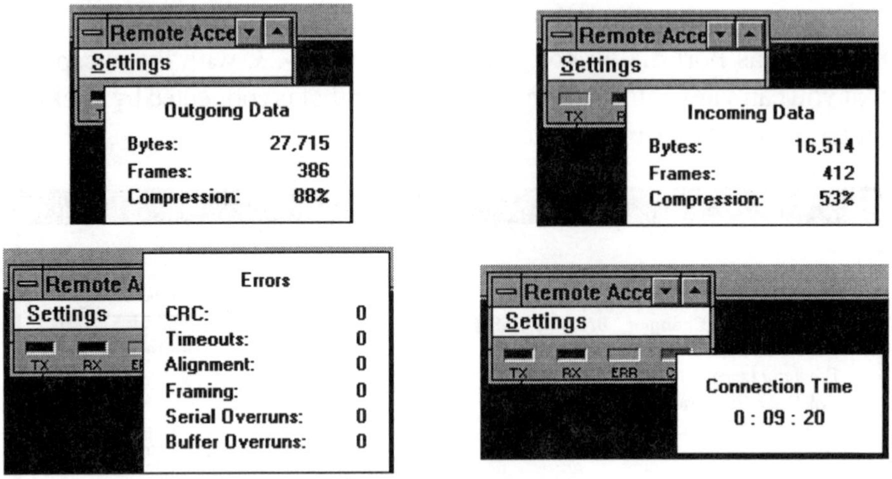

Outgoing Data	
Bytes:	27,715
Frames:	386
Compression:	88%

Incoming Data	
Bytes:	16,514
Frames:	412
Compression:	53%

Errors	
CRC:	0
Timeouts:	0
Alignment:	0
Framing:	0
Serial Overruns:	0
Buffer Overruns:	0

Connection Time
0 : 09 : 20

Figure 9-28
Communications Session Statistics

As you can see from the Incoming and Outgoing data statistics, compression is activated. The communications for this illustration are taking place over two 2400-bps modems which do not have compression technology on-board. The compression is a function of the RAS software, not hardware. Hardware compression such as MNP 5 can also coexist with the software-level compression of RAS.

Connecting to a Remote RAS Service

To place calls to a RAS service you use the Remote Access application, also located in the Remote Access Service group. The very first time you run the RAS application, Windows NT will tell you that there are no entries in the phone book.

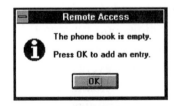

Figure 9-29
First-Time Start-up of RAS

Windows NT stores potential RAS connections in what it calls a phone book within the Remote Access application. The phone book stores the parameters for establishing a connection with a named RAS host and what communications device to use when making the connection.

After you click on the **OK** button for the first-time warning, Windows NT presents you with the dialog box for adding new phone book entries as shown in Figure 9-30.

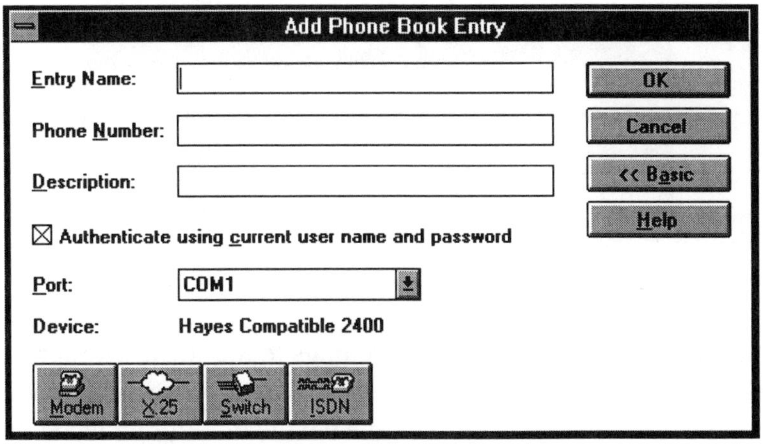

Figure 9-30
Adding a New Phone Book Entry

This dialog box shows the advanced options turned on, so you can see the **X.25**, **ISDN**, and **Switch** options. For our illustration, the modem is the area of focus. The Remote Access application has correctly identified the port that I wish to use for the service I want to call. All that's left to enter is the name, description, and phone number to dial. The number should include local access digits, such as "9" to get an outside line, and long distance codes if necessary.

User Authentication

The option to **Authenticate using current user name and password** passes your current logon name and password at your

local NT machine to the remote RAS machine. The remote RAS machine must have a user account with your name and password if you want to log on remotely. If you are connecting to a machine that will give you access to a domain rather than a workgroup, then the user name and password must exist in the domain user accounts database.

This is a good time to point out that if you want to be a member of a domain or workgroup, connected remotely, your network setup should include the workgroup or domain name that you want to connect to.

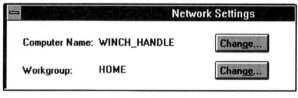

Figure 9-31
Setting Local Membership for Remote Access

If the machine you are calling belongs to the **HOME** workgroup and that is the workgroup you want access to when you connect remotely, then your local network setup should have the workgroup name defined as **HOME**. Whether you are on a workgroup physically or not makes no difference; when you connect, it will.

If you elect not to authenticate using your current logon name and password, when you establish a connection with the remote RAS, you'll be prompted for a logon name and password. This, like the other option, must be a user name and password that is either found in the remote machine's user accounts database or in the domain user accounts database.

Controlling Access to the RAS Server

As you already know, you must have a user account on the RAS server or on the domain you want to log onto remotely. This however, is not the end of the security checking. Each user must also be granted permission to access the machine or domain remotely. As an administra-

tor, you can grant or deny privileges to RAS from the Remote Access Admin utility. From the Users menu, select **Permissions**.

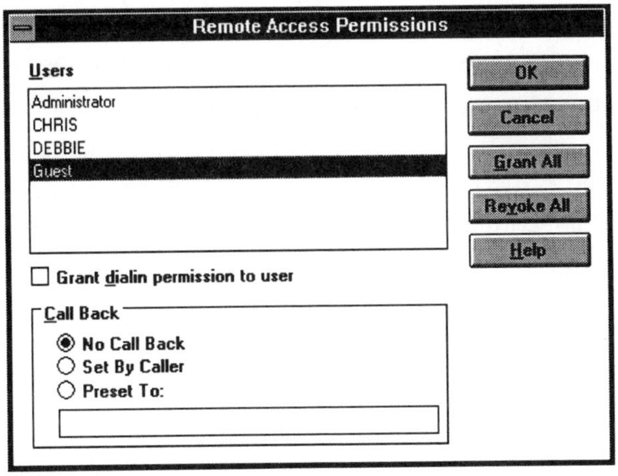

Figure 9-32
RAS Security

The list box shows all users in the user accounts database. If you are running RAS from an Advanced Server, the list of user names will come from the domain user accounts database. For NT machines, the list will be from the local user accounts database.

Once you have completed the settings for your first phone book entry and set all relevant security parameters, click on **OK** and you're ready to dial

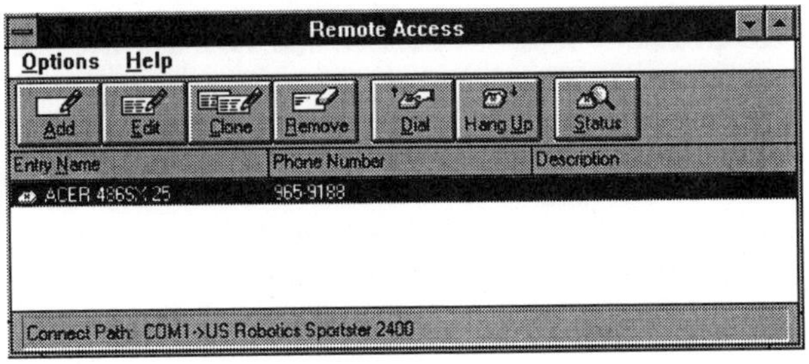

Figure 9-33
Ready to Dial Out

The OPTIONS menu allows you to turn on and off software compression, turn on and off the modem speaker, and set minimize functions. RAS can be set to automatically minimize on dial-up or on hang-up. From the OPTIONS menu you can also invoke operator-assisted or manual dialing, where you can pick up a phone on the modem line and manually dial the number. After clicking **OK** in the dialog box, Windows NT will go off-hook and attempt to connect to the service that was dialed. One other option available is the Redial Settings. This option lets you set the number of times that a connection will be retried if it is unsuccessful and how many seconds between attempts. Additionally, you can configure RAS to redial in the event of a link failure. A link failure is any event that causes an abnormal termination of a RAS session, such as a cut line or electronic noise on a line.

To place a call to a RAS server, click on the **Dial** button and you're on your way. After the connection is completed, RAS will notify you if no option has been set for the minimize function with the dialog box shown in Figure 9-34.

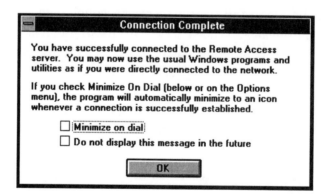

Figure 9-34
Setting RAS Minimize Options on Connect

From this point forward, you are connected and can function as if you are just another workstation on the LAN or another user on the RAS host. At times, due to the speed of communications, you may wish to use standard UNC naming for gaining access to shares, printers, and other resources. It speeds the process up since Windows NT will not have to retrieve a list of machines, domains, workgroups, or user names from the RAS host. Several of the Windows NT applications such as the Event Viewer contain a menu bar option for Low Speed Connection. If you are communicating with a modem, it's wise to turn this option on and use UNC naming.

```
\\SAIL\CDRIVE
```

SAIL is the name of the computer and **CDRIVE** is the share name. By typing out desired share names rather than browsing for them, your operations will be faster. It takes much longer for RAS to retrieve browse lists and send them to a remote machine.

The effects of compression on connectivity are pretty good, but depend heavily on the files you are accessing or the services you are using. I transferred four 150-KB files in under two minutes over a 2400-bps line. Not bad at all!

Other Communications Adapters

In addition to modem-to-modem connections, RAS can connect to another RAS with X.25 communications adapters, modem-to-PAD-to-X.25, ISDN adapters, and can utilize modem pooling equipment through a switch.

The procedure to install an X.25 smart card or an ISDN adapter varies with each manufacturer, so it isn't possible to cover those situations. Once the card or cards have been installed, setting RAS up to use it is another story.

RAS automatically recognizes the existence of communications ports. X.25 and ISDN are no exception. Usually, the drivers that accompany communications cards such as these will automatically configure RAS for the new card.

X.25

There are two methods of connectivity with an X.25 RAS server. At the host end of the network, i.e., the computer that a remote machine will dial into, the RAS service must be configured with an X.25 smart card and an X.25 line running right into the back of the machine.

The remote end of the equation is a different story though. To facilitate easy access to X.25 networks and to lower communications and equipment costs, remote users can connect to an X.25 network with a regular modem. The process involves routing your modem connection through an X.25 Packet Assembler/Disassembler (PAD) which converts the modem packets to X.25 packets before sending them to the RAS host on the other end of the X.25 network. You can of course, also use an X.25 smart card in the remote machine, rather than the modem-to-PAD solution, but it's more expensive.

You should know that the best way to guarantee good results from a X.25 PAD connection is to acquire the exact same type of modem that the PAD is using. This information can be obtained from your X.25 service provider.

If you are going to be using a PAD to connect to an X.25 network, you need to know about the **PAD.INF** file. This file controls the connect parameters and is located, by default, in the **C:\WINNT\SYSTEM32\RAS** directory. It is a text-based script file that is executed when a connection to a remote PAD is established. Of special interest in the file are the X.3 settings. These 22 parameters determine how to communicate effectively with the RAS. Here are the parameters that are best suited to communication with a RAS server:

Parameter Number	Parameter Name	Parameter Value
1	PAD Recall	0
2	Echo	0
3	Data Forward Character	0
4	Idle Timer	1
5	Device Control	0

6	PAD Service Signals	1
7	Break Signal	0
8	Discard Output	0
9	Padding after Carriage Return	0
10	Line Folding	0
11	*Not Set*	0
12	Flow Control	0
13	Linefeed Insertion	0
14	Padding after Line Feed	0
15	Editing	0
16	Character Delete	0
17	Line Delete	0
18	Line Display	0
19	Editing PAS Service Signals	0
20	Echo Mask	0
21	Parity Treatment	0
22	Page Wait	0

When establishing an X.25 entry in your phone book, there are two ways to go. If you will be using a PAD, your communications will take place with a modem.

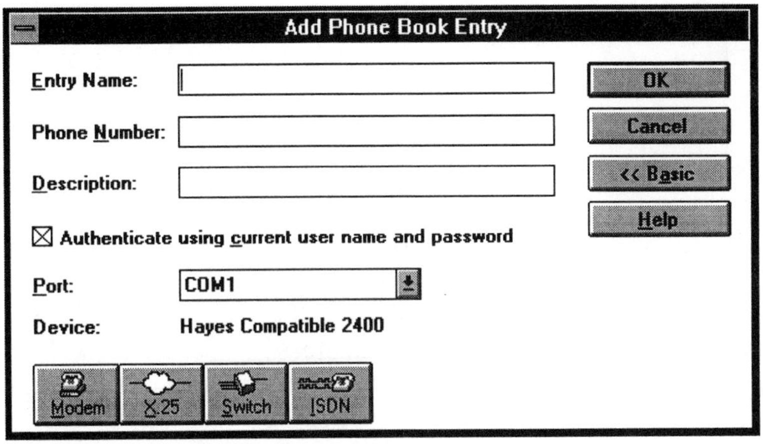

Figure 9-35
Adding a New Phone Book Entry

You should select the appropriate port and specify the phone number to the PAD, including any outside line and long distance codes. You should also check the modem settings by clicking on the **Modem** button.

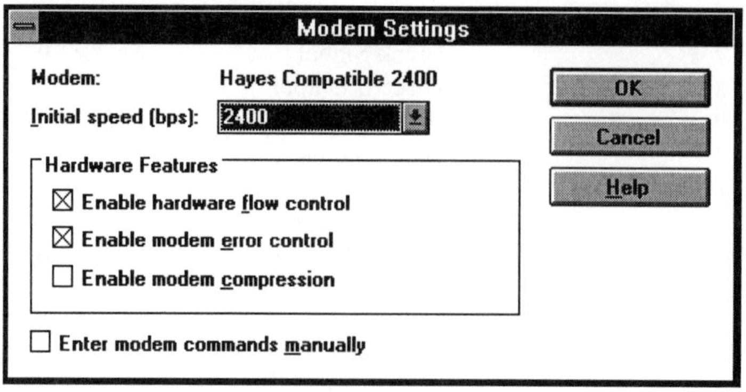

Figure 9-36
Configuring Modem Settings

Once the modem is set correctly, you need to enter the X.25 parameters for the PAD. Click on the X.25 button and enter the proper configuration information for X.25 network.

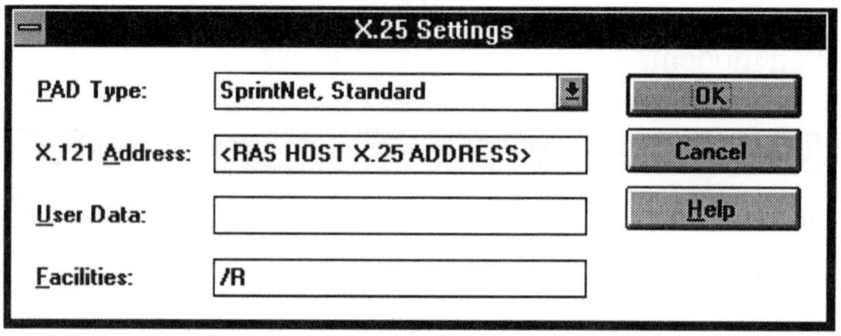

Figure 9-37
Configuring X.25 Settings

You must specify the type of PAD you will be connecting to and supply an X.121 address. The X.121 address is essentially the X.25 destination port for your RAS server. This information can be gained from your X.25 service provider. Your X.25 service provider may also have additional information requirements, such as the **User Data** and **Facilities** text boxes of the X.25 configuration. These fields can specify parameters for charging and other miscellaneous information.

If any information is entered in the X.25 dialog box when using a modem port to communication, RAS will assume that you are connecting to a PAD and thus proceed through the PAD.INF. If you forget to enter X.25 information, RAS will view the phone book entry as a standard modem-to-modem entry.

If you are connecting directly to X.25 with the use of an X.25 smart card, you would select the port from the Ports list box of the phone book entry dialog box and specify your X.25 communications parameters.

ISDN

ISDN is a high-speed wide-area network communications standard that utilizes digital communications and compression to achieve very fast long distance transfer speeds. ISDN, which stands for Integrated Service Digital Network, works on channels. Typically, a single ISDN line contains three channels:

> D Channel — 16,384 bits per second
> B Channel — 65,536 bits per second
> B Channel — 65,536 bits per second

The D channel is used to control the communications of the other two channels. You can configure the two B channels to act as a single line with a throughput of 131,072 bits per second or to act as two independent channels. The former configuration is called aggregate channeling. Aggregate channeling can also be a dynamic process that the user can configure. This is the most efficient and flexible use of ISDN channels. By allowing the user to configure the channeling dependent on the number of available channels, a remote user can get the best possible communications rate.

When you install your ISDN adapter, depending on the card and drivers, you may or may not have the option to configure it for dynamic aggregation. You should spend some time thinking about ISDN implementation because that ability to dynamically configure aggregation can also lead to trouble, like a single user having several ISDN cards using all available channels. While the single user will have terrific throughput,

nobody else will be able to connect to the RAS server. You can monitor all of these conditions with the Remote Access Admin utility.

Once your ISDN adapter or adapters are installed, you can begin making calls to ISDN RAS servers and receiving calls from remote ISDN users. When calling with ISDN, the RAS server you are calling must also be using ISDN.

To place a call to an ISDN RAS server, you have to create a new phone book entry in the Remote Access application. Make sure that the **Advanced** button has been pressed so that you can see the configuration buttons for various types of adapters.

```
┌─────────────────────────────────────────────────────────────────┐
│ ─                      Edit Phone Book Entry                      │
│                                                                   │
│  Entry Name:    │ISDN TO CEDAR HQ            │      ┌─────────┐   │
│                 └───────────────────────────┘      │   OK    │   │
│  Phone Number:  │555-7829:555-7829          │      └─────────┘   │
│                 └───────────────────────────┘      ┌─────────┐   │
│  Description:   │Cedar HQ ISDN Line         │      │ Cancel  │   │
│                 └───────────────────────────┘      └─────────┘   │
│                                                    ┌─────────┐   │
│  ☒ Authenticate using current user name and password│ << Basic │  │
│                                                    └─────────┘   │
│  Port:          │Any ISDN port           │ ↨│     ┌─────────┐   │
│                 └──────────────────────────┘      │  Help   │   │
│  Device:                                           └─────────┘   │
│                                                                   │
│       ┌──────┬──────┬──────┬──────┐                              │
│       │  📞  │ ☁─  │ ─◇  │ 🖧   │                              │
│       │Modem │ X.25 │Switch│ ISDN │                              │
│       └──────┴──────┴──────┴──────┘                              │
└─────────────────────────────────────────────────────────────────┘
```

Figure 9-38
ISDN Phone Book Entry

You may notice that there are two phone numbers listed in the phone book entry. We'll get to that in a moment. For now, select the port type you wish to use, either **Any ISDN port** or a specific ISDN port.

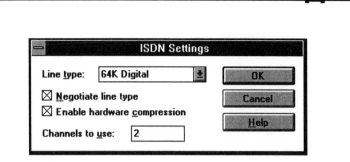

Figure 9-39
Configuring ISDN Settings

The ISDN configuration dialog box lets you tell RAS how you want to use ISDN services and what type of service to use. First select one of the three available line types. The selection here will depend on the type of ISDN service you have in your area as well as the cost of different modes of service. The information can be provided by your ISDN service provider. The highest quality line type is 64-KB digital and the lowest is 56-KB voice. Rates and communications speed vary with each line type.

Negotiating line type allows RAS and your ISDN card to determine the line type to use and can occasionally negotiate a lower line. In doing so, you may be charged more for your service because of the amount of traffic you put out over the wire. In most situations, turning off line negotiation allows you to know exactly what line you're using and how much it costs. Also, if 56-KB voice is the only available level of line service in your area, there's no point to having line negotiation on, since it will never get anything different; all it will do is waste time and connection charges.

The number of channels to use is dependent on your ISDN installation as well, but this information you can enter with the help of your service provider. For each ISDN line you have coming into your machine, you have two communications channels. Those are the B channels discussed earlier. If you have three ISDN cards in your machine, you can configure this phone book entry to use all six available ISDN channels for the connection. This would be very expensive, but it can be done. Gener-

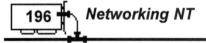

ally speaking, you should keep your entry to one or two. The number will also depend on how ISDN is implemented at your server site, the number of available ISDN channels at the server and whether or not aggregate channeling is available.

Once the specific ISDN parameters are configured, click on **OK** and you're back to the basic phone book entry. This is where the phone numbers come into play. Remember that each ISDN line has two usable communications channels. In order to use more than two channels for a single connect, you must specify a phone number for each one. As you can see from the figure on the previous page, the phone number is the same for both channels. That means that I will be using both B channels of the ISDN line at 555-7829. If I want to use six channels, then I have to enter six phone numbers. The numbers must be separated by a colon and no spaces. When specifying the phone numbers, keep in mind that some ISDN service providers require a single phone number for each channel. You should check that out before entering the numbers.

Keep in mind that if you are using more than two channels, you cannot specify a single port for the phone book entry and must select **Any ISDN port**, so that RAS can allocate as many ports as are needed.

Modem Pooling and Switches

Windows NT and RAS can support the use of switches and modem pooling for communications services. A *switch* is a directable device which can select a communications device based on parameters entered in the **SWITCH.INF** file in the **C:\WINNT\SYSTEM32\RAS** directory. You can use a switch with a group of modems so that multiple communications sessions can take place on a single machine. The manufacturer of the switch will provide drivers for the equipment and instructions for installing, as this can vary with each switch vendor.

Modem pooling which also applies to X.25 and ISDN adapters is the ability of RAS to use any available resource of a particular type. In a phone book entry, there are three static entries in the **Port** type list. The entries, **Any modem port, Any X.25 port** and **Any ISDN port** allow RAS to sequentially locate an available communications adapter of the selected type. If you have four ISDN cards in your machine, you can ask RAS to use any available card, so you don't have to keep track of which communications devices are currently in use.

To use a switch in conjunction with a communications method, such as modem or X.25, you simply specify the switch parameters to direct RAS to use the appropriate device. It is a bit more complicated than that, and a switch cannot be used in conjunction with ISDN.

A switch can be just about anything. It's just a generic term to describe a device that you either pass through on your way to a communications device or a device that you pass through once you get connected to a server service. Microsoft uses a security device in their own examples of another type of switch. In that case the post-connect script may pass special passwords or other security-related information. Another option for the security device may be to request an additional authentication word from the user when the connection is established or to pass coded information from a credit card type security card from a slide reader at the remote site across the wire to a security authentication device. The possibilities for this gem are really endless.

Let me give you an example of a switch: If you have four modems in a pool, all connected to a switch that is then connected to your machine, you would continue to configure your RAS phone book entries with the COM port that represents the switch, but in addition to selecting the parameters for your COM port, you would also set the script for the switch. In this case, it would be **Pre-connect Script**: since the switch comes before the call is made. By doing this, RAS, when making a call, will negotiate the switch and run the session through the proper communications device as selected in the switch configuration.

```
┌──────────────────────────────────────────────────────────┐
│ ─                    Switch Settings                       │
├──────────────────────────────────────────────────────────┤
│                                              ┌──────────┐  │
│                                              │    OK    │  │
│  Pre-connect Script:   [none]        │ ±│    └──────────┘  │
│                                              ┌──────────┐  │
│                                              │  Cancel  │  │
│  Post-connect Script:  [none]        │ ±│    ├──────────┤  │
│                                              │   Help   │  │
│                                              └──────────┘  │
└──────────────────────────────────────────────────────────┘
```

Figure 9-40
Configuring Switch Settings

The entries you make in the Switch dialog box, shown in Figure 9-40, depend on the type of device you are running through and the script options available when drivers for a switch are installed. The dialog box allows both pre-connect and post-connect scripts depending on the source of the switch. If, for example, you are calling out from a single COM port in your machine, but the receiving end has a switch that must be negotiated, you would place your script selection in the **Post-connect Script:** field since the script must run after the connection is made, in order to negotiate the switch on the other end—just the opposite if the switch is on your end and the receiving machine does not have a switch.

If it seems that this information is a little vague it's because so much of it depends on the implementation by individual vendors of NT-compatible switch equipment.

As you can see, RAS is very powerful and relatively easy to use. Microsoft intends to make RAS communications possible for Windows 3.1 and Windows for Workgroups based computers as well. In the past, the implementation of high-end communications services has been a patchwork of standards and incompatibilities. Windows NT and Advanced Server have smoothed many of the edges and made the power of wide area networking available to the end user.

Part Four

Step-by-Step
Managing
Windows NT

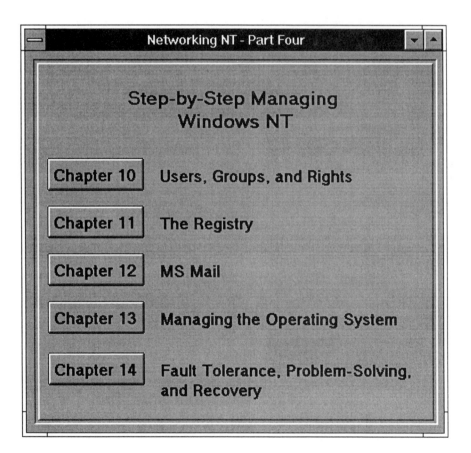

Networking NT - Part Four

Step-by-Step Managing
Windows NT

Chapter 10	Users, Groups, and Rights
Chapter 11	The Registry
Chapter 12	MS Mail
Chapter 13	Managing the Operating System
Chapter 14	Fault Tolerance, Problem-Solving, and Recovery

Chapter 10

Users, Groups, and Rights

Well, if you haven't already noticed, Windows NT places a pretty hefty emphasis on security. Windows NT is, in point of fact, the most secure shrink-wrapped operating system ever, and the footprint of security implementation can be found at every level of the NT OS. The real question is "How can users manage that security?" Let's face it—you could have the most powerful and secure operating system in the world but if a person can't effectively manage it, who needs it?

A while back, when I was running my own Novell consulting firm, I thought I could make a million bucks or more coming up with a graphical program for Windows that could manage a NetWare server. The project never got off the ground, but then came Windows NT. Guess what? The very concept that I envisioned for NetWare can be found in Windows NT. Maybe I ought to file a mental patent infringement case for the same look and feel as the intellectual property I had in my head. . . . Maybe not. Anyway, the tremendous security arsenal that Windows NT can bring to bear is quite happily the easiest to manage of any I have ever seen. All that Windows NT can do with security can easily be managed by graphical utilities such as the User Manager and File Manager.

If you read one or more of the Step-by-Step chapters, you learned that when connecting to a server such as NetWare or LAN Manager, you have to have a user account on the host that matches an account in Windows NT. In this chapter, I'll show you how to set up and manage user accounts, implement groups, and manage rights to files and directories. Before we get to it, I want to cover some of the conceptual models that computer and network-based security subsystems operate from.

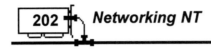

The User

At the heart of any system is the user; and what that user is allowed to do is dependent on a multitude of factors, ultimately culminating in the establishment of a user account that defines the limits of that user's functionality within the system. In order to allow some users more access to the system than others, user accounts are established and granted to individuals who must use the system. The amount of control that an administrator has over a user account is complete. There is literally no factor of access that an administrator cannot control. Users are the first order of the security model.

Groups

The next level is the group. Groups are a way of grouping users together. If, for instance, you have multiple users—all of whom have similar security requirements—then you can implement the security restrictions on the group and simply make users members of the group. This may be getting a bit too abstract, so allow me to illustrate the point.

Let's say you have Excel installed on your NT machine and several people who use the machine must have access to the program while others should not have access. To save time, you can create a group called EXCEL with the proper security limitation that allows the group EXCEL to access the Excel directory. Once this process is completed, any time you make a new user who must have access to Excel, you just make the user a member of the group. You don't have to set up each user to have access to each individual directory or file. As a member of the group, the users automatically take on the rights defined for that group. Groups are a real time-saver, and you'll see that when we get further into the creation and management of these users and groups.

Rights

Users and groups are controlled by way of rights. Just because a user has an account on an NT machine does not automatically allow that user to access anything. Each user or group must be given certain rights for operation. For example, User A has the right to create and delete files in directory X while user B only has the right to view files in that directory. Windows NT can control the access to all resources in the machine.

- Files
- Directories
- Printers
- Sharing directories
- Sharing printers
- Using backup devices
- Using communication ports

At the file, directory, and printer levels of security control, there are different attributes that you can assign.

Directory Access

- `No access`   (No Access to files)
- `Read`   (Read-only on files)
- `Write`   (Write changes to, read, delete, execute)
- `Full control` (All privileges)

File Access

- `Read`   (R)
- `Write`   (W)
- `Execute`   (E)
- `Delete`   (D)
- `Change permissions`   (P)
- `Take ownership`   (O)

Printer Access

- `No access`   (No access to printer)
- `Print`   (Print to queue)
- `Manage documents` (Promote, demote, and delete)
- `Full control`   (All privileges)

You may have noticed two special attributes that are available at the file level. Change Permissions and Take Ownership offer special capabilities to the users who have them. First and foremost is the Change Permissions right. This right allows the user to set which users are allowed what levels of access and control to a file. The right is accorded to the owner of the file, i.e., the person who created the file or copied it to the system, and can be granted to other users as well at the owners discretion. The other right is Take Ownership. This one needs some explanation since it's probably unlike anything you have ever encountered before.

In Windows NT, the administrator or a user that is a member of the administrator group is not all-powerful on the machine. This is a little bit of an ego hit for those of us who called NetWare and several other operating systems home; where admin privileges meant that you were all-powerful on the LAN. This is not so anymore. Users have rights, and the privacy of files that a user may create are not infringable by the administrator of the LAN—almost. To start with, every file that is created in or copied to a directory inherits the rights of the directory. If you place a file in a directory that has the group Everyone granted Full Control then the file will have the same attributes. If a user places a file within his or her own directory, then an administrator cannot access the file at all—almost. The file will inherit the rights of the directory and therefore be accessible only to the owner of the file—almost. Administrators cannot even see into a private directory—almost. Additionally, if a user creates a file and saves it to a public directory where many people have access, that user can use the file manager to restrict access of the file beyond the inherited rights of the directory. The key here is *ownership*. A user who owns a file can control all aspects of access to that file, including denying access to administrators—almost.

The *almost* in all of these statements is tied to the ability to take ownership of a file or directory. This privilege is automatically granted to administrators for all files and directories and can be given to an individual user or group on a single file or directory basis at the discretion of the owner. The kicker here is that once a person takes ownership of a file or directory, the original owner is not automatically granted rights to it. If you take ownership of a user's personal logon directory, the next time the user attempts to log on, he or she will be notified that the user directory is no longer accessible. If, after taking ownership of a file or directory, the administrator goes back to grant rights back to the original owner, the original owner can still check the ownership of the file and see that it is now owned by the administrator.

There is a loophole, however. If you take ownership of a file or directory, you can then grant access to the original owner with full control, then log on as that user and take back ownership. This will still leave the admin with full control to the file or directory. The catch is that if the user bothers to check the permissions for the file or directory, he or she will see that in addition to his or her own full control, the administrator has full control as well. The user can delete that permission because they are now again the owner of the file. It's complicated I know, and the best bet is not to fool around with other people's files and directories. With the amount of legal work being spent on trying to establish laws concerning privacy of computer documents, it's best to ask or leave it alone. The one time when this really comes in handy is when an employee is fired, quits, or moves, and the user files must either be deleted or transferred to a new user directory. That's when taking ownership would be a normal course of action.

A final note about the ability to control rights of users to files and directories: You must be using the NTFS file system in order to set the attributes of files or directories. When you create a share for other users on a workgroup to access, you can grant access at the user and group level, but the individual files and directories of a local NT machine will not be protected from other users of the machine unless you are using NTFS. Both FAT and HPFS do not contain the necessary structure to accommodate the attributes that NT can control. If you are running FAT or HPFS, you'll get a message not unlike the one shown in Figure 10-1.

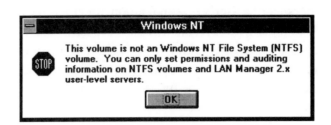

Figure 10-1
Unable to Set Permissions

The solution to this problem is *not* a complete reinstallation of Windows NT. If you need to change from FAT or HPFS to NTFS after NT is installed there is a relatively easy method to accomplish this.

Converting to NTFS

Step 1:   Locate and execute the Command Prompt icon in the Main group of the Program Manager.

Step 2:   Determine the drive that you want to convert (C usually).

Step 3:   Type the following:
        CONVERT C: /FS:NTFS
  where **C:** is the drive to convert.

Step 4:   Restart Windows NT.

If the drive you want to convert is also the drive that NT resides on and boots from, you must reboot your system, at which time Windows NT will convert the system. Don't be alarmed if the system reboots several times in the process of making the conversion; this is normal. Once the process is complete, you are ready to begin setting permissions on files and directories for the machine.

Control of Users

Users are authenticated to use a system after passing security checks that define who, what, when, and where. Not all facets of authentication are available for local NT users versus users who log onto an Advanced Server and there are several other factors at work here. First let's look at the attributes that users are authenticated on:

    User Name
    User Password
    Logon Station*
    Time Of Day*
    Day of the Week*
    Specific Dates*

Those are the primary specifications for user security. The entries with a * next to them apply only to users who are logging onto an Advanced Server network. As noted in Chapter 8, when you connect to an Advanced Server network, your user account doesn't reside on the local machine, but on the domain controller. The domain controller is responsible for the authentication of users and the levels of security are obviously higher given the multitude of factors that affect users in a LAN environment.

At the NT machine connected to a LAN Manager, NetWare, Workgroup, or other network, the security is handled at the local level, with workgroup rules. That means that each NT machine is responsible for its own security. Rather than centralized administration of users, groups, and rights, each NT machine has its own user accounts database and users logging on with administrative privileges have the responsibility of defining what users of the machine and other users on the net can and cannot access and with level of access each may have. If I have a directory called EXCEL and I want only two other users to use it, I can define that. Other NT machines on the net will have similar abilities to grant or not grant rights to resources on their PC to users on the net.

So, we know that in an AS environment, the user accounts are on the domain controller, and other network connections such as Novell and LAN Manager require that you have an account on the NT machine that matches an account on the network. By the way, the amount of "matching" only applies to the password and user name. The rights that a user has on the local NT machine do not have any affect on the granted rights on the network. In accordance with this, you cannot manage the access of a local NT user to resources of the network. The access that a user has on the LAN in question is controlled by that network's own user-management software, such as SYSCON.EXE for NetWare or NET ADMIN for LAN Manager. The matching user name and password just provide a way for the network to identify the user account that the NT machine is attempting to use.

In a workgroup, every machine is in charge of itself. With a workgroup of NT machines, the other machines do not need to have user accounts for users that do not log onto their local machine. In a workgroup of NT machines you can grant users of other NT machines the rights to your resources. This is because NT machines in a workgroup can access each other's user accounts databases.

Creating and Managing Users

When Windows NT is first installed, two users are automatically created: Guest and Administrator. The Guest user account has no password and the administrator account has whatever password you specified during the installation. In addition, you set up a user during installation who has administrative privileges and assigned a password at that time. So, by default, Windows NT has three established users.

To begin the process of setting up new users, locate the administrative tools group of the Program Manager. You should be logged on as Administrator or a member of the Administrative Tools

 User Manager

Administrators group. You will not be able to create users unless you are. Open the group and double-click on the User Manager icon to launch the program that allows

you to create users. Once you open the User Manager program you'll get a screen like the one shown in Figure 10-2.

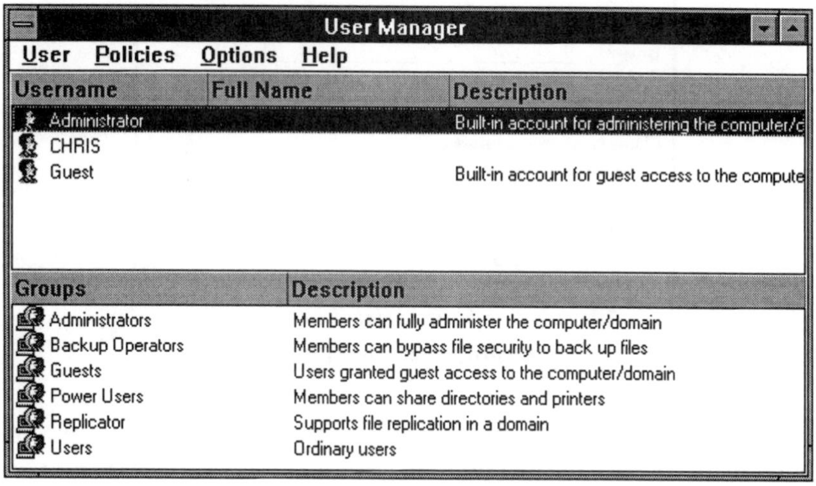

Figure 10-2
User Manager

This is the main screen for the management of users. The existence and basic attributes of every user are controlled from this program and nowhere else. The rights that a user has are completely separate from the actual user. The program does not directly control access rights. What it does control are things like the user name, password, logon directory, and so on. We're going to cover every function of the program as it applies to real administrative duties.

To start, let's create a new user. Select the User menu from the menu bar and select the **New User...** option. Once you have done this you get the dialog box shown in Figure 10-3.

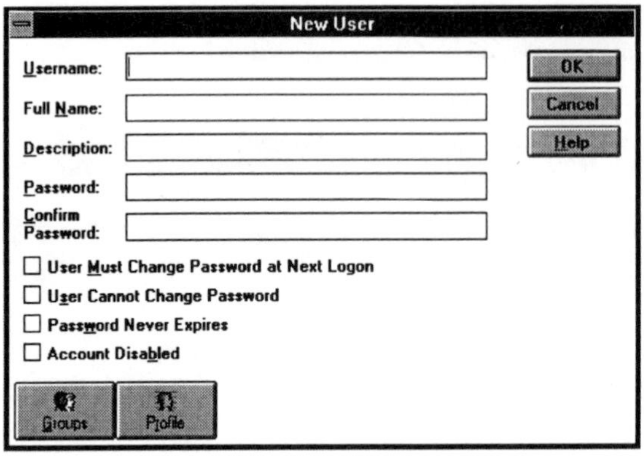

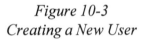

Figure 10-3
Creating a New User

The entries on this form are pretty self-explanatory. The password management options allow you to determine how your users and you, as administrator, handle passwords. The first option:

☐ User **M**ust Change Password at Next Logon

You use this if you have no desire as an administrator to manage everybody's passwords. You enter a default password which the user will be forced to change when he or she logs on next. From that point forward, you don't know the password. This is perhaps the most secure method of password management.

☐ U**s**er Cannot Change Password

Use this option when you do want to manage passwords and don't want the users changing them. It's an extra liability to have to keep a record of every user's password.

☐ Pass**w**ord Never Expires

Use this option if you want to override the regular expiration term of a password. The setting for expiration terms and other system-wide password settings are located in another part of the User Manager. We'll get to them in a few minutes.

Once you have entered the appropriate information in the entry boxes, you can select **OK** from the dialog box and the user will be set up. If, however, you wish to specify a home directory, logon script, or membership to NT groups, then you can go further. The **Groups** button brings up the dialog box shown in Figure 10-4. The illustration was taken from a new installation of Windows NT.

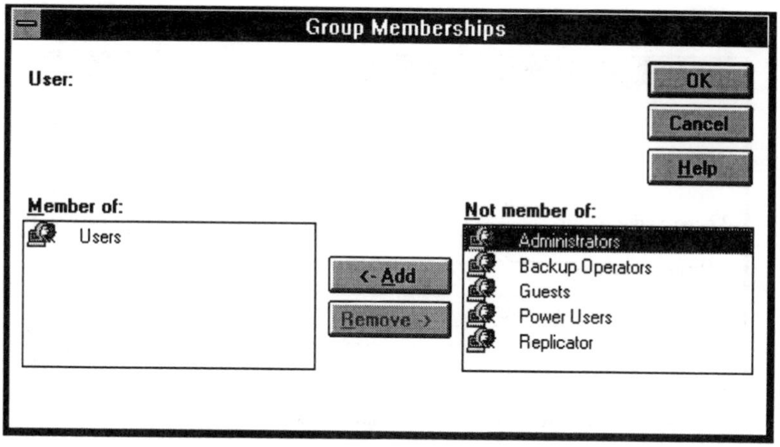

Figure 10-4
Setting Group Membership

If you are unsure about which groups your new user should belong to, relax. We can change all of this later. When we get to the segment about groups, we'll cover what all of the default groups do. Any new user that is created will automatically become a member of the **Users** group and a member of the global group **Everyone,** which is not shown.

The **Profile** option is next. The profile specifies whether or not the new user will have a logon script and what directory, if any, will be his or her home directory.

Logon Script

In Windows NT, a logon script is any executable program. That includes batch files from DOS, CMD files from OS/2, and EXE files. The most likely use will be the batch file, so that you can custom-design the logon process for users. The strange thing about this is the place that Microsoft chose for the location of logon scripts. It could not possibly be any further down in the directory structure. The directory for a default installation of Windows NT is:

```
C:\WINNT\SYSTEM32\REPL\IMPORT\SCRIPTS
```

```
┌────────────────── User Environment Profile ──────────────────┐
│                                                    ┌────────┐ │
│ User:                                              │   OK   │ │
│                                                    └────────┘ │
│                                                    ┌────────┐ │
│                                                    │ Cancel │ │
│ Logon Script Name: [                            ]  └────────┘ │
│ ┌─ Home Directory ──────────────────────────────┐ ┌────────┐ │
│ │                                                │ │  Help  │ │
│ │ ◉ Local Path: [                              ] │ └────────┘ │
│ │                                                │            │
│ │ ○ Connect [  ] [↕] To [                     ] │            │
│ └────────────────────────────────────────────────┘            │
└───────────────────────────────────────────────────────────────┘
```

Figure 10-5
Setting Logon Parameters

The text entry box for a logon script name is not for entering a full path. It is a relative entry box, allowing you to only enter the name of a script or the name of a subdirectory and then a script name. I have a logon script that I use for all users of the machine that is called **LOGON.BAT**. This file is located in the default location. To tell Windows NT about it, I just type **LOGON.BAT**, not the whole path. The obvious downside of this is that you cannot specify scripts that are located anywhere else. If you decide to create subdirectories, say for instance **SAILLOFT**, then in the logon script the entry should read **SAILLOFT\LOGON.BAT**. Windows NT will interpret this as:

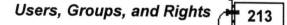

C:\WINNT\SYSTEM32\REPL\IMPORT\SCRIPTS\SAILLOFT\LOGON.BAT

There is no way that I know of that you can change this. Another rather annoying problem is the absence of a **Browse** button. Look for that to be added in a maintenance release of NT. The logon script can make use of Windows NT and DOS variables if the script is a batch file. The most important variable, which is set by NT during logon, is the **%USERNAME%** variable which, when included in a batch file can make decisions based on the logon name. Another variable is the **%SystemRoot%** variable which for a default NT installation amounts to **C:\WINNT**. These variables come in handy when you are creating custom batch files. Here's a complete listing of the variables that are available along with their values on a default installation of Windows NT with the user CHRIS logged on:

```
ComSpec=C:\winnt\system32\cmd.exe
HOMEDRIVE=C:
HOMEPATH=\USERS\CHRIS
HOMESHARE=
OS=Windows_NT
Os2LibPath=C:\winnt\system32\os2\dll;
Path=C:\winnt\system32;C:\winnt
PROCESSOR_ARCHITECTURE=x86
PROCESSOR_LEVEL=4
PROMPT=$P$G
SystemRoot=C:\winnt
temp=C:\temp
tmp=C:\temp
USERDOMAIN=WINCH
USERNAME=Chris
windir=C:\winnt
```

While some variables such as the day of the week or time are missing, all in all, these variables are pretty useful for robust batch files. You can, of course, create your own variables using the standard DOS **SET** command.

Home Directory

Next stop is the home directory. With most network installations, every user on the network has his or her own home directory. The home directory is a place to store data files and personal applications that do not affect other users. Larger corporate installations occasionally abandon the single-user directory in lieu of the group directory, where all people of a particular type work out of the same home directory, like **SALES** for instance. The user directory by default is located at **C:\USERS** and has one subdirectory called **DEFAULT**. When setting up a new user, you can just type in the name of the path to that person's home directory. In my default system, that's **C:\USERS\CHRIS**. You must type the full path, and it cannot be a directory that is already owned by someone else, unless you have already granted rights for the new users to access the directory.

Just as with the batch files, you can use the **%USERNAME%** variable in the home directory entry. Unfortunately, Windows NT does not place a default entry in the entry box with the new user's name in it. Look for that to change in a maintenance release.

Another option that I personally find very useful is the ability to specify another machine in the workgroup as the location of my home directory. This way I can have one NT machine that holds all the user directories for easy backup. You specify the destination with standard UNC or Universal Name Convention notation. The NT machine that holds all my home directories is called **SAIL** and the share name is **CREW**. After that I specify the **%USERNAME%** variable and all is well. The entry looks like this:

\\SAIL\CREW\%USERNAME%

Now, I have to tell you about a little quirk of NT and home directories. According to its manual and the help files, Windows NT helps user file management by using the user's home directory as a reference point when opening or saving a file. If you select open from an application menu, Windows NT will place you at your home directory by default. At least that's what it's supposed to do. In reality, something very strange is going on. If you specify `C:\USERS\CHRIS` as your home directory, according to the manuals and help files, you should be placed at `C:\USERS\CHRIS` when you want to open or save a file. The truth is that you get put at `C:\USERS\DEFAULT`! which makes no sense at all. The really weird part about it is that if you specify `C:\WIN32APP` or any other directory name that isn't the user subdirectory, it works fine. Using my example, when I try to save a file, Windows NT would open the Save dialog box pointing to the `C:\WIN32APP` directory. If you use the `Connect To` option instead of the `Local Path` option, there are no problems.

Multiple User Management

Once you have created users, you can go back and make changes to anything that you specified, and as a bonus, you can select more than one user from the list of users if you want multiple users to have the same logon script or to use the same home directory. Unfortunately, you cannot create multiple users at once; you can only modify them after they exist. Remember that you can use the `%USERNAME%` in the home directory field, and that gives you the flexibility to select many users at once and standardize all of their home directories in one shot. You can also, by way of multiple selection of users, add multiple users to a group all at once. To select multiple users, just use your mouse and hold down the `CTRL` key while you click on each user you want to edit. While still holding the `CTRL` key, double-click on one of the selected users. You'll get a dialog box like the one shown in Figure 10-6.

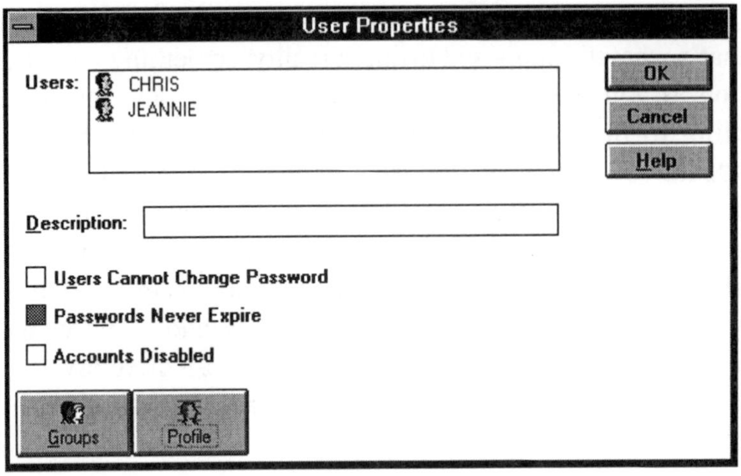

Figure 10-6
Multiple User Modification

You'll notice that one option is missing from the check boxes. You cannot force multiple users to change passwords at the next logon.

Groups

This part of the User Manager is really rather simple. You create groups for one of two reasons: to group users by physical location and job duties, or to group them by resources such as an application directory. Any user who is a member of a group takes on the access permissions of that group.

Windows NT has six default groups, shown in Figure 10-7.

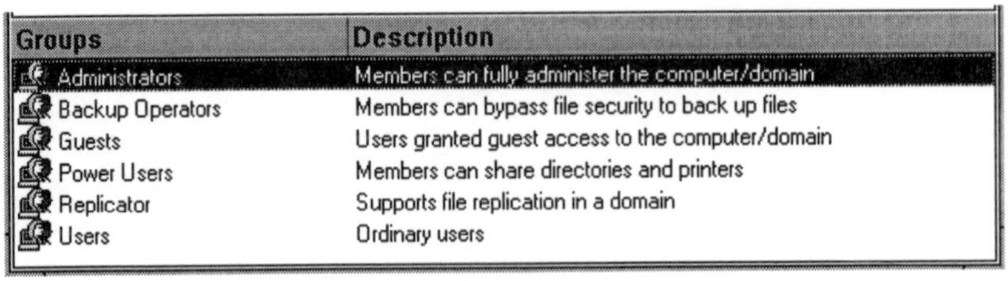

Groups	Description
Administrators	Members can fully administer the computer/domain
Backup Operators	Members can bypass file security to back up files
Guests	Users granted guest access to the computer/domain
Power Users	Members can share directories and printers
Replicator	Supports file replication in a domain
Users	Ordinary users

Figure 10-7
Default Groups Created by NT During Installation

Each of these groups, as their names clearly define, have special privileges. The default groups cannot be deleted. The replicator group is the only one that deserves some explanation. With Windows NT, when connected to an Advanced Server domain, a user can have files replicated on the server. It's a kind of real-time backup for fault tolerance.

The only attribute that groups have in User Manager is the members of the group. To create a new group just select the User menu from the menu bar and select the **New Local Group...** option. You get a dialog box like the one shown in Figure 10-8.

```
┌─────────────────────────────────────────────────────────────┐
│ ──                    New Local Group                        │
├─────────────────────────────────────────────────────────────┤
│  Group Name:  │Sheet Handlers              │      ┌────────┐  │
│                                                   │   OK   │  │
│  Description: │All Jib and Mainsail Sheet Handlers│ └────────┘  │
│                                                   ┌────────┐  │
│                             ┌──────────────────┐  │ Cancel │  │
│                             │ Show Full Names  │  └────────┘  │
│  Members:                   └──────────────────┘  ┌────────┐  │
│   ☻  CHRIS                                         │  Help  │  │
│   ☻  JEANNIE                                       └────────┘  │
│                                                              │
│                                                   ┌────────┐  │
│                                                   │ Add... │  │
│                                                   └────────┘  │
│                                                   ┌────────┐  │
│                                                   │ Remove │  │
│                                                   └────────┘  │
└─────────────────────────────────────────────────────────────┘
```

Figure 10-8
Creating a New Group

You may be wondering why the menu option is to create Local groups. This is in contrast to the Domain User Manager used by Advanced Server domain administrators which allows the creation of domain and local groups. Domain groups can encompass users and resources throughout the entire LAN and are available for all users of a domain.

As you can see from the dialog box, there really isn't much to do with groups except name them and add members to them. The real configuration of a group takes place in the File Manager. As shown in Figure 10-9, I have both types of groups operating on my system: Application and Job type.

Groups	Description
Administrators	Members can fully administer the computer/domain
Backup Operators	Members can bypass file security to back up files
Crew	All crew members
Excel 4.0 (WIN)	Windows 3.1 version of MS Excel
Guests	Users granted guest access to the computer/domain
PageMaker 5.0 (WIN)	Windows 3.1 version of Aldus PageMaker 5.0
Power Users	Members can share directories and printers
Replicator	Supports file replication in a domain
Sail Loft	All Sail Loft Workers
Skippers	All boat captains
Users	Ordinary users
Word for Windows 2.1c (WIN)	Windows 3.1 version of Word for Windows 2.1c

Figure 10-9
Groups for Applications and People

Copying a User or Group

The User menu also lets you copy existing users and groups to new ones. You can create a template user that has all your standard options selected and you just use the **Copy** command to make a new user with the same options. Understand that copying a user does not duplicate any other settings beyond what is stored in the User Manager. Configurations like printers, desktop configuration, colors, etc. are not copied to the new user. Copying a group simply duplicates the membership of the copied group and you give it a new name.

Renaming a User

The **Rename** option deserves some explanation. In Windows NT, the operating system was designed to protect against object reuse. You see, in the NetWare environment, objects in the Novell bindery are stored by name. A user called **IVY** is stored in the bindery as **IVY**. Any resources that **IVY** creates, such as files and directories, are accessible by the user by name. This means that if you delete the user **IVY** from the bindery, but leave her files intact, creating a new user called **IVY** later will give that user access to those same files. NetWare doesn't see that it is a different user, and so any object or resource that is identified as being owned by **IVY** is therefore controlled by this new user. As you can imagine, that is not good.

In Windows NT, users that are created are not internally referenced by their names. Instead, each user is given a Security Identifier, or SID. The SID identifies the user and cannot be duplicated. The number of possible SIDs for a single NT machine numbers in the billions. Resources such as files and directories are controlled by the SID, and therefore, a new user with the same name will not have the same SID and thus not have access to any other resources. If you wish to assign a new user to have access to an old user's files and other resources, you use the **Rename** option from the User menu to change the logon name of the user. The SID will still be the same but the logon name and at your option the password, full name password options, and all other points of user configuration can be changed, but the user will have access to the files created under the old user's name. You cannot rename a group.

User Manager Policies

There are several other control points for the creation and management of users on an NT machine. The Policies menu of the User Manager is the place where all other configuration points are controlled because they don't fit neatly into one category or another. They probably should have called it **Misc** instead.

Account Policy

The account policy option sets up the default configuration for passwords on your NT machine. The options are mostly self-explanatory. The only one that may need some explanation is the **Password Uniqueness** option. What that does is store X number of previously used passwords to ensure that duplicates are not being used. If you have implemented password security with passwords that expire, it makes little sense to allow users to keep using the same password over and over again. I usually set this to 5 with a 30-day expiration date.

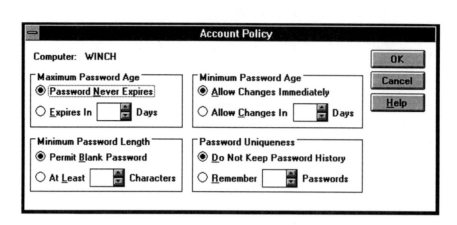

Figure 10-10
Setting Account Policies for Passwords

User Rights Policy

The User Rights Policy area is an interesting one, especially to administrators who like maximum flexibility in the control of users. There are certain functions of the system that do not fall neatly into an access right for a file or directory. Certain functions have to be handled as special rights of the system.

To the right is shown a list box containing all of the possible special rights that can be granted to a user or group of users.

Access this computer from network
Act as part of the operating system
Back up files and directories
Bypass traverse checking
Change the system time
Create a pagefile
Create a token object
Create permanent shared objects
Debug programs
Force shutdown from a remote system
Generate security audits
Increase quotas
Increase scheduling priority
Load and unload device drivers
Lock pages in memory
Log on as a batch job
Log on as a service
Log on locally
Manage auditing and security log
Modify firmware environment values
Profile single process
Profile system performance
Receive unsolicited device input
Replace a process level token
Restore files and directories
Shut down the system
Take ownership of files or other objects

To see which people have access to these rights, just select a right from the drop-down list. Windows NT will display the users or groups that can perform the functions.

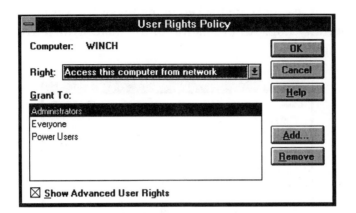

Figure 10-11
Setting System User Rights

To add or remove users and groups to or from a particular right, use the **Add...** and **Remove...** buttons. Pretty simple. The dropdown list shown previously displays the advanced rights. Many of these rights are of no use to you, and apply more to an application process or thread than to users and groups. The situation that would require the use of some of these advanced functions depends on the type of application you are running, and none of them are needed at this time. If you acquire an application that needs these rights, your documentation will specify it.

Only one of the advanced rights is of real concern to administrators. **Bypass traverse checking** is the ability of a user to travel through the directory structure, possibly passing over directories he or she does not have access to, in order to reach a subdirectory that can be accessed.

Audit Policy

For security or troubleshooting purposes, it is often necessary to keep track of what users are doing, such as logon and logoff events so you can tell when somebody is working, or when users make changes to the security of files. For this reason, Windows NT has extensive logging capabilities. Any events that you want to track can be configured from the Audit Policy dialog box shown in Figure 10-12.

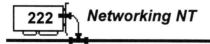
All of these events are tracked in the Event Viewer under the Security Log. All events for all users are written to the same log file.

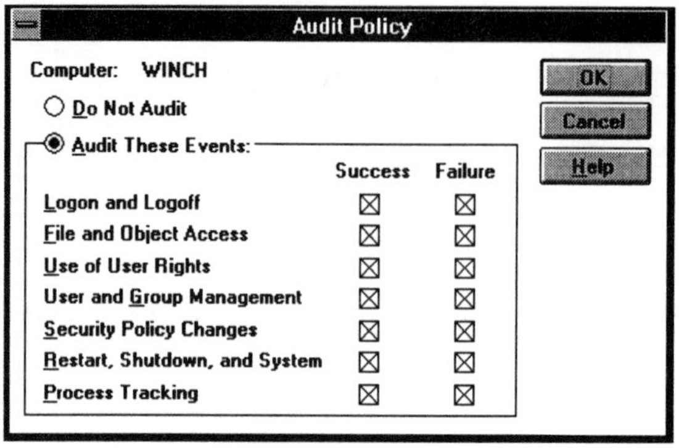

Event Viewer

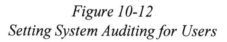

Figure 10-12
Setting System Auditing for Users

Figure 10-13 shows some examples from the Security Log with all events tracked for success and failure.

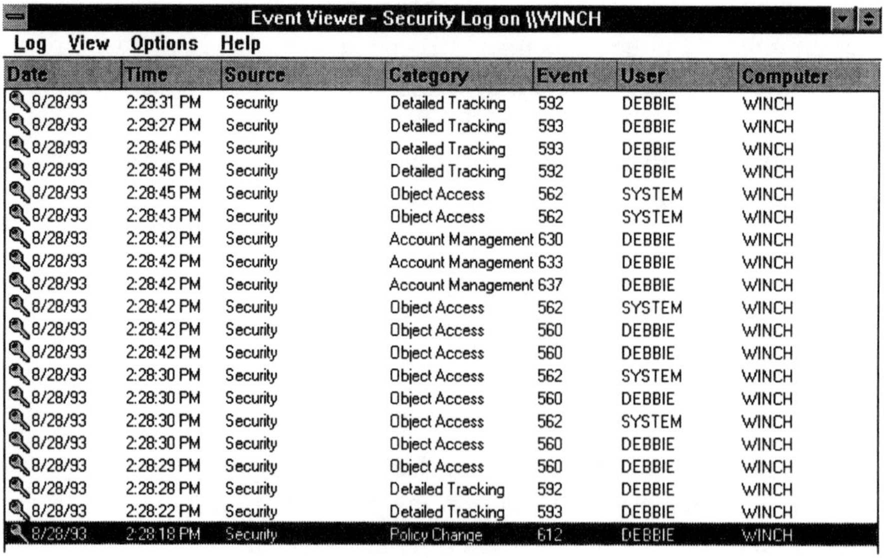

Date	Time	Source	Category	Event	User	Computer
8/28/93	2:29:31 PM	Security	Detailed Tracking	592	DEBBIE	WINCH
8/28/93	2:29:27 PM	Security	Detailed Tracking	593	DEBBIE	WINCH
8/28/93	2:28:46 PM	Security	Detailed Tracking	593	DEBBIE	WINCH
8/28/93	2:28:46 PM	Security	Detailed Tracking	592	DEBBIE	WINCH
8/28/93	2:28:45 PM	Security	Object Access	562	SYSTEM	WINCH
8/28/93	2:28:43 PM	Security	Object Access	562	SYSTEM	WINCH
8/28/93	2:28:42 PM	Security	Account Management	630	DEBBIE	WINCH
8/28/93	2:28:42 PM	Security	Account Management	633	DEBBIE	WINCH
8/28/93	2:28:42 PM	Security	Account Management	637	DEBBIE	WINCH
8/28/93	2:28:42 PM	Security	Object Access	562	SYSTEM	WINCH
8/28/93	2:28:42 PM	Security	Object Access	560	DEBBIE	WINCH
8/28/93	2:28:42 PM	Security	Object Access	560	DEBBIE	WINCH
8/28/93	2:28:30 PM	Security	Object Access	562	SYSTEM	WINCH
8/28/93	2:28:30 PM	Security	Object Access	560	DEBBIE	WINCH
8/28/93	2:28:30 PM	Security	Object Access	562	SYSTEM	WINCH
8/28/93	2:28:30 PM	Security	Object Access	560	DEBBIE	WINCH
8/28/93	2:28:29 PM	Security	Object Access	560	DEBBIE	WINCH
8/28/93	2:28:28 PM	Security	Detailed Tracking	592	DEBBIE	WINCH
8/28/93	2:28:22 PM	Security	Detailed Tracking	593	DEBBIE	WINCH
8/28/93	2:28:18 PM	Security	Policy Change	612	DEBBIE	WINCH

Figure 10-13
Auditing Entries in the Event Viewer

If you don't need logging, don't turn it on because it does take up space on the hard drive and it uses up processor resources while writing, making the processor(s) take a little longer to complete tasks. The performance hit is almost nothing, but it is there.

Each of the events that the log tracks holds complete information on what happened. To zoom in on a particular event, just double-click on the entry in the log. This will produce a dialog box like the one shown in Figure 10-14.

```
┌─────────────────────────────────────────────────────────┐
│ ▬                      Event Detail                       │
├─────────────────────────────────────────────────────────┤
│  Date:     8/28/93          Event ID:  630                │
│  Time:     2:28:42 PM       Source:    Security           │
│  User:     DEBBIE           Type:      Success Audit      │
│  Computer: WINCH            Category:  Account Management  │
│                                                           │
│  Description:                                             │
│  ┌──────────────────────────────────────────────────┬─┐  │
│  │ User Account Deleted:                             │▲│  │
│  │      Target Account Name:      JEANNIE            │ │  │
│  │      Target Domain:      WINCH                    │ │  │
│  │      Target Account ID:                           │ │  │
│  │ S-1-5-21-97720808-889461693-429528154-1003        │ │  │
│  │      Caller User Name:   DEBBIE                   │ │  │
│  │      Caller Domain:      WINCH                    │ │  │
│  │      Caller Logon ID:    (0x0,0x53C6)             │▼│  │
│  └──────────────────────────────────────────────────┴─┘  │
│                                                           │
│  Data:   ● Bytes  ○ Words                                 │
│  ┌──────────────────────────────────────────────────┬─┐  │
│  │                                                   │▲│  │
│  │                                                   │ │  │
│  │                                                   │▼│  │
│  │◄│                                              │►│  │  │
│  └──────────────────────────────────────────────────┴─┘  │
│                                                           │
│  ┌────────┐  ┌──────────┐  ┌────────┐  ┌────────┐         │
│  │ Close  │  │ Previous │  │  Next  │  │  Help  │         │
│  └────────┘  └──────────┘  └────────┘  └────────┘         │
└─────────────────────────────────────────────────────────┘
```

Figure 10-14
Audit Entry Zoom from the Event Viewer

As you can see, the detail of each event is quite sufficient to describe everything that happened.

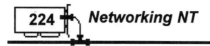
File Manager

The File Manager contains all the tools to set permissions for files and directories. It is, in point of fact, the only place that you can do this. If you are not using the NTFS partition type on your machine, you cannot set access permissions. At the end of the File Manager tool bar is an icon for controlling permissions for files and directories.

The same function can be accomplished by selecting the Security menu from the File Manager menu bar and selecting **Permissions**. The options for file and directory permissions are different. We'll start with the file permissions.

File Permissions

To start, select a file for which you want to adjust the permissions. Let's say you have a graphic in the **WIN32APP** directory that you want to be sure that nobody can delete. First, locate the file.

Next, click on the file and then on the Permissions icon in the tool bar. You'll see a dialog box like the one shown in Figure 10-15.

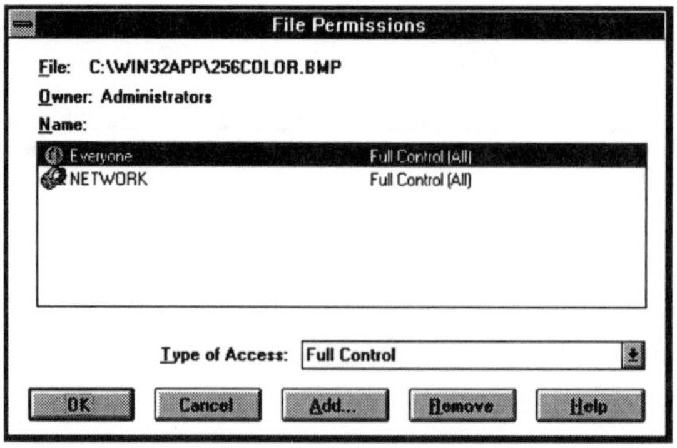

Figure 10-15
File Permissions List

This is a good time to talk about global groups. Notice the **NET-WORK** group listed in Figure 10-15? Wonder why that wasn't covered in the section on groups? That's because the membership in that group as well as the others listed in Figure 10-16 changes frequently, depending on where a user is accessing the machine from. The **SYSTEM** group is for the operating system itself.

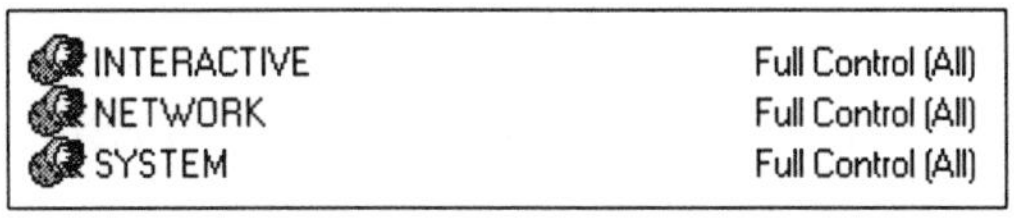

INTERACTIVE	Full Control (All)
NETWORK	Full Control (All)
SYSTEM	Full Control (All)

Figure 10-16
Windows NT Global Groups

The Interactive group defines all users who are logged on locally and the Network group is for all users who are logged on remotely from other workgroup machines. If there are other users or groups that you want to have access to a file, just click on **Add...** You can also browse the users and groups of other NT machines and add them to the permissions list for a file.

There are four standard attributes that can be granted to a user or group for a file. These rights, also listed at the beginning of the chapter, are the most common rights granted. In addition, you can grant special access privileges, by selecting the **Special Access...** option from the **Type of Access** list box.

Standard Access
- **No Access** (None)
- **Read** (R)
- **Change** (RWXD)
- **Full Control** (RWXDPO)

Special Access
- **Read** (R)
- **Write** (W)

🖥	Execute	(E)
🖥	Delete	(D)
🖥	Change Permissions	(P)
🖥	Take Ownership	(O)

Directory Permissions

Directory permissions are handled in a different way from file permissions. When setting the access permissions for a directory, you have the option of redefining the permissions of all files and subdirectories under the selected directory to match the permissions you choose.

This makes the process both easier and more complicated at the same time. Take a look at Figure 10-17. Do you see how the access rights are listed twice. Next to **Full Control** is listed **(ALL) (ALL)**. The first set of brackets is for the type of directory access. The second set is the file access permissions for files in that directory.

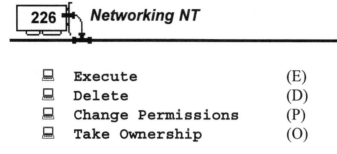

Figure 10-17
Setting File and Directory Access Permissions

Directory Permissions comes with its own set of standard and special access rights. The standard rights define both directory and file level access:

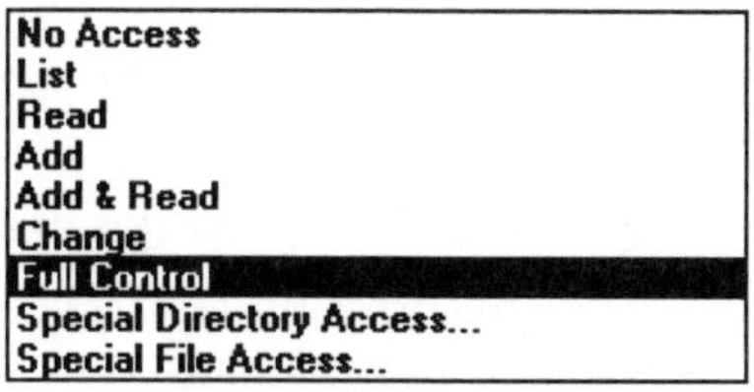

```
No Access
List
Read
Add
Add & Read
Change
Full Control
Special Directory Access...
Special File Access...
```

Figure 10-18
Access Rights

Standard Access		Directory	File
🖥	No Access	(None)	(None)
🖥	List	(RX)	()
🖥	Read	(RX)	(RX)
🖥	Add	(WX)	()
🖥	Add & read	(RWX)	(RWX)
🖥	Change	(RWXD)	(RWXD)
🖥	Full Control	(RWXDPO)	(RWXDPO)

Special File Access		
🖥	Read	(R)
🖥	Write	(W)
🖥	Execute	(E)
🖥	Delete	(D)
🖥	Change permissions	(P)
🖥	Take ownership	(O)

Special Directory Access		
🖥	Read	(R)
🖥	Write	(W)
🖥	Execute	(E)
🖥	Delete	(D)
🖥	Change permissions	(P)
🖥	Take ownership	(O)

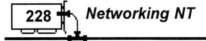

There's one last thing I need to tell you about the Directory Permissions. Directory Permissions has one very different type of user that can be added to the permissions list for the directory. It is called the Owner Creator user and it's a variable user that identifies the current owner or original creator of the directory you are granting permissions for.

By using the check boxes at the top of the dialog box, you can replace all file and directory permissions under the selected directory. This is a powerful feature for complete implementation of security.

Granting Rights

Keep the group model of security in mind when setting up your permissions. Make as few permissions as possible dependent on a single user; this will make the creation of new users easier. If all your security is tied to groups then all you have to do is add users to those groups when you want a user to have more or less access.

Remember that when you grant rights, the lowest available rights will be the rights granted to the user or group. For instance, you have, group called CREW and they have the right to delete files in a directory. Another group, SALES, can only look at a file. If the user Shawn is a member of both groups, she will not have delete rights to the file. The lowest available rights prevail.

A Word About Shares

Just because you have granted rights for a user or group to access files and directories on your machine does not mean they are available to users on other machines in a workgroup. The only way a user on another machine may gain access to your files is if you establish a share for a directory on your system. For more information on shares, see Chapter 6.

That's all there is to managing users, groups, and rights.

Chapter 11

The Registry

VB	INI	WINHELP	INI	WINBENCH	INI	MSACCESS	INI	MMTOOLS	INI
DCASYNC	INI	CORELCHT	INI	MSMAIL	INI	PCAW	INI	NETMETER	INI
VIEWER	INI	ANSEL	INI	COMMENCE	INI	WPS	INI	ENTPACK	INI
SETSCAN	INI	WINCHAT	INI	CONTROL	INI	DLGEDIT	INI	ICONMAN	INI
ENCARTA	INI	ONLINE	INI	ODOMETER	INI	LAUNCH	INI	WINMINE	INI
MCSINIT	INI	CLOCK	INI	NETWATCH	INI	MBROWSER	INI	SMETER	INI
SOL	INI	PPTVIEW	INI	MPLAYER	INI	DOSAPP	INI	HELPREQ	INI
PASINI	INI	PHONE	INI	WINFILE	INI	EXCEL4	INI	MSD	INI
MOUSE	INI	CLIPBRD	INI	SETUPWIZ	INI	SHED	INI	MV	INI
PAS	INI	PROGMAN	INI	ODBCINST	INI	VUEPOINT	INI	QTW	INI
QEX	INI	ODBC	INI	MCSDFALT	INI	WINGIF	INI	SYSTEM	INI
NDW	INI	MTFONTS	INI	WINAW	INI	TBEDIT	INI		
SETUSER	INI	FISH!	INI	CEDAR	INI	WINMETER	INI		
PROTOCOL	INI	SCHDPLUS	INI	WIN	INI	WINCOLOR	INI		

Does this look familiar? This is the list of INI files from one of my Windows machines. This doesn't include the INI files that are stored in the directories with the applications. Some applications also store configuration information in the **WIN.INI** and some in **DAT** or **CFG** named files. When you want to adjust the configuration of a Windows application, or the environment itself, good luck! It takes 15 minutes just to figure out where the information is stored.

In reality, the **WIN.INI** file, when originally conceptualized, was supposed to hold all information about all applications. The idea was to have a single place to adjust configuration information. It was an excellent idea that didn't work because Independent Software Vendors (ISVs) decided to go it alone, creating their own INI files. As you can see, it got out of hand.

Registry Purpose and Structure

Enter the registry. In as few words as possible, the Windows NT registry is a database that was designed to hold all configuration informa-

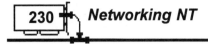

tion for everything. There is little chance that ISVs will forge ahead on their own, leaving the registry behind. It is the perfect structure for storing configuration information. In addition, with the multiple-user capabilities of NT, the registry can hold multiple configurations for an application, depending on the user who is logged on. Every possible point of configuration can be stored in the registry, from screen colors to the last four files you had open in Excel to your arrangement of program groups in your Program Manager to your favorite date format.

Another big strength of the registry design is that it is completely secure and security-enabled so that administrators can define which users can edit entries in the registry. To top it all off, the registry is an accessible network resource, which allows a remote administrator to open the registry of a network machine to view and modify values, operating on the remote registry as if it were the local registry.

Accommodating Non-Conformists

There is a catch to all of this, though. Although it is unlikely that ISVs will go it alone in regards to the registry, it is equally unlikely that there will be a mass exodus to the registry in the first year or so. Applications must be written to use the registry, and that requires a lot of recoding of current applications. For the time being, configuration of applications in Windows NT will be an amalgam of **INI**, **CFG**, and **DAT** files as before, while other newer or recently converted applications will write configuration information directly into the registry. You can be certain that everything you can configure in the environment itself will use the registry and Microsoft will probably be releasing all their existing applications in WIN32 form, thus using the registry. For now though, you'll have to deal with both methods.

To accommodate the older applications, especially those written for Windows 3.x, Windows NT does have a **WIN.INI** and a **SYSTEM.INI**. During the installation of a Windows 3.x application, many install programs will write some information to the **WIN.INI** and **SYSTEM.INI**. It wouldn't work very well if the **WIN.INI** did not exist. When running one of those Windows 3.x applications, the app can still look to the **WIN.INI** for configuration info, just as though it were running in a native Windows 3.x environment.

Registry Data Types

Up to this point, I've only mentioned software configuration information; however, the registry also stores all hardware information for the machine. You see, the registry is made up of two different types of data, volatile and stable. Hardware data, such as installed cards and configuration, is volatile. Every time Windows NT boots, the **NTDETECT.EXE** program executes and determines the hardware configuration of the machine. Depending on what NT finds, drivers are disabled, enabled, or enabled with different settings. In order to accommodate the regularly changing configuration of your system, all hardware information in the registry is repopulated every time the system is booted. Stable data is the type of configuration information, like the color of your desktop background, that you change when you want to, but which should stay in place until you change it. The values are the same from one boot to the next, until you change them.

The existence of a volatile data type assists Windows NT in recovering from faulty configuration information. Since NT rebuilds the hardware information every time it boots, the registry stores the "Last Known Good" configuration of hardware, so that if drivers are loaded that don't work or aren't configured properly, Windows NT can load the last working configuration. Most drivers that come with NT not only load like they should, but they also report back to the system that they loaded and what resources they are using. The registry uses the status of the drivers loaded to determine that the system has properly booted. If everything is okay, then Windows NT places that configuration into the registry as a known good configuration.

We'll look more closely at how information is stored in the registry when we start working with the registry editor.

Manipulating the Registry

As I said earlier, everything for the NT environment is held in the registry, but is far easier to manipulate using control panels and applications. In most situations, the registry does not need to be manipulated directly. When you use the Control Panel to change your screen colors, you are actually changing values in the registry. The user interface for changing colors or other desktop configurations through their respective control panels or applications is a lot easier to understand than changing numeric values in the registry directly. Without a decent reference, changing a value from **00001C2** to **00001F3** could do awful things to your desktop, but using the Control Panel to change the border width of your windows is easy.

Now that I have given you the long-winded disclaimer/warning about the registry, I'll show you everything you need to know. The first thing you need to know is where the registry editor is. During the installation of Windows NT, the registry editor is not added to any of the program groups in the program manager. Even if you elect to have Windows NT search for application during the install, Windows NT has been programmed to ignore discovery of the registry editor. It's just not the type of application that most people should know about and have access to.

Accessing the Registry Editor

Locate the Administrative Tools program group in your Program Manager and place the focus on it, so that it's the front group. Next, select **New...** from the File menu of the Program Manager. You'll be adding a new program item, so select that option from the dialog box and proceed. The application we want to add is called **REGEDT32.EXE** and is located, at least on a default NT installation, in the **C:\WINNT\SYSTEM32** directory.

Once the addition of the registry editor is complete, you'll have a new icon in your Administrative Tools group. The application is added to a personal program group, which means that it will not appear in any other user's program groups. If you want to make the application available to others, consider adding the registry editor to a common group instead. Let's fire it up and take a look.

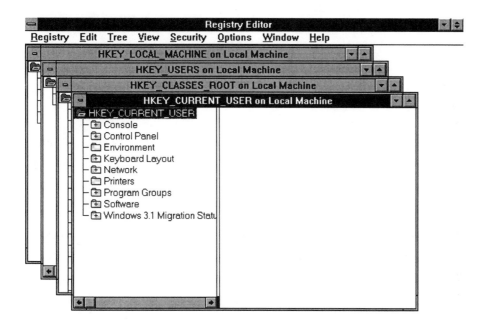

Figure 11-1
The Registry Editor

The most striking feature of the registry editor is its similarity to the File Manager. To make this complex database of configurations easier to navigate and understand, all entries in the registry are stored in a hierarchy like "directories" and "files." In the registry editor, the items listed next to folders that appear as directories are *registry keys*. The information stored in the folders, which in the metaphor represent files are *registry values*. Keys and values make up the entire registry database.

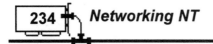

The database is divided into four key handles, covering the major components of the operating system.

```
HKEY_LOCAL_MACHINE
HKEY_CLASSES_ROOT
HKEY_USERS
HKEY_CURRENT_USER
```

Under each of these four keys there are sub-trees holding more keys and values.

There are limits to the registry, however. The registry can hold anything, from files to bitmaps to purely numeric configuration information. With this open ability, the registry can be abused by programmers who want to take shortcuts. Instead of placing a reference to a bitmap in the registry telling an application where to find the file, the logic may be: "Why not just store the whole bitmap in the registry?" If enough applications store unnecessary information or take up wasted space, the database grows too large, taking up too much space and making access to it slower. To prevent possible abuse, the registry database cannot be any larger than 32 MB and no value entry in the registry can be larger than 1 MB. These are not system limitations, but Microsoft-inspired logical limits. The registry could in fact, be quite larger if it were not governed with an arbitrary limit.

Let me stress again that this information does not need to be directly manipulated, as almost every setting in the registry is tied to some configuration application whether it's a control panel or an application or just simply how you last left your program groups arranged in the Program Manager. The only time you need to manipulate registry data is when you are managing your system and users, as you'll see when we get to the practical application segment in this chapter and in Chapter 12.

HKEY_LOCAL_MACHINE

This key handle is probably the most important of the four, since it contains so much critical data to the system and its operation. There are

five keys in the **HKEY_LOCAL_MACHINE**
handle. These five keys are predefined and cannot be added to. The registry editor will not
allow any additional keys at the first level of
this handle unless they are loaded as a *hive*.
(We'll get to hives in a few minutes.) The
HARDWARE key is the volatile data. It is pos-
sible to delete the entire **HARDWARE** key and all subtrees of the key, shut
down the machine, and come back up without skipping a beat. Windows
NT rebuilds this portion of the registry every time the computer starts up.

HKEY_LOCAL_MACHINE
- HARDWARE
- SAM
- SECURITY
- SOFTWARE
- SYSTEM

The entire key handle holds all machine-specific settings for the
machine, including such things as the type of processor, video card, and
parallel controller type, as well as configured data such as the computer
name and installed printers. None of the information held in this key is
user-specific, and any user accessing the registry editor with sufficient
rights will see the same information. Another key handle, the
HKEY_CLASSES_ROOT handle, gets its data from the
HKEY_LOCAL_MACHINE handle when you log on. It duplicates the class
information into its own key handle. When you get a chance, browse
through the handle to get an idea of how information is stored here and
what the handle stores. I would have been more than happy to insert a
printout of the handle and all sub-trees, but the text file representation of
the handle is nearly 1 MB in size and would take up approximately 807
pages. I don't think that would be a very good use of paper.

HKEY_CLASSES_ROOT

The **HKEY_CLASSES_ROOT** key handle contains information related to Object Linking and Embedding (OLE) as well as file association
information. File extensions are listed as keys and the values associated
with the keys tell NT what application should be launched to handle the
file type. If you are familiar with Windows 3.x, this is the same thing as
the associations in the Windows 3.x File Manager. Additions to this key
handle are permitted and you can do them manually or you can select a
file from the File Manager and then click on the **Associate...** menu

option of the File menu. This will automatically create a new key for the selected file type, say **XLS**, and the application you associated the **XLS** files with will be the value stored in the **XLS** key.

In addition, the classes root handle also stores specific OLE operational commands for installed applications. These values define what commands NT should execute to perform a particular function for an OLE object.

One example of this is the Print command for text files. If you drag a text file from the File Manager to a printer or select **Print...** from the File Manager's File menu while you have a text file selected, Windows NT will look in the **HKEY_CLASSES_ROOT** key handle for the commands to print the file. In this case it would be **notepad.exe /p %1** where **%1** is the name of the file which Windows NT inserts during the operation. You can verify that Windows NT uses this parameter to perform the function requested by changing the value and watching what happens. Let's give it a try.

Locate the **HKEY_CLASSES_ROOT** key handle and goto the following key:

HKEY_CLASSES_ROOT\txtfile\shell\print\command

In this key, you find the value:

```
<No Name> : REG_SZ: notepad.exe /p %1
```

Double-click on the value and change it so that the actual value portion reads:

```
notepad.exe %1
```

All we've done is remove the **/p** parameter. Now, try printing a text file from the file manager. Do you notice a problem? All that happens is that Windows NT loads the file into Notepad. The **/p** parameter tells NT to print the file and without it, all you're doing is loading the file. Let me remind you to change the key back to its original value, including the **/p** parameter.

As I said when talking about the **HKEY_LOCAL_MACHINE** key handle, it's really the most important handle of all, and any changes you make to the information in the **HKEY_CLASSES_ROOT** handle is automatically written again into the **HKEY_LOCAL_MACHINE** and vice versa.

You may be wondering, if the information is already in the **HKEY_LOCAL_MACHINE** key handle, why does it need to be duplicated into another key handle all its own? The reason is quite simple. To provide compatibility with Windows 3.x applications that use OLE, Windows 3.x has a registration database that all OLE apps must belong to in order to operate properly. When a Windows 3.x OLE-enabled application goes looking for the registration database while running in Windows NT, they will get to **HKEY_CLASSES_ROOT**, which appears the same as the Windows 3.x registration database.

HKEY_USERS

There are only two primary keys in the **HKEY_USERS** handle, and you cannot add more unless you are loading a hive. Hives are discussed next in this chapter. **DEFAULT** and the SID (security identification) for the currently logged-on user are the only available primary keys from the handle. This handle *does not* list all users of the system.

Everything about a user's configuration, from colors to program groups and everything in between is stored in the **HKEY_USERS** handle. The **DEFAULT** configuration has two purposes. The first is the **DEFAULT** desktop and color configuration values of the machine which are used when the system is waiting for someone to log on. This can be very useful for setting a company logo to display at the logon screen or to display some other useful bitmap. The other purpose of the **DEFAULT** configuration is to accommodate the existence of user profiles that exist on other machines. According to Microsoft, there are utilities that will be available that allow you to store the user profile information on another machine. In the event that Windows NT cannot access the remote user profile because of a LAN problem or other complication, the system will use the default configuration. Understand that this does not have any bearing on security or other settings, only those that are stored in the user profile: colors, preferences, and other such information.

HKEY_CURRENT_USER

The **HKEY_CURRENT_USER** key handle is a duplication of the settings in the **HKEY_USER** handle. The settings listed in the key will either represent the SID of the currently logged on user or the **DEFAULT** user, depending on the logon. Just as with the **HKEY_CLASSES_ROOT**, all information in this key is linked both ways with the **HKEY_USER** handle and a change in one will cause a change in the other. The exception to this is that if you logged on and got the **DEFAULT** configuration because the user profile for your SID was unavailable, any changes you made would be made to the user profile with your SID. You would not be making changes to the **DEFAULT** configuration.

Do You Have Hives?

Yes, you do. What is a hive, you ask? Well, a hive is a file equivalent to keys in the registry. Hives are files that can be unloaded and loaded in the **HKEY_LOCAL_MACHINE** and **HKEY_USERS** handles. Hives can exist in one of two forms: native and backup. The native form of a hive depends on the key or keys in question. For example, the **DEFAULT** user profile is actually a file called **DEFAULT.LOG** which is located in the **C:\WINNT\SYSTEM32\CONFIG** directory. This is considered a hive and contains all the information that you see in the **DEFAULT** user profile. When you make a change to information in the keys beneath **DEFAULT**, the changes are being made in the hive file.

Other hives, also located in the **C:\WINNT\SYSTEM32\CONFIG** directory include the **SOFTWARE**, **SYSTEM**, **SAM**, and **SECURITY** keys of **HKEY_LOCAL_MACHINE**.

The other format is for a key or set of keys that you save as a file. From the File menu, you can select a key and save the key and sub-tree as a file. At a later time, you can restore the key to your system or load it somewhere else in the registry. I'll give you some practical examples to help illustrate the point and purpose of hives, but first some rules.

There are five things you can do with a hive. You can load a hive, save a key as a hive, unload a hive, restore a volatile hive, and restore a hive.

Load a Hive

Loading a hive allows you to add a key with possible subtrees into either **HKEY_USERS** or **HKEY_LOCAL_MACHINE**. The purpose is to add registry information to your registry database. You could, for instance, load a key for a new application into the **HKEY_LOCAL_MACHINE** handle. Applications that have NT-style installation programs may actually do this to add new configuration information to the registry by loading a hive from the installation disks into the **HKEY_LOCAL_MACHINE\SOFTWARE** key. Once a hive is loaded, the file that represents the hive is attached to the registry database. Any changes you make to values in the hive are reflected in changes made to the file that represents the hive.

Save a Key as a Hive

Saving a key as a hive is applicable to any of the four handles. You would have a key as a hive by using the **Save Key...** option of the registry editor's File menu. This creates a file on your hard drive or on the network that contains all the information stored in the selected key, including all sub-trees. This is a way to do a backup of the information stored in the registry. For instance, you could select the **HKEY_CURRENT_USER\Network** key and save it to a file. This would place all information in and below that key into a file. The file can later be used as a loadable hive or used to restore information back into a key.

Unload a Hive

Unloading a hive means that you are telling Windows NT to disconnect from the loaded hive. A loaded hive is a file that has been attached to the registry. If you unload it, the hive and hence the configurations contained within will not be part of the registry anymore. You should know that this does not delete the hive, it just disconnects it from the registry. You can use this feature with the load feature to temporarily load another user's profile into your registry, make some changes and then unload it. All the changes will be reflected in the hive you loaded and unloaded. Remember all hives are files but not all files are hives. All user profiles are hives but not all hives are user profiles.

Restore a Hive and Restore a Volatile Hive

Restoration of a hive simply tells Windows NT and the registry editor that you want to replace the currently selected key with a hive on your disk or on the network. The information that you are replacing may not be a hive, but simply entries in the registry. When you restore this information, Windows NT does not link the information to the file you restored it from, it just updates the registry values and keys. The file that you restored from can be discarded after the procedure is complete.

Let's say that you want to back up your Control Panel key. You would save the key using the **File** menu option and give it a descriptive name. Remember that NT can use 255-character file names. At a later time, you decide that you want your old configuration back. You would select the Control Panel key from your SID in the **HKEY_USERS** handle and restore the key, giving NT the name of the file you saved earlier. NT would replace all configuration information and keys in the selected key with the values in the hive/file you select. Control Panel itself is not a hive, but the information saved in the file is a hive by itself. When you restore the hive to the Control Panel key, the values and keys in the saved hive are integrated back into the key you selected.

Restoring volatile hives simply tells the registry to hang on to the hive only until the next reboot and then get rid of it. The file will still be there, but the registry will no longer consider it a part of the registry database.

Practical Applications of Hives

Aside from the fact that Windows NT depends on some hives, such as those found in the `C:\WINNT\SYSTEM32\CONFIG` directory, you can use hives to ease administration.

1) Control User Profiles

By adding user profile hives, which can be found in the `C:\WINNT\SYSTEM32\CONFIG` directory, you can control the registry-based configuration of users on your system. To do this, bring the **HKEY_USERS** handle to the front. Next, select the very top key in the window: **HKEY_USERS**. Then, select the **Load Hive...** option from the **File** menu of the registry editor. Locate the `C:\WINNT\SYSTEM32\CONFIG` directory and select any file in the directory that represents the user you want to control. The file must be one that ends with no extension. The files that end in **LOG** are not hives.

After selecting the appropriate hive, the registry editor will ask you for a name. Give it a descriptive name so that you know which user it represents. Once complete, all the user profile information for that user will be accessible to you in the registry editor. When you make changes to the keys, the changes will be written back to the user's profile. The next time that user logs in, he or she will have the changes that you specified.

2) Modifying Users with a Backup Hive

Another very useful use of the hives is to duplicate the configuration of one user to another user. You can load the hive of the user you want to change and then simply restore a hive or hives representing the values you want to change. I use this at times to replace the control panel settings of certain users. I keep a backup of a pre-configured Control Panel key as a file. I select the Control Panel key of the user I want to change

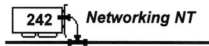
and then perform a restore from my backup hive/file. The user now has a duplicate of the backup hive for his or her Control Panel settings.

3) Controlling the Creation of New Users

There is a hive in the **C:\WINNT\SYSTEM32\CONFIG** directory which is not attached to the registry at any time but can easily be added to control the configuration of new users added to the system. The file is called **USERDEF** and can be loaded as a hive into your **HKEY_USERS** handle. In and under this key, you'll find the same keys that you have in your user profile, but they are the values used to create new users. If you want all new users to display the same bitmap as a background, the **USERDEF** hive is the place to do it. Anything you put in or change in this hive will affect the configuration of all new users created. This is useful if you have to create a thousand users and don't want to spend three days changing their desktops around.

Remember that restoring keys can be performed on any key in any key handle. Loading and unloading of hives can only be performed on **HKEY_USERS** and **HKEY_LOCAL_MACHINE** handles. Also remember that you can set security for any key in the entire registry. The implementation of security in the form of permissions is the same as setting directory permissions in the File Manager. If you need to, review Chapter 10.

You cannot set permissions on individual values in the registry editor. Also, much like you can in the File Manager, you can set up auditing on a particular key, and that information will be written to the security log that you can view in the Event Viewer. Finally, you can also take ownership of a key or hive, just like you can with a file in the File Manager. The cautions for this and the reasons for it are explained in Chapter 10.

Use the Registry Editor carefully and take time to learn how it works. Making a mistake in the editor can destroy your system, rendering it useless. As you'll see in the next chapter, although most everything can be configured using user interface applications and control panels, there are some other uses of the registry editor that can make management easier.

Chapter 12

MS Mail

To instantly create a network with all the features you need, Microsoft has elected to add MS Mail to Windows NT. MS Mail is based on workgroup post offices that you place on your LAN. Each user of the network is a member of one of the post offices, and all of the user's mail is routed through it.

Creating and sending mail is relatively self-explanatory and it's not what we're concerned with here. What we want to do is discuss the creation and administration of an MS Mail system on your LAN. As I said above, the Mail system is based on a workgroup post office, which is usually referred to as a WGPO. In a workgroup, two WGPOs cannot communicate with one another, and thus, two users who belong to different WGPOs cannot send mail to one another. The version of Mail that comes with Windows NT and Windows for Workgroups is not the full-blown version of MS Mail. This version of Mail is designed specifically for workgroups, not enterprise LANs or WANs.

To start off, we need to create a post office. The post office will be the central "mail drop" for users communicating in the workgroup. To create a WGPO, double-click on the Mail icon in the Main program group of the Program Manager.

The first time you run Mail from any workstation and any user on the LAN, from a WFW or NT machine, Mail needs to know what to do. Any Mail installation must be connected to a WGPO and if the system

you are working on will not be the WGPO, then you have to connect to an existing WGPO located somewhere else on the LAN. If you make an error and accidentally establish a new post office when one already exists on the LAN, we can fix that. It takes a bit of work but I'll show you how at the end of this chapter.

The first thing you'll see is MS Mail asking you what to do. Select the option for creating a new post office.

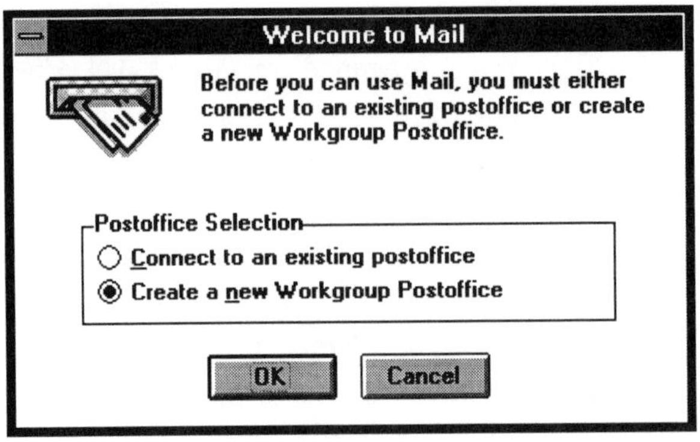

Figure 12-1
Running MS Mail for the First Time

Windows NT will warn you about the existence of multiple post offices. Remember that you can have more than one post office but users from the two post offices will not be able to exchange mail. In keeping with the multi-user structure of NT, each user of the NT machine has their own mail setup and one user from the system may be attached to one post office in the accounting department while another user may manage a post office on the machine itself. The Mail configuration is user-dependent, not machine-dependent. Every user who runs Mail for the first time will see the same dialog box as shown in Figure 12-1. Depending on how you set up mail on your system, you can automate the process. We'll get to that later, though.

When establishing a new WGPO, you must select a location for the files. I usually put my WGPO in the **WIN32APP** directory. Mail will create a WGPO directory wherever you tell it to, assuming you have rights

to the directory and will then build a ton of subdirectories to hold the
WGPO structure. Once complete, you need to create a user account at
the WGPO for your mail.

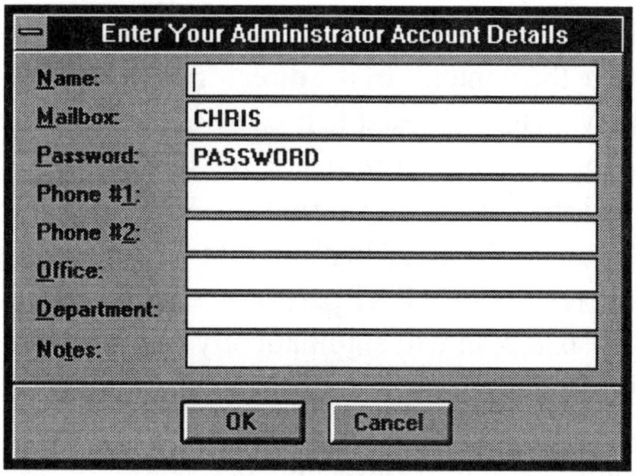

Enter Your Administrator Account Details
Name:	
Mailbox:	CHRIS
Password:	PASSWORD
Phone **#1**:	
Phone **#2**:	
Office:	
Department:	
No**t**es:	
OK   Cancel

Figure 12-2
Creating an Administrative Account for the Post Office

The first three entries in the dialog box shown in Figure 12-2 are not
optional. The password is optional but you don't want to have a mailbox
without a password, because anyone can access your messages if your
mail box isn't password-protected. The user account you are creating
will be the Post Office Manager account, which gives the user access to a
utility in the Mail menu of MS Mail for managing users and shared folders in the system. After you have created your user's account, Mail will
tell you that everything is set up and you have one more step to complete
before other users can access the post office (Figure 12-3).

Figure 12-3
MS Mail is Installed

The directory that was created for the post office must be available to all users who want to join. For users in the workgroup the WGPO directory should be shared with a minimum of **CHANGE** access to the directory. This allows workstations in the workgroup to share the WGPO. Users on the same machine where the WGPO resides should have permission to change the contents of the directories in the WGPO. You have to use the File Manager to establish each of these parameters. If you neglect to do so, the WGPO will not be seen by other users in the workgroup. For information on sharing the WGPO and setting permissions, refer to Chapter 10. Bear in mind that you cannot set permissions for a WGPO that resides on a FAT partition, only an NTFS partition. The WGPO on a FAT partition will automatically be available to users of *that* machine. You will still have to establish the share for remote users.

You are now ready to begin using MS Mail. All users who will be using Mail must run through the same process. When the Option dialog box appears, they will choose to connect to an existing WGPO rather than create a new one. The dialog box for entering the location of the WGPO is amazingly poor. There is no browse command and you must enter the location of the WGPO in UNC format. UNC (Universal Naming Convention) puts the computer name first and then the path, whether it is a share name or a directory.

\\MAST\WIN32APP\WGPO

When you are connecting to a remote WGPO, you should specify the computer name of the computer that has the WGPO, then specify the share name that points to the WGPO directory on that machine. If you are connecting to a WGPO that resides on the machine that you are currently running on, you would specify the name of your machine, then the directory that contains the WGPO.

Now, you're probably thinking that there is no way you can accurately ensure that all users on your network will enter the right information and therefore get to the right WGPO. Guess what? I've found some little tricks that can really make things easier.

Using the Registry to Manage Mail

If you'll recall, in Chapter 11 I told you about the default user configuration hive called **USERDEF**, which is located in the **C:\WINNT\SYSTEM32\CONFIG** directory. We're going to use this hive to automate part of the mail installation process.

Step 1 — Get a Valid Mail Configuration

Before mail is set up for a user, the registry has a single key and set of values for Mail. They are located in the following key and are shown in Figure 12-4.

HKEY_USERS*SID*\\Software\\Microsoft\\Mail

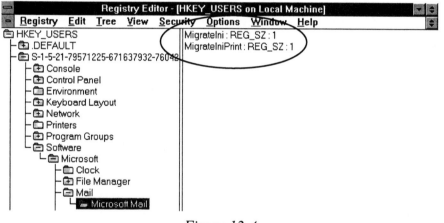

Figure 12-4
Using the Registry to Manage Mail

What we're most concerned with is the two items circled. The values are an indication that no MS Mail configuration has taken place yet. The values trigger Mail to go through the setup phase of Mail for this user. Run Mail and set it up. If you are creating a new post office, do that. If you will be connecting to a remote WGPO, do that. Whatever steps you need to take to get Mail up and running, including sharing or setting permissions for the directory, you should do them.

Step 2 — Copying the Mail Configuration

The next step is to get a copy of the configuration you just set up when you configured yourself for Mail. All of the information that you specified for getting Mail running is now in the registry. Your Mail key in the registry has changed significantly as shown in Figure 12-5.

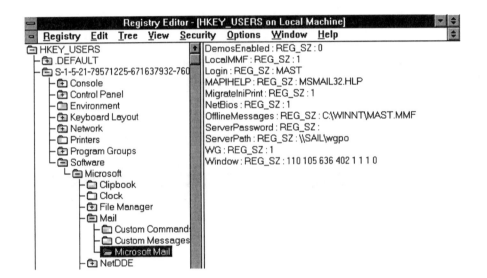

Figure 12-5
Setting Default for the USERDEF Hive

As you can see, several new keys have been added and the values in the Microsoft Mail key have been modified and added to. We want to focus on a couple of the values in the Microsoft Mail key. First, notice that the **ServerPath** value points to your WGPO. The information is there, and since new users will point to the same WGPO, we can use this value in the default user profile. The other two values we need to look at are the **Login** value and the **OfflineMessages** value. We need to make a copy of the entire **Mail** key before proceeding. Click on the **Mail** key just below the **File Manager** key in the **Software\Microsoft** key of your SID. Make certain that the Mail key contains information similar to the values shown above. Your individual installation path and other parameters may be different, but if it looks like the values shown in Figure 12-4, you're not looking at the right Mail key. Once you know you have selected the Mail key of a user who has already set up Mail and the parameters are already entered, select **Save Key...** from the Registry menu of the registry editor. Select a location and file name for your saved key. Make it descriptive so that you can remember what it is. For instance, **MAILKEY.SET**. Go ahead and save the key.

You now have a file on your hard drive that represents the settings found in the Mail key.

Step 3 — Load the User Default Hive

Bring the **HKEY_USERS** handle to the front and place the highlight on the first key in the handle also called **HKEY_USERS**. Next select **Load Hive...** from the Registry menu. Next, locate the directory that holds the default user profile, which is usually **C:\WINNT\SYSTEM32\CONFIG**. Select the **USERDEF.** file to load. Do not select the **USERDEF.LOG**; only the one without an extension.

The registry editor will ask you for a name. I usually just call it **New User Defaults**. This action attaches the **USERDEF** hive to your registry, so that you can make changes to it. Any changes you make will be reflected in every new user you create.

Step 4 — Replace the Mail Key

When you open the Mail key of the new hive you loaded for **USERDEF**, it will most likely appear like this:

Figure 12-6
Empty Registry Entry for MS Mail

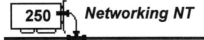

There will be only one key below mail and it will have the default values that signify a user that has not been configured for Mail. Select the **Mail** key, not the Microsoft Mail key, just the **Mail** key. Then, **Restore...** from the Registry menu of the editor. Locate and select the file name you saved the **Mail** key as. The editor will request confirmation on the action you wish to take. Please, make sure you have followed the instructions to the letter. Proceed with the action. When the editor completes it, you have replaced the default "No Mail Setup" with the configuration of your mail setup. The next new user will have the exact same configuration for mail as you have, including the same messages file. At this point, you have two choices.

Step 5 — Set the Configuration

If you will be using mail with a single, shared mailbox, where everybody's messages all go to the same place, you can elect to leave the key values as they are. This will ensure that every new user will point to and use the same messages file. You should also be certain the file, indicated in the **OfflineMessages** value, is set with the proper permissions to allow everyone access to it.

If, on the other hand, you want all new users to have their own mailboxes, you need to remove the values for **OfflineMessages** and **Login**. Double-click on the **Login** value and delete the entry that is listed in the box. In my example from Figure 12-5, that is **MAST**. Do the same for **Offline Messages**.

Once you have completed the appropriate steps, you can unload the hive using the Unload Hive command from the Registry menu while you have selected the default user hive. Mine was called **New User Defaults** so I select this key from the **HKEY_USERS** handle and unload it. The changes I made are saved and any new user attempting to run mail for the first time will not be asked what method to install or where the post office is. The user will receive a dialog box asking if he or she is a user in the WGPO. All the user has to do is answer no and Mail will ask for new user information. This gets rid of a lot of management problems.

Cleaning Up After an Accidental Installation

If you proceed though an installation of Mail, creating a new post office, then decide you want to change everything and start over, you can do that. Locate the **Mail** key of a user who has not been set up for mail, like **GUEST**. The **Mail** key will look like the one shown in Figure 12-6, with only one key under **Mail**. Save this key using the **Save Key...** command from the Registry menu. Next, open the **Mail** key of the user that you want to take back to square one. All you have to do is select that **Mail** key and do a restore of the key you saved as a file. Any information in the **Mail** key will be replaced with the keys and values in the file. The next time the user runs Mail, it will be as if he or she had never run it before.

Managing Size

This version of MS Mail does not include some of the more advanced features and one of the features that is missed is the management of old mail. With certain options in Mail, you can have all mail that you send copied into your Sent Mail folder. After a few weeks or even days, the contents of that folder can become rather significant. It is important that you monitor mail usage and make your users aware of the need to delete old mail when it is no longer needed. Unfortunately, you cannot manage their personal messages, so users must do this for themselves.

One area you can manage is shared folders. If you establish a shared folder, you can delete anything in the folder. In addition, you can grant other users the right to delete messages in the shared folder. As a post office manager, you can use the manager utility in the Mail menu of MS Mail to view the resources used by shared folders. It isn't very complete information but it does tell you the basics. It is up to you to find out where the largest shared mail folders are and delete messages.

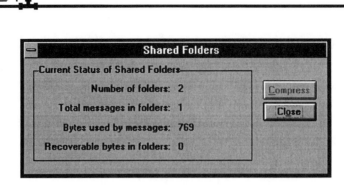

Figure 12-7
Checking Usage of Shared Mail Folders

The dialog box above shows very little usage of the shared folders and no need to administrate at this time.

Managing and Maintaining a Post Office

Only the person who established the WGPO can run the post office management utility. If you sign onto Mail with one user name and want to log on as another, you must use the **Exit and Sign Out** option from the File menu of Mail. Otherwise, the next time you run mail during the same logon session, Mail will assume the same name. Signing out will force Mail to ask you for a logon the next time you start it.

Finally, keep in mind that the machine that is running the post office should be on at all times. If the machine is off, and you are running Mail from a remote computer, the Mail application on the remote PC will ask you if you want to work offline, since it cannot access the post office. Mail will use your message file, which ends in MMF, to temporarily store your messages until you connect with the post office again. You are free to create new messages and perform other tasks that do not require connectivity with the post office. When you attempt to send your messages, they will simply be placed into the Outbox and the next time a connection can be made to the WGPO, the mail will be sent.

Chapter 13

Managing the Operating System

Up to this point, I've showed you how to do nearly everything you need to get NT running the way you want it. Once you are up and running, maintaining the system is another issue. Windows NT comes with several utilities and control panels to assist in managing your system.

When your system is running properly, there is little need to adjust anything, but network conditions, disk space available, memory available, and many other factors can require occasional management. In addition, there are times that you need to change the way that Windows NT operates, in order to perform a function or to track down a problem. Modifying NT to improve performance is also very important. In this chapter and the next we'll look at all the utilities and functions that help you to accomplish these tasks.

In this chapter we'll cover some basic monitoring and configuration tools. The tools we'll cover are shown below. One utility that should be included in the lineup is the Event Viewer, but since that utility plays a larger role in problem-solving than it does in basic management, the Event Viewer is included in the next chapter.

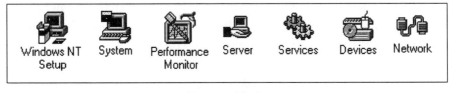

Figure 13-1
Tools for Managing NT

Window NT Setup

You probably already know what setup is for. In Windows 3.x, it is used to change the display drivers, mouse, keyboard, and network option installed. Well, we already know that the network options are all controlled from the control panel, but what you may not know is that the menu for the setup program contains two very needed functions that do not fit neatly anywhere else.

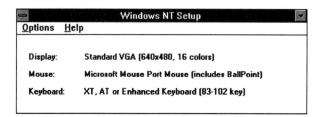

Figure 13-2
Windows NT Setup Utility

If you read the chapter on the registry, then you're already familiar with the volatile data type for hardware configurations and the fact that **NTDETECT.COM** runs everytime you start NT to rebuild that hardware configuration to accommodate new hardware. Now, think back to the installation of Windows NT. Do you recall that during the first disk of the installation, NT began searching for SCSI adapters? Have you noticed that it doesn't do that everytime you start NT? The process of detecting the SCSI adapter is time consuming and deals with functions that can be harmful to the stability of the system under "non-installation" conditions. As a result, the addition of a SCSI adapter to your system will not cause NT to do anything. You must configure it yourself. From the Options menu of the Windows NT setup program, you can:

```
Add/Remove SCSI Adapters...
Add/Remove Tape Devices...
```

Figure 13-3
Adding New SCSI Devices

As you can see, the option for adding a tape backup driver is located here as well. The only reason these options are here is because they don't neatly fit into any other control panel or category of control.

System Control Panel

Another place where you'll find some relevant configuration controls is in the system control panel. This screen covers the miscellaneous configuration information that defines how NT and the DOS application subsystem run. Your first option is to configure the multi-boot option of Windows NT which allows a DOS, OS/2, and Windows NT operating system to exist on the same machine. Users who have multi-boot partitions can configure the default boot configuration and the length of time that the multi-boot option menu is displayed before the default start-up OS is loaded automatically.

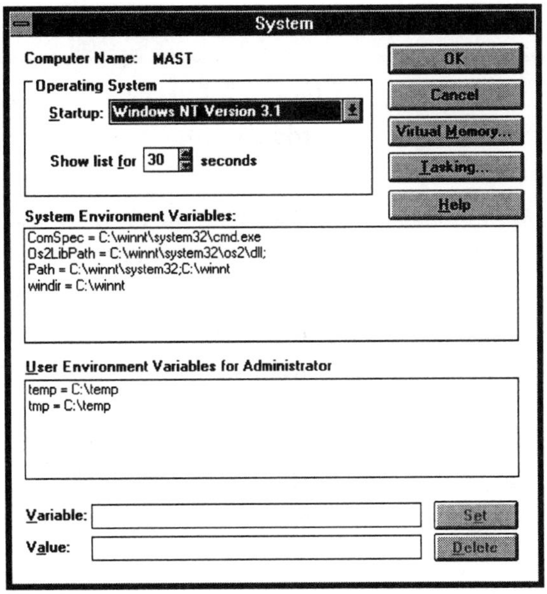

Figure 13-4
Windows NT System Settings

If you recall the discussion on user logon scripts, you'll probably remember the segment on variables. Some variables such as the user name and so forth are part of the system itself and not configurable, but other variables for DOS, OS/2, and Win32 applications can be declared here. The variables that you add are user specific. Adding a variable for one user will not make it show up in another user's environment. If you are interested in creating default variables for all new users by way of the registry and the **USERDEF** hive, the variables are stored in **HKEY_USER***Hive Name You Specified***Environment**

The other really important feature of the system control panel is the **Tasking...** button. It is one of the few ways in which you can affect the performance of your system.

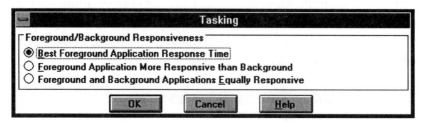

Figure 13-5
Setting System Performance Options

The available options are pretty easy to understand but what isn't said is that if foreground applications have priority, the networking functions, such as a remote user running an application from your machine, will not have the highest priority and therefore, when you are running an application, the networking performance of any users connected to you will slow somewhat. The actual amount of degradation in performance depends on a whole multitude of factors such as network cards, protocols, resources in use, and much more. If your machine will be a server and not much else, set the background to have equal priority.

Performance Monitor

Did you ever wish you could see how your system was handling a particular load? Applications running, network requests, printing, hard drive space, processor load, packets or bytes transmitted. All of these things and many more can be monitored with the Performance Monitor located in the Adminstrative Tools group of the Program Manager.

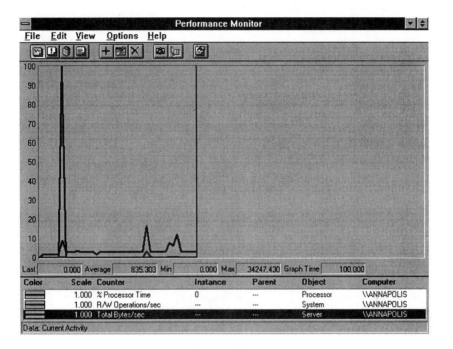

Figure 13-6
Windows NT Performance Monitor

As shown in Figure 13-6, the Performance Monitor is running three independent performance graphs. Adding a new object for the Performance Monitor to keep tabs on is as easy as clicking on the **+** button from the Performance Monitor menu bar.

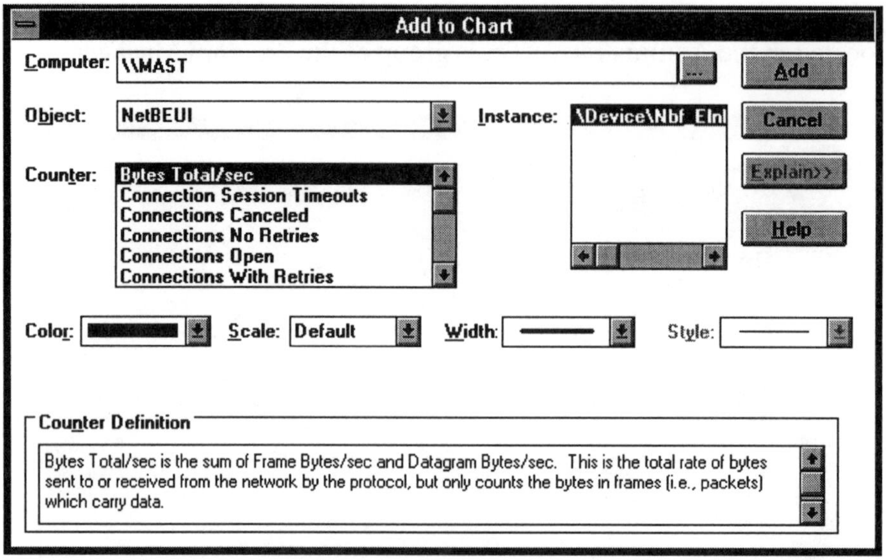

Figure 13-7
Adding Objects to the Chart

The dialog box shown is using the **Explain>>** option which reveals the **Counter Definition** text box at the bottom. There are so many settings; and so many objects that you can monitor that it isn't practical to list all of them. The beauty of the utility is that it can be used to monitor the traffic and stats of another machine across the room or across the world. From the menu bar, you can elect to save the chart stats into a file that can then be used in a spreadsheet or charting program to demonstrate increased load over time. If, for instance, you are running TCP/IP on your LAN and you want to show the progressive increase in network traffic over a six-month period, you could save chart stats each week at a particular time and then compare the data.

The Performance Monitor is not just a pretty graph that shows you the stats you want to see. There are four modes to the monitor that perform all kinds of useful functions. The most common mode is the graph mode, but the PM also has an alert mode, a log mode, and a report mode.

Graph Mode

The graph mode allows you to select a resource to monitor, and the graph will chart the rise and fall of the resource usage as it changes in whatever time slices you want to use. You can track as many resources as you want and all graphs will run simultaneously. Use the Chart Options menu command or the Chart Options button to modify the appearance of the chart, including grids, labels, legend, style, and other options.

Alert Mode

The alert mode allows you to monitor resources using alert values. You can set alerts for any value and any resource. For example, if you're using 16-MB of RAM and a 27-MB paging file you can find out when the memory gets too low. This could help determine that it's time to make a larger paging file or add physical RAM to your machine.

If you have an alert where one of your monitored resources drops below or rises above a particular level while you are looking at one of the other three modes, the Performance Monitor will display the alert count at the bottom of the window.

The illustration above shows that my red-keyed alert has occurred seven times since I last viewed the alert list.

When setting up an alert, you can also specify a program to run when the alert condition is met. You may want to broadcast a message to all users when the available disk space on your machine is low, or when the network traffic reaches a certain point, you can send a mail message indicating the condition to an administrator.

Report Mode

The report mode allows you to specify resources you want to monitor in real-time, at a specified interval which is displayed as a simple numeric value. This is really an alternate to the graph, allowing you to focus on exact numbers, not the overall trend or flux of values.

Log Mode

The log capability allows you to record the performance values into a file. You specify a file name to send the values to and then start the log. While viewing other performance modes you will be kept apprised of the growing size of the log as it collects values with the indicator shown below.

You can stop the log at any time. The log file creation is interesting because it can be used to show data in the Performance Monitor that happened at a previous time. In the Options menu of the Performance Monitor there is a menu option called **Data From...**. In the subsequent dialog box you can tell Performance Monitor to take information from either current activity or from a log file. When Performance Monitor is using a log file as a source for information, you can use the other three modes to research conditions during the time that the log was collecting data. If, after loading a log file, you go into the alert mode and specify an alert to monitor for one of the resources that the log file was tracking, the alerter will show you all the times and conditions under which the alert would have occurred. For instance, let's say I create a log file for processor utilization. I collect five minutes worth of data about it and then close the log file. After telling the Performance Monitor that I want to use a log file as a source for data, I can go into the alerter and enter an alert for any processor utilization that went above 35%. Every instance in the log file that the utilization rose above 35% would be shown in the alerter.

While using a log file as a source, you view the graph of logged resources and set the time interval to view in the graph.

As you can see, the Performance Monitor is a fine way to keep on top of your systems and keep an eye on potential problem areas before they get to be real problems.

Server Control Panel

Where the Network Control Panel manages the configuration of your network services, protocols, bindings and so on, the Server Control Panel lets you view and manage the network resources that your computer offers to the LAN. From the Server Control Panel, you can view data about users connected to your machine and using your shares. You can disconnect a user from one of your shareable resources or disconnect all users connected. You can view what files a particular user is using. The Server Control Panel also lets you manage directory replication and the list of users and machines that should receive administrative alerts from the system.

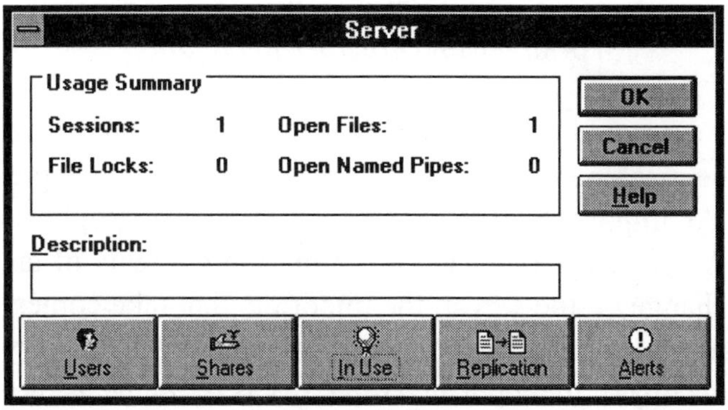

Figure 13-8
Monitoring Server Operation and Connections

The option buttons shown in Figure 13-8 let you perform the different functions listed above. Most are self-explanatory, but two of them, **Alerts** and **Replication**, deserve some explanation.

Replication

Directory replication is quite simply the ability of an NT machine to hold a duplicate of a directory that resides on a Windows NT Advanced Server machine. This option applies only to NT machines participating in a domain-based LAN.

Directory Replication

○ Do Not Import

⦿ Import Directories

To Path: Manage...

nnt\System32\Repl\Import

From List:

SAIL

Add...   Remove

OK

Cancel

Help

Figure 13-9
Working with Directory Replication

There are two roles in replication: exporter and importer. The exporter is the machine that has a directory that should be copied to other locations. An importer is a receiver for the directory. Replication works from the Advanced Server, and any time the contents of an exported directory change on the server, the importers that take copies of the directory will also receive the changes. This ensures that every machine that holds a copy of the replicated directory is the same as the server.

If export replication is active on an Advanced Server machine in your domain or a domain that you can access, you can become an importer of the replicated directories. One use for this is to keep a copy of the logon scripts from a domain controller. Although authentication occurs at the domain controller or a backup domain controller, the execution of a logon script is faster if it does not have to go across the network to run it. By replicating the logon script directory of the domain controller, the importer can keep a copy of the logon scripts locally, thus allowing faster execution.

In order to establish an import relationship with an Advanced Server machine, you must have a user account established that can use the replicator service. To do this, a user account must exist that is a member of the **Backup Operators** group, the **Password Never Expires** option must be turned on, and there cannot be any restrictions in the times that the user can log on. The user is created using the User Manager for Domains that accompanies Advanced Server.

The export relationship is established at the Advanced Server machine, and you simply select the machine or domain from which you want to receive replicated directories. If you turn on the import option but do not specify any objects in the From list, the replication is assumed to apply only to the local domain in which the import computer resides. After configuring the options, you still have one more step to complete replication.

The directory replication function is controlled by a service that can be stopped and started or set to automatically start when the system starts up. We'll cover the service control panel shortly, but for now, I can tell you that you must open the Services Control Panel and locate the Directory Replication service. By default, this service is manually started and stopped. When you become an import receiver, the replication service must be running at all times so that the machine can receive updates whenever they are made on the export server. You must change the start-up mode to **Automatic** and in the **Log On As:** text entry box, you should specify the user name and password of the account you created on the Advanced Server for replication.

Alerts

This option allows you to specify what users or machines in your LAN will receive administrative alerts from the system. These alerts include UPS warning of loss of power, printer problems, and low resource

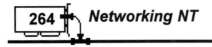

levels such as low memory or hard disk space. They do not include the alerts that you configure in the Performance Monitor.

Services and Devices Control Panels

I've included both control panels in the same segment because they are so similar. The Services Control Panel (Figure 13-10) manages software-related services while the Devices Control Panel (Figure 13-12) manages the hardware drivers and resources.

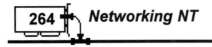

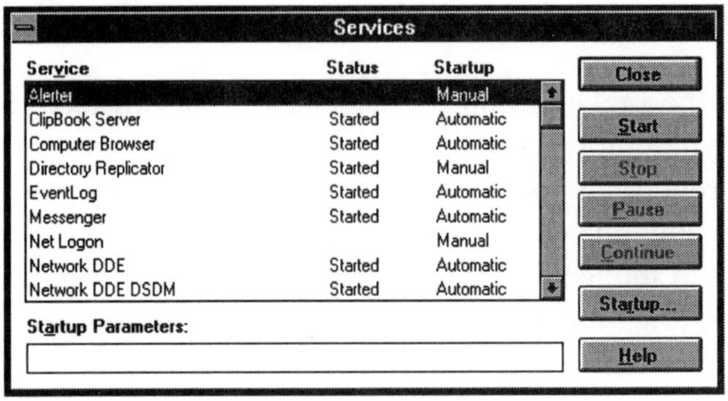

Figure 13-10
Checking and Changing Software Services Start-up Mode

Software-related services have three states: stopped, started, or paused. The loading of a driver is managed in three different modes: automatic, manual, or disabled.

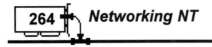

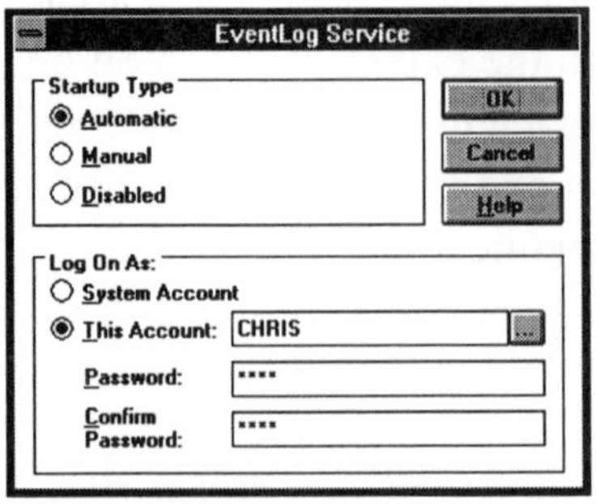

Figure 13-11
Modifying Start-up Mode

As you just read in the section about directory replications, it is sometimes necessary to modify the services of the machine for particular situations. When setting a service to load automatically that must communicate with a domain, you must use the Log On As option and specify the user account on the domain that the service should log on as. If you recall from the discussion on User Rights in the User Manager, the ability to log on as a service is one of the available rights that can be granted to a user. When you set up a service to load with a name and password in which the user does not already have the right to log on as a service, the Services Control Panel will automatically grant the user that right and notify you that the right has been granted.

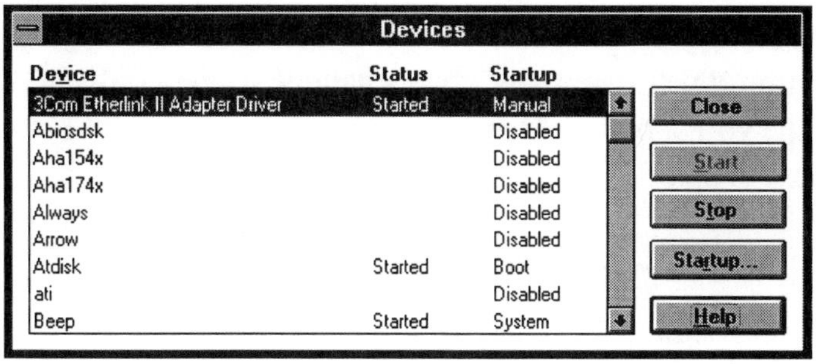

Figure 13-12
Hardware Device Start-up Mode

Device-related services have two states: stopped or started. The loading of the driver can be managed in five different modes: boot, system, automatic, manual, or disabled.

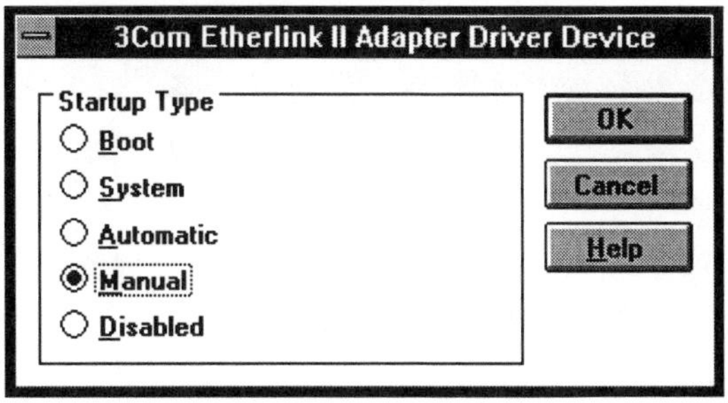

Figure 13-13
Modifying Device Start-up Mode

The modes of loading are in order of priority. Some devices such as a disk controller must be started at the time that the system boots, so that the OS can load from a hard disk. It is integral to the operation of the OS. System-level drivers are critical to the system and must be loaded in order for the OS to load properly. These drivers include the floppy controller and parallel controller. Automatic, manual, and disabled drivers are not critical to the systems' operations. They may need to be started in order for a feature to work, but the operating system will load without them.

CAUTION: You must use caution when modifying load parameters for hardware drivers. If you modify a boot-level driver to be automatic, the system will likely be hung and require a boot with the Last Known Good configuration, thus losing any other changes in the configuration since the last time you booted. For more information on the Last Known Good see the next chapter.

Network Management for Performance

There are very few places in Windows NT where you can tell the OS how to perform so that you can gain performance. One of these places is in the Network Control Panel. The performance modifications are only for machines that act as servers in a LAN environment. To adjust network performance, double-click on the Network icon in the Control Panel. From the **Installed Network Software** list box, select **Server** and click on **Configure....** It brings up the dialog box shown in Figure 13-14.

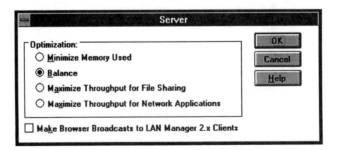

Figure 13-14
Setting Server Performance Ratio

Chapter 14

Fault Tolerance, Problem-Solving, and Recovery

Protecting your system and getting it running again after a problem has happened are not fun tasks but they are very critical to ensuring the long-term productivity of your systems. *Fault tolerance* is the ability of the system to handle problems that occur without disrupting normal operations. Windows NT includes two specific utilities to handle fault tolerance. *Problem solving* for faulty configurations and errors is handled by a single NT utility. *Recovery*, or the ability to get back up and running after an event has occurred that couldn't be handled without interrupting normal operations is handled by two different features of NT, depending on the circumstances. This chapter discusses these features in greater detail.

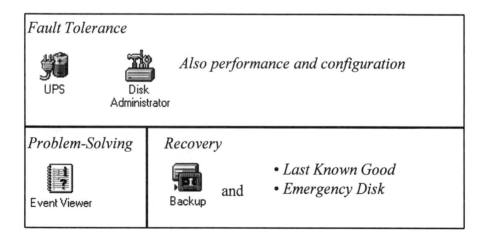

UPS

UPS, or Uninterruptable Power Supply, is a battery backup device that detects the loss of power in an AC line and switches automatically from AC power to battery power. The very nature of a UPS means that eventually, the battery will lose its juice and will no longer be able to supply enough power to keep the PC operating. Since the PC will eventually go down if AC power is not restored, at least with a UPS you have some warning of the impending doom.

```
┌─────────────────────────────────────────────────────────┐
│ ─                         UPS                             │
├─────────────────────────────────────────────────────────┤
│                                                          │
│ ☒ Uninterruptible Power Supply is installed on: [COM2: ±] [  OK  ] │
│                                                          │
│ ┌─UPS Configuration──────────────────────────┐  [ Cancel ] │
│ │                    UPS Interface Voltages:  │            │
│ │ ☒ Power failure signal   ◉ Negative ○ Positive│ [  Help  ] │
│ │                                             │            │
│ │ ☐ Low battery signal at least ◉ Negative ○ Positive│    │
│ │   2 minutes before shutdown                 │            │
│ │ ☒ Remote UPS Shutdown    ◉ Negative ○ Positive│         │
│ │                                             │            │
│ │ ┌─☒ Execute Command File─────────────────┐ │            │
│ │ │ File Name: [closeall.bat             ]  │ │            │
│ │ └────────────────────────────────────────┘ │            │
│ └─────────────────────────────────────────────┘          │
│ ┌─UPS Characteristics──┐ ┌─UPS Service──────────────────┐ │
│ │Expected Battery Life:[2 ⬍] min│ │Time between power failure [5 ⬍] sec│ │
│ │                      │ │and initial warning message:  │ │
│ │Battery recharge time [100⬍] min│ │Delay between warning [120⬍] sec│ │
│ │per minute of run time:│ │messages:                     │ │
│ └──────────────────────┘ └──────────────────────────────┘ │
└─────────────────────────────────────────────────────────┘
```

Figure 14-1
UPS Configuration

The UPS monitor program in Windows NT is based on an industry-standard connectivity method through a serial port on the machine. The UPS is connected to the PC by a serial cable which transmits information about the status of the battery backup to the machine. When the AC power fails, the UPS sends a message to the PC that the power is lost and the battery is draining. Some more advanced UPSs, can also transmit status information, such as the internal temperature of the UPS, current load levels, percentage of full charge available, and other useful information. In keeping with Microsoft's strategy to provide only bare essentials for functionality, the UPS monitor control panel is not a full-fledged UPS management utility. Third-party vendors like APC (American Power Conversion) will provide better, full-featured UPS management applications in time. For now, if you have a serial UPS, you can hook it up and at least get this protection and be warned in case of a power failure. If your UPS is not serial-based for communication with a PC, then you will have to rely on indicators on the front of your UPS and your own knowledge of the UPS to prepare for a power failure. Without a serial cable to the PC, Windows NT will not know that the power has been lost.

To configure your system to communicate with a UPS, locate the UPS control panel. The options are relatively easy to configure. After enabling the UPS and selecting the port that the UPS serial cable is connected to, you can select the features that apply to the features your UPS provides. You will certainly need the manual that came with your UPS, since it's unlikely that you will remember the voltages for UPS signaling.

The most important option allows the UPS to signal that the power has failed. This will initiate an administrative message to designated recipients that the power has failed. Some UPS systems can also generate a signal when the charge level of the battery has fallen below a certain level. If the UPS has been running for 15 minutes, it's nice to know that the UPS cannot hold out much longer. The second voltage option is for a UPS-generated warning that the battery is almost dead. If your UPS doesn't generate a low charge signal, you can use the **UPS Characteristics** frame to tell NT what the battery life is normally. NT will use the configured time and subtract from the power loss signal to determine when the battery is low. You should estimate on the low side, so that you don't overestimate the amount of life left in your battery.

The third option allows for UPSs that reach an extremely low state of battery power and signal the connected machine to shut down.

As you can see from Figure 14-1, you can also have NT execute a program when the UPS kicks on.

Disk Management

Another way of protecting your system from unexpected problems is to configure your disks to duplicate one another. Working with the configuration of your disk can also improve performance and maximize the available space on your drives. First, let's talk about protecting your data.

In a system, four things can kill your operational status: system board, power supply, hard-disk controller, and hard disk. Granted, other components can fail, such as your video controller or network card, but they usually do not affect the functionality of the actual system itself. If the machine is a server, then a network card failure can cause you all kinds of trouble, but you can guard against that by using multiple network cards. If the system-board or power-supply fails, you're up a creek, and no feature of Windows NT allows system-level fault tolerance. Fortunately, system board and power supply problems are rare, except on an aging machine. The most common problem with system integrity is the media. Hard drives fail, sometimes very often. Everything affects hard drives; movement, alignment, heat, dust, and a host of other internal problems. System boards don't usually fail because there are no moving parts. Hard drives are chock full of moving parts. How do you protect your data stored on hard drives?

The industry-standard term for having two drives that contain the same information is *mirroring* and *duplexing*. Windows NT treats them as the same thing, but in reality, one is more secure than the other.

Mirroring

The first and least expensive method of disk-drive protection is *mirroring*. Mirroring uses two hard drives of similar size and duplicates one to the other. If one drive should fail, the other drive in the mirrored set takes up where the dead drive left off. It is dependable and stable. The obvious disadvantage is that you use twice as many hard drives for half the space. There's always a cost to protecting your data.

Duplexing

The other, more complete option is to not only make your disks redundant, but to make your controllers redundant. With mirroring, if one drive fails, you use the other, but what happens if the drive controller fails? Both drives are gone and your mirroring is worthless. Disk *duplexing* puts a hard drive of similar size on two different controllers. If either disk or controller fails, the other will kick in to provide service to the system until the problem can be fixed.

RAID

RAID, which stands for Redundant Array of Inexpensive Disks, has five levels, and not all of them are fault-tolerant. Windows NT is not capable of supporting the fault-tolerant levels of RAID but for completeness, we'll cover them anyway.

RAID level 1 is the same as the mirroring and duplexing that we discussed above.

RAID level 0 allows you to connect up to 32 drives together as a single drive and create a *stripped set*. With a stripped set, a block of data is divided and written to the array simultaneously. It is a great way to increase performance on your system. Let me show you why. Let's say that you have ten disks configured as a stripped set. You wish to save a 100KB file to your drive. Windows NT will split that file into ten pieces and write 10KB to each drive. Instead of waiting for your system to write 100KB to a single drive, you wait for a 10K file, and all drives write and read simultaneously. It's fast and gets faster with every disk that you add to the set, thus reducing the size of any piece of data that must be written to the individual disks. Performance is the only reason to implement this strategy, because it is not at all fault-tolerant. If any one of the disks in a stripped set fail, all data on all drives is lost.

RAID levels 2, 3, and 4 do offer a level of fault tolerance by using an additional drive to write error-correction code about data that resides in the array.

RAID 5 is the most popular fault-tolerant disk array implementation. Level 5 essentially works the same as level 0, but parity information is also written to the disk along with the data pieces. If one drive in the array fails, the parity information stored on the other drives can be used to "rebuild" the information on the dead drive. A simple example of this is in order. Let's say you write a file to the drive. Your array is made up of four disks. The file is split into four pieces and in addition to writing the data to each disk, an additional piece of code is written, representing the parity value of the data. If your parity value is:

Disk	Value
0	7
1	8
2	3
3	14

The total value is 32, and if disk 2 dies, a simple calculation can replace the data stored on the drive. **MISSING DATA = TOTAL VALUE - VALUE on DISK(x)**. That's basically it. It is slightly "slower" than RAID 0 because of the additional information that must be written, and when a dead drive is in the array, performance drops again because the missing data must be calculated every time you access the drive. If, while one drive is dead, another drive dies, it's all over. There is no calculation that can recreate two values for the data stored on two missing drives.

In order to implement level 0 or 5, you must have at least two or three partitions respectively, that reside on different physical drives. When creating the set, Windows NT will configure the partitions so that they are the same size. If your physical drives differ in size, NT will leave some space unpartitioned. Sometimes this can be a very small amount like 1 or 2 MB and sometimes it can be a great deal of space. If you combine an 80-MB, 120-MB and a 170-MB drive, Windows NT will create three partitions of approximately 80-MB on each of the disks. That leaves an extra 40 MB on the second disk and 90-MB on the third disk. It would be a pain to have that many separate drives, so you can combine the available space of multiple drives and partitions together to form a single drive called a volume set.

Windows NT *does not* have the ability to support RAID 2, 3, 4, and 5. Windows NT Advanced Server can use RAID 5, but with Windows NT, you must use either level 0 or 1. As you know, level 0 offers no fault tolerance and therefore, it's not a great choice unless you keep a good backup and you can live with losing a day's worth of data.

Let's summarize. Mirroring and duplexing, which Windows NT can do, offer the best protection of your disk data but are slower than RAID solutions. RAID level 0 or stripped sets offer the best performance but no protection of data. RAID levels 2, 3, 4, and 5 cannot be configured on Windows NT. Finally, volume sets allow you to utilize leftover space on multiple drives and combine them. The performance of volume sets is equivalent to a single-drive system or a mirrored set, as no simultaneous writing or reading takes place.

Partitioning

To set up any of the disk options, you use the Disk Administrator, which is located in the Administrative Tools group of the Program Manager. Be aware that if your system is set up with the dual boot option for OS/2 or DOS, any disks or partitions set up with any of the features we've talked about, such as stripped sets, will not be available or visible to DOS and OS/2 operating systems. Only disks configured with regular partitions and compatible formatting will be usable in other operating systems. This brings me to my next point: the Disk Administrator utility gives you the ability to create new partitions for unformatted free space on your drives. If you are using dual boot with Windows NT and DOS, you must use the `Create Extended...` menu option, not just the `Create...` option. DOS, as an operating system, expects to see a primary active partition and subsequent partitions are "extended." The `Create Extended...` option creates another primary partition in addition to the one you are using to boot from. In Windows NT, that is a valid configuration, but DOS doesn't know what to do with it. The `Create Extended...` option will partition the drive in a such a way that DOS can understand it. All of these limitations for DOS and OS/2 are only for the operating systems themselves, not the DOS and OS/2 subsystems that run under Windows NT.

The reason that you may want two partitions set to primary is the ability to boot two different NT systems on the same machine. The partition that Windows NT boots from must be a primary partition and it must be marked active. You can install two sets of Windows NT, each on a different primary partition, and then by selecting one or the other to be the active drive, you can boot two different Windows NT environments.

The one thing that is missing from the Disk Administrator is the ability to format partitions, or sets. Once you create a partition or set, you have to use the command-line prompt to format it. The command looks like this:

FORMAT E: /FS:NTFS

The **FS** option allows you to specify what type of file system to use on the new partition. Your options include NTFS, HPFS, or FAT. Remember the security implication of not using an NTFS partition. You cannot give access permissions to files and directories in a FAT or HPFS partition.

There is one last option in the Disk Administrator that you should know about. You can load, save, and restore disk configuration information. Windows NT stores configuration information as an object and the object can be loaded from other installations of NT. If you have two copies of NT installed on your machine, and one of them is already configured with the disk arrangement for this machine, you can load the arrangement to the unconfigured NT install. Windows NT does not immediately recognize the existence of stripped sets, volume sets, and mirroring. It relies on configuration information in the registry to set up the disks. Rather than creating all new definitions for the drives in the system, which would destroy the existing structure, loading from another installation will simply tell NT how the drives are currently configured. This leaves the partitions and sets intact.

You can also save the configuration to a disk. If your installation of NT includes complex drive configuration with mirrored sets, volume sets, or stripped sets, I emphatically recommend that you save your disk configuration information to your emergency disk whenever you change your configuration. If you don't do this and the boot drive crashes, you'll have a real problem. Let's say you have a stripped set of four drives and a boot partition. The boot partition dies so you have to reinstall NT. The new installation of NT will not know about the drive configuration and you cannot ask NT to figure it out. It looks like four separate drives. The only way Windows NT can recognize the four drives as a stripped set is if you can use a backup of the drive configuration. Otherwise, all data on the set is lost and you'll have to recreate the set manually. Not fun!

Problem-Solving

Though Windows NT is a very complex operating system, figuring out where a problem is has never been easier. Unlike older and less-sophisticated operating systems, the messages that Windows NT generates for problems are dead-on accurate, and the drivers and components of the OS are designed to communicate with the system regularly so that status is always available.

Whenever a problem arises, assuming that you can at least get NT to start, your first and usually last—place to look is in the Event Viewer. The EV is a special utility that lets you look at everything that happens to not only *your* system but the events that occur on anybody else's system as well. You can be halfway across the world and look at the event log of another machine to perform troubleshooting.

Use the EV as your starting point and take any messages seriously. When a problem occurs in NT, the results can cascade into tons of messages. If one service doesn't start, then another can't start, and so on, until NT has recorded a whole bunch of things that have failed. This may be the only cumbersome thing about EV. Sometimes it gives you too much information. The most common error that you get is an improperly configured hardware device. If that hardware device happens to be the network card, you'll get a flood of messages as network services, protocols, and drivers fail to load because the network card device driver failed

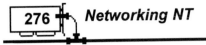

to load. You can arrange for the EV to list the messages from first to last or last to first. You can save error logs and reload them later.

Messages that appear in the system log come in three categories: Information, Warning, and Error. When a document is printed, the log records the print event as an informational message. Warnings are messages about the system that do not directly affect functionality but are areas for concern. When the system is getting low on hard-drive space, the EV will write a warning message into the log. Errors are events that caused an interruption in service. The absence of a network driver and subsequent failures of other components are errors and are so noted in the log.

For problems that are not related to the functionality of the system but may involve a user or an application, the EV actually has three different logs that it maintains. You can elect to view the security log, which shows events that occurred to objects in the system that have been configured for auditing. If you turned on auditing in the User Manager, you can view all audited functions in the security log. When a user tries to create another user and fails, you can see the failure in your log and determine that the user did not have sufficient rights to perform the function.

The third log, the application log, tracks messages from applications. The system log records only errors from the system itself but if an application generates an error, the message and cause will be written to the application log.

Experience has taught me that the vast majority of errors that NT will generate are due to pilot error, usually involving hardware problems such as improperly configured devices or a hardware failure. The second most likely occurrence of errors is due to limited resources. If your hard drive is low on space or you don't have enough memory, the errors in the log will start to pile up. Anything that is a resource-driven error can be monitored in the Performance Monitor utility.

Recovery

Getting back up and running after something disastrous has happened is not an easy task and the quality and speed of the recovery will depend greatly on the steps you took before your system died. When fault tolerance fails to keep you going or the error is related to a component that was not protected by fault-tolerant features, you have to rely on a couple of things in NT. First and foremost is data protection. I have no sympathy for people who lose all their data and haven't done a backup for six months. Computer systems are volatile and occasionally undependable. If you don't use a backup because you think your system is perfectly configured and won't have any problems, think again. Nature doesn't care if your registry is in order when it sends down a lightning strike.

Backup

Because of the mission-critical role that NT will likely play at many sites, a rudimentary backup program was included with NT. The program is not an enterprise-wide backup solution and does not contain some of necessary features like timed backup and loadable backup templates. The backup program can perform basic backup and restore functions, however, and that is better than nothing. Windows NT does support QIC-40 and -80 floppy controller tape drives, as well as many SCSI-based 4mm DAT drives and several proprietary controller tape devices, including Wangtek. You should consult the hardware compatibility guide to determine if your tape drive is supported. Please, make sure you have a regular backup.

Last Known Good (LKG)

If you read the chapter on the registry, you are partially familiar with the LKG already. The LKG is a configuration that is stored by Windows NT after a successful boot. From the last chapter you know that drivers can be loaded in one of four modes: boot, system, automatic, and manual. A known good configuration is any configuration in which a boot or

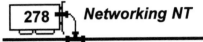

system-level driver does not fail and the system was able to come up properly. Automatic drivers may fail and prevent a feature or service from loading but they do not impact the core functionality of the OS the way boot and system drivers do. The boot and system-level driver load is conditional, though, because some system-level driver may fail to load and the system will still start. One example of this is the tape device driver. The tape device driver is loaded as a system-level driver but the system will still start without the tape drive being present. If your system boots up and you can log on, Windows NT will take that as a known good configuration. Windows NT stores the LKG in a branch of the registry and the LKG can be used to boot the system when the current configuration would prevent a proper boot sequence.

A good way to test the LKG functionality is to go into the Device Control Panel and turn a boot-level device into a disabled device, especially a disk driver. The system will fail to boot and you'll wind up with the BSOG or Blue Screen of Garbage. It's a diagnostic screen that assists Microsoft engineers with troubleshooting a system problem. Whenever you get a BSOG, you should use the LKG. During the boot process, you'll notice NT telling you to press the spacebar to bring up the LKG menu. From the menu you can tell NT to use the current configuration, use the LKG configuration, or just reboot the system. Assuming that the moon still revolves around the earth, the LKG will get you back to the logon screen. Any changes you made to the system as far as configuration will be nullified, but at least you boot. You can then inspect the system for errors using what?. . . That's right, the Event Viewer! I think you're getting the hang of this.

Emergency Disk

If using the LKG does not solve your problem, then you are dealing with another type of problem, most likely derived from a hard-drive error where some of NT's files have become corrupted or have been deleted. The only solution to this type of problem is to use the coveted Emergency Repair Disk. You should use the disk only as a last resort. It can return your system to the state that it was in when you first installed NT. User accounts and other configuration information may be returned to zero. The emergency disk procedure will analyze your files and replace any of them that do not match the installation specifications to ensure that the system files of your installation are not corrupt. The emergency disk method will not overwrite any files on your system that you created for applications or anything like that. Its only concern is the system itself, not applications and data files.

To use the emergency disk to restore a corrupt system installation you must get out your Installation Disk number 1 and the emergency disk that was created when you installed NT. If you installed NT with a CD-ROM, then get the CD boot diskette. If you also used the emergency disk to store the disk configuration information as I advised you to do in the disk management section of this chapter then the disk configuration information will also be restored. Without it, your restored NT installation will not recognize or be able to use the configured disks in your system if they are volume sets, mirrored sets, or stripped sets.

Reboot your system with the installation disk in the floppy drive and wait until the opening screen appears. One of the options available is **R**. Type the letter **R** and NT will look for SCSI adapters just like in a normal install. After the search for SCSI adapters, you will be asked to insert the Emergency Repair Disk into the floppy drive. Press Enter and away you go. The installation program will then ask you what parts of your installation should be checked. You should usually check all three, which is the default. Windows NT will then start checking everything. The file sizes and dates will be checked to ensure that all system files are not corrupt. Next, NT will ask you what parts of the registry should be replaced with the defaults. If your registry or a part of it has become corrupted, select the options that you want to restore to defaults. The SAM, which represents the user accounts database, when restored to defaults will wipe out any users you have on the system, and the files that belong to them will be orphaned, thus requiring the newly created users of the system to take ownership of them.

All I can do is tell you to be certain that the registry is completely corrupted before you replace it. A lot of work may be going down the

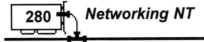

tubes. You will have to reconfigure many facets of the OS as a result of replacing the registry. Think of it as starting over. All your MS-Mail configurations will be lost, and essentially everything you configured since you installed the system. If parts of the registry, such as particular hives, are still okay, try to get copies of them so that you can load them into the registry to transfer values from the old configuration to the new one. Remember that NT protects against object reuse so a new user created with the same name as a user that existed before the disaster will not have rights to file(s) that the original user may have created. Ownership will become critical. Also remember that things like directory replication and auditing will be erased and must be set again.

NT, by default, will not select any of the registry options because of the severity of replacing any of them. If you are forced to replace any part of the registry, I want to know about it. Please send me E-mail on CompuServe at 74250,1327. Problems of this type are, as I said, usually tied to hard-drive failures and cannot be prevented except for the implementation of mirrored sets to make the data redundant.

If, after you have restored the system to a functional status, you have a backup that contains a good copy of the system from sometime before the error occurred, you can restore it and return your system to its former level of integrity and functionality. I must stress again the need to back up disk configuration information with the Disk Administrator utility if you are using any of the complex disk arrangement features. If your system dies and you must use the emergency disk to restore your system and do not have the disk configuration information, your complex configured disks will not be accessible and you won't be able to restore backups to them.

Glossary

API, See Application programming interface

Application programming interface
A set of functions or procedures used by a program to perform lower-level operations.

ASCII
American Standard Code for Information Interchange. ASCII is standard method of identifying characters, numerals, and punctuation marks, so that, for instance, an ASCII code 65 is a capital a (A).

Auditing
A security precaution where events are recorded and stored for later review. These events can be system oriented, such as a hard drive failure, or a security breach such as a non-authorized user attempting to log onto the system.

Authentication
A procedure that the Windows NT operating system performs to verify that a user is allowed to access the system. Windows NT is always performing authentication services, from the initial log onto continued access to objects such as files and printers.

Basic input/output system
The hardware device which interprets calls from the operating system when the operating system needs to work with devices in the computer. In order for the operating system to write a file to a diskette, the operating system must pass its commands to the BIOS; the BIOS then actually talks to the floppy drive.

Binding
The combination of multiple drivers that, as a whole, form a functional service. Windows NT uses binding to combine a network card driver, and protocol drivers, which produces a functional network service.

BIOS, See Basic input/output system

Certified NetWare Engineer
A certification program offered by Novell Inc. that certifies a certificate holder as knowledgeable in the installation and maintenance of Novell NetWare network operating systems.

CNE, See Certified NetWare Engineer

Command-line options
Additional characters or symbols added to a command that tells the program how to execute. Many programs offer help information by adding a forward slash and question mark to a command (SETUP /?).

Computer profile setup
A method of installing Windows NT with pre-selected options to speed installation on large quantities of computers. In order to use a profile setup, all machines must be identical.

CPS, See Computer profile setup

Data link control protocol
A Windows NT provided protocol that primarily allows connectivity with IBM mainframes as well as directly attached network printers such as the Hewlett-Packard LaserJet 4si.

Department of Defense Trusted Computer System Evaluation Criteria
A US Government publication, referred to as the "Orange Book" which determines the attributes that a computer system must meet in order to meet specific DoD system ratings. C-2 is one of these ratings.

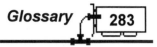

Directory permissions
Security rights assigned by an administrator to allow or prevent access to directories on a hard drive.

Discretionary access control
A conceptual function outlined in the DoD C-2 security specification that requires the operating system to limit user access to system objects such as files and directories as well as system functions such as auditing, user database modifications and so on.

Disk mirroring, See Mirroring

Disk striping with parity
This hard disk partitioning and control method places a stream of data across multiple drives and uses a mathematical calculation to compute a parity data stream. The parity data is written to a single drive. If one of the data drives fails, the parity data can be used to reconstruct missing data.

DLC, See Data link control

DoD C-2 security rating
A security specification implemented by the U.S. government which defines the functions, components, and environment for a secure computer.

Domains
A Microsoft inspired network structure which separates large networks into smaller more manageable segments. A domain can be made up of multiple servers and thousands of workstations. All user, resource, and security configuration for the domain can be handled from a single location.

DoubleSpace disk compression technology
A utility offered in Microsoft's MS DOS v6.x operating system packages that allows a user to increase the capacity of a hard drive by compressing files when they are not in use.

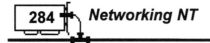

Dual cursor

A Windows NT cursor that displays an hour glass icon in addition to another icon. This signifies that Windows NT is able to accept input, and this is currently doing some background processing.

Dual-boot

This feature allows a single computer to boot up with multiple operating systems by selecting the desired operating system from a menu as the computer is starting up.

Duplexing

The configuration of hard disks in a computer where two disks are mirrored and controlled by separate hard drive controllers so that a failure of either hard drive or controller will not disable the system.

Emergency disk

A disk created during the installation of Windows NT which can assist in the recovery of a crashed system. If system files, registry objects or other malfunctions occur, the emergency disk may be able to salvage the system.

Environment subsystems

Parts of the Windows NT operating system that are used to run applications made for different operating systems such as DOS and OS/2.

Extensibility

The ability of an operating system to accept additions such as new device drivers, and other system level modifications.

FAT, See File allocation table

Fault tolerance

The ability of a system to overcome or minimize the effects of a failure. This is usually in reference to hardware configurations such as mirrored disks.

File allocation table
A method of disk formatting in which all files that occupy a disk are mapped in a table, showing location, size, and other attributes. This formatting offers the least secure environment for Windows NT.

File permissions
Security rights assigned by an administrator to allow or prevent access to files on a hard drive.

File name conversion
A process that Windows NT performs to convert native 254 character file names in the DOS compatible 8.3 format so that DOS applications can see and read Windows NT file names.

Flat memory
A method of looking at and working with memory in a non-segmented manner, unlike DOS which has regions of memory such as conventional, expanded, and extended. Windows NT views memory as a large pool which can be interacted with in any way necessary.

Frames
A quantifiable segment of data that is sent over a network medium such as a cable or laser. Frame size and content is dependent on the protocols and services used.

Gateways
A device used to connect different types of systems, often using different communications methods together. Users of IBM mainframes can access the mainframe services from a LAN through a gateway.

Groups
A logical grouping of users in network management that allows for simplified administration. Users of a similar type or in the same department can be grouped together. Grouping can also be used for application access by creating groups that only have security to a particular application and then *making users of the application members of that group.*

HAL, See Hardware abstraction layer

Hardware abstraction layer
   A translation layer of the Windows NT operating system that presents a generic view of system hardware to the operating system. Each different type of hardware architecture has a HAL which is provided by Microsoft or the hardware manufacturer.

High performance file system
   A disk formatting method used in IBM's OS/2 operating system

Hives
   Files which hold keys, subkeys, and values from the registry.

Home directory
   The directory on a system in which a user is granted full permission to files and directories for data and applications, if needed. It is a method of administration that separates users files for security and privacy.

HPFS, See High performance file system

IEEE, See Institute of Electrical and Electronics Engineers

INI files
   Files used by an application to hold configuration information such as the last four files opened or your preferred screen colors. Used primarily with Windows. Their purpose and functionality is replaced by the Windows NT registry if the applications are written for Windows NT.

Institute of Electrical and Electronics Engineers
   A standards body that determines the electrical standards that the computer and other industries use based on technical merit and other factors. Ethernet 802.3 and 802.2 are IEEE standards.

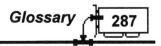

International Standards Organization

A standards body that organized and documented the OSI reference model for computer connectivity.

Internationalization

The structure of a program, operating system, or system so that it can be easily ported to another language.

IPX/SPX

The proprietary protocol used by default on Novell networks for LAN communications.

ISDN

ISDN or Integrated Services Digital Network is a method for Wide Area Network (WAN) communications utilizing vendor supplied connections. MCI is one ISDN vendor.

ISO, See International Standards Organization

LAN Manager

Microsoft network operating system which was the predecessor to Windows NT Advanced Server.

Last known good

The Windows NT term for the last system configuration which resulted in a successful launch of the operating system. This is stored in the registry in the event that a system configuration error occurs, allowing the user to boot Windows NT with the last known good configuration.

LLC See Logical link control

Logical link control

An IEEE standardized segment of the Data Link Layer of the OSI model which was originated under the IEEE's 802 project.

MAC, See Media Access Control Layer

MCP, See Microsoft Certified Professional

Media Access Control Layer
An IEEE standardized segment of the Data Link Layer of the OSI model which originated under the IEEE's 802 project

Message queues
A method by which Windows NT and other operating systems communicate with applications running on the system. In Windows NT message queues are established for each application that is running and allow the application to carry on a two-way communications session with the operating system.

Microsoft Certified Professional
A program established by Microsoft to certify knowledge in particular Microsoft products and product lines.

Mirroring
The process of duplicating the contents of one hard disk onto another during system operation so that if one hard drive fails, the other can continue to provide services. This is not as secure as duplexing because it does not protect against a controller failure.

Modem pooling
The configuration of multiple modems in a common pool so that if one modem is in use, another can be allocated for a task.

Monolithic protocol stack
A design of network driver which combines the protocol and hardware specific functions together and which occupies many or all of the theoretical layers of the OSI model.

Multitasking
The performance of multiple threads of execution by the operating sys-

tem by allowing each thread to execute for specified amount of time before yielding to another thread. This function is generally known as time-slicing.

Multiprocessing

The execution of multiple threads and processes on multiple processors. The existence of a second processor in a computer will effectively double system performance by sending tasks to a second processor when the first is busy.

NDIS

Network Driver Interface Specification which was created by Microsoft as a way to modularize the drivers that make a protocol stack so that they more closely conform to the OSI model.

NetBEUI

NetBIOS Extended User Interface used as the primary protocol in Windows NT and Windows for Workgroups.

NetBIOS

An application programming interface which defines functions for communicating with other computers.

New technology file system

A disk formatting structure in Windows NT which allows for features such as 254 character file names and extended security attributes.

NTFS, See New technology file system

Object reuse protection

Part of the DoD's C-2 security specification which requires the operating system to protect against the possibility that, for instance, a user could be created with the same identification as a previous user, thereby possibly allowing the newly created user to access system objects the deleted user had access to.

ODI, See Open datalink interface drivers

Open datalink interface
  A Novell specification for modularizing a protocol stack, similar in most respects to the Microsoft NDIS structure.

Open system interconnection model

OSI, See Open system interconnection model
  A ISO conceptual model of what services should be provided in the connection of two or more computers and how those services should be laid out and interact.

Packets
  A quantifiable package of data which is transmitted over a network medium.

Partition
  A segmentation of hard disk resources to form a logical unit. A partition may divide a single hard drive into multiple logical partitions, or a partition may be made up from multiple hard drives.

Portability
  The ability of an operating system or application to be used on multiple hardware platforms without a complete rewrite of the software. This feature is available in Windows NT through the use of the hardware abstraction layer or HAL.

POSIX
  A standard being built by the IEEE that will standardize operating system functions such as the interface, security, networking, and management. This specification will be a public domain standard rather than the proprietary structure of Windows NT which is of great interest to the U.S. government.

Preemptive multitasking
  The assignment of priority levels to threads which allow the operating

system to determine which threads should execute first and in what order.

Protocol

A set of rules that govern the communication between two computers which defines such functions as error checking, routing, and security.

RAID

Redundant Array of Inexpensive Disks is a means of configuring hard disks in such a way so that the drives act as a single unit and in most cases provide fault tolerance.

RAS, See Remote access service

Registry

A system-wide configuration database used in Windows NT which stores everything about the operating system options, installed devices, application preferences, user configuration, and more.

Remote access service

A Microsoft application that allows remote users to dial into a system and act as if they are just additional workstations connected to the LAN.

Remote procedure call

A call to a procedure that does not reside locally to an application. This function, if written into an application, allows the application to call procedures on other computers. It's a way of asking remote computers to do the work for a local computer.

RISC-based computers

Reduced Instruction Set Computer is a hardware design for a processor which reduces the number of instructions that need to be sent to the processor to perform functions. Rather than sending massive quantities of instructions to the processor as in the Intel x86 architecture, RISC computers process smaller numbers of more powerful messages.

RPC, See Remote procedure call

Scalability
   The ability of a system or operating system to increase its processing power through the addition of option such as multiple processors.

SID
   A Windows NT security identifier which is unique to every user on a network.

Simple network management protocol
   A protocol for monitoring, controlling, and taking inventory of networked devices such as hubs, bridges, routers, printers, and workstations.

SNMP, See Simple network management protocol

Streams-TCP/IP protocol
   A wrapper for ported protocols. TCP/IP is implemented as a streams protocol in Windows NT.

Structured exception handling
   Error handling in an application or operating system that allows the system to respond and correct errors before they can harm the system's stability.

TCP/IP, See Transmission control protocol/Internet protocol

TDI, See Transport device interface

Transmission control protocol/Internet protocol
   A DoD/Internet inspired network protocol for connectivity with many different types of computers.

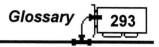

Transport device interface
   A layer in the Windows NT network design which provides a common interface to applications communicating at the session layer of the OSI model.

Trojan horse programs
   Programs that are designed to deceive the user while preforming unseen functions. They appear to be harmless but may be destroying your system or stealing information such as passwords.

UNC, See Universal naming convention

Unicode
   A character table similar to ASCII which can hold significantly more characters for standardization across multiple languages.

Universal naming convention
   A standard method of referring to network resources by placing names which identify the resources in a hierarchical format. The format begins with a double backslash and each subsequent resource in the hierarchy is separated with a single backslash.

Virtual memory
   Memory that is used by the operating system that is not represented by true RAM chips. Hard disks can be used as virtual memory where the operating system uses part of the empty space in the disk as a place to store items that are in memory while they are not currently being used.

X.25
   A wide area network protocol

Bibliography

"Windows NT Resource Guide, Volume 1" Published by Microsoft Press, Copyright 1993. ISBN 1-55615-598-0

"Microsoft Windows 3.1 Resource Kit" Produced by Microsoft Corporation, Copyright 1991.

Custer, Helen **"Inside Windows NT"** Published by Microsoft Press, Copyright 1993. ISBN 1-55615-481-X

Index

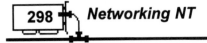

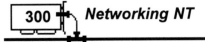

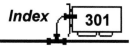

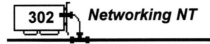